Stanford Fleming

An appeal to the Canadian institute on the rectification of

Parliament

Stanford Fleming

An appeal to the Canadian institute on the rectification of Parliament

ISBN/EAN: 9783337153281

Printed in Europe, USA, Canada, Australia, Japan

Cover: Foto ©Suzi / pixelio.de

More available books at **www.hansebooks.com**

AN APPEAL

TO

THE CANADIAN INSTITUTE

ON THE

Rectification of Parliament

BY

SANDFORD FLEMING, C.M.G., LL.D., Etc.

———————

TOGETHER WITH THE CONDITIONS ON WHICH THE COUNCIL OF THE INSTITUTE
OFFERS TO AWARD

ONE THOUSAND DOLLARS FOR PRIZE ESSAYS.

TORONTO:

THE COPP, CLARK COMPANY, Limited.

1892.

MEMORANDUM BY THE COUNCIL.

Early in the present year a letter was received from a member of the Society, Dr. Sandford Fleming, bringing to the attention of the Institute the importance of an enquiry into the possibility of rectifying our electoral and parliamentary system, with the view of averting many evils now attending it. He appealed to the Institute as a body which, while non-political in its corporate character, is representative through its members of all shades of opinion. The object expressed was to awaken an interest in a difficult problem, which vitally concerns the whole community, in the hope that some practical and beneficial solution may be obtained.

The Council has had the matter under serious consideration for some time ; meanwhile an old friend of the Institute, deeply impressed with its importance, and the great public need of a satisfactory solution, has placed at the disposal of the Council the sum of one thousand dollars to assist, as far as possible, in the attainment of the desired end.

The matter was formally brought before the Institute, at a largely attended meeting, on the 20th February last, when after the reading of Dr. Fleming's communication and the discussion on the " Note " attached, the following resolution passed with substantial unanimity :—

" That the generous offer of a friend (who does not wish his name to be known) to contribute the sum of $1,000 to aid in obtaining a satisfactory solution of the problem referred to in Dr. Sandford Fleming's paper, be accepted with the best thanks of the Institute, and that the Council be empowered to take the necessary steps to obtain essays or treatises, and award the premium to the best workable measure, which, if made law, would give the whole Canadian people equal representation in Parliament, and each elector due weight in the government through Parliament."

The Council thereupon appointed a special committee to carefully weigh the whole subject, and consider how best to deal with the matter and carry into effect the wishes of the meeting and the authority and trust conferred on it by the Institute.

After many meetings and conferences, the Council has adopted the recommendations of the special committee, and now appeals to every member of the Institute and to all thoughtful persons within the Dominion, for their assistance in obtaining a complete solution of the problem.

While the Institute addresses Canadians as being specially interested in the good government of their own land, the prize competition is extended to all persons of whatever country, on equal terms, as set forth in the conditions issued herewith.

ARTHUR HARVEY,
President.

ALAN MACDOUGALL,
Secretary.

Canadian Institute,
Toronto, April 4th, 1892.

CONDITIONS

On which The Canadian Institute offers to award prizes for essays on "ELECTORAL REPRESENTATION AND THE RECTIFICATION OF PARLIAMENT."

The sum of one thousand dollars ($1,000) has been placed at the disposal of the Council of the Canadian Institute to be awarded in whole or in part by the Institute for the best workable measure (Bill or Act of Parliament) which, if made law, would give the whole Canadian people equal representation in Parliament and each elector due weight in the Government, through Parliament.

The Council of the Institute accordingly invites essays on Electoral Representation and the Rectification of Parliament, accompanied by a draft bill applicable to countries with a Parliamentary System similar in general features to that of Canada.

The essays will be received by the Council before the first day of July, 1893. As the Transactions of the Institute are printed in English, it is desirable the essays should be in that language. They are to be signed with a motto, and the name and address of the writer are to be enclosed in a sealed envelope, endorsed with that motto; the whole under one cover, to be addressed

---

ELECTORAL REPRESENTATION.

TO THE SECRETARY,

CANADIAN INSTITUTE,

TORONTO, CANADA.

The sealed envelopes to remain unopened until final adjudication by the Council of the Institute.

The Council will, immediately after the 1st July, 1893, examine all the Essays received.

All treatises of merit, to which an apparently "workable measure" is appended (in which considerable latitude must necessarily be allowed), will then be referred to an independent tribunal for a report. It will be the aim of the Council to have this tribunal composed of men of the highest standing in their several spheres, comprising persons learned in political science, law and practical politics.

The Council proposes that one award be given of not less than five hundred dollars ($500), and others, proportionate to the merits of the works submitted.

If the essays and draft bills shall not be thought by the above tribunal of sufficient merit to entitle them to receive the principal or any premium, or if the Council on receiving the report shall be of that opinion, the Council reserves to itself the right not to award any premium.

The Canadian Institute reserves to itself the right to publish the successful essays and draft bills to which premiums may be awarded.

CANADIAN INSTITUTE,
Toronto, April 4th, 1892.

ALAN MACDOUGALL,
Secretary.

Alan Macdougall, Esq.,

 Corresponding Secretary Canadian Institute, Toronto.

SIR.—I am desirous of bringing to the attention of the Canadian Institute a subject of more than ordinary importance, and to my mind, especially so at this period in our history. I beg leave to refer to the accompanying " Note" by which it may be seen that the design in view is the removal of certain evils which unfortunately beset us as a people.

I cannot resist the impression that the examination of the facts presents a scientific problem, in no way unworthy the consideration of the Institute ; and if a solution of the difficulties presented be possible, it can best be obtained by bringing the subject to the attention of properly qualified minds. It is the duty of us all to seek the best means of serving our country, and on this ground I appeal to the Institute to extend its consideration to the matter which I respectfully ask permission to lay before its members. The Institute, from its recognized character as a scientific and literary body, holds a peculiarly favourable position to entertain the consideration of the subject. It may be briefly described as an inquiry into the possibility of rectifying our electoral and parliamentary system, with the view of averting many evils now attending it, and of promoting the common happiness by terminating party conflict, and assuring political peace and freedom, by the removal of the painful and depressing influences from which we suffer.

I feel therefore warranted in appealing to the Institute, as a body nonpolitical in its corporate character, but which, nevertheless, is representative through its members of all shades of opinion, to give the weight of its name in directing public attention to the subject.

I trust I am not too sanguine in expressing the hope, that by the weight and influence of the Institute, so great and so general an interest in the subject may be awakened, as to lead to important and beneficial results. Should a practical solution to the problem be obtained, it will be attended with the happiest consequences, and the Institute will have conferred a lasting benefit on the Dominion.

Along with the accompanying " Note" I enclose a list of writings bearing on the subject of this communication, some of which are of deep interest.

 I have the honor to be, Sir,

  Your obedient servant,

   (Signed)   SANDFORD FLEMING.

NOTE ON ELECTORAL REPRESENTATION AND THE RECTIFICATION OF PARLIAMENT.

There are in Canada few men past middle age, who have not long felt the unsatisfactory condition of much which appertains to public life in the Dominion. There are not a few who have from year to year hoped that the unfortunate features in that which we call "politics" would in some way disappear. Recent revelations have, however, rudely dispelled such hope, and have confirmed the fears of those who foresaw that as the tendency of the evils was progressive, we could not reasonably look for an improvement.

Thoughtful persons, having the welfare of the country at heart, are thus impelled to give serious attention to the subject, with a view of considering the possibility of securing some beneficial change. The examination naturally takes the direction of an enquiry into the origin of the evils with which we are confronted, and the causes which persistently keep them associated with government, which, therefore tends to become mis-government.

The objects of government may be thus defined : To maintain peace and security, to increase prosperity and wealth, to advance moral and intellectual development, and generally to promote the good and the good-will of the people.

With us the universal belief is, that the representative system is best calculated to attain these ends. In other countries the representative system has long been a constitutional reality, and from time to time modifications have been made in the system to render it more workable and more beneficial ; but, notwithstanding the various changes which have been made, it cannot be held that its full and complete development has yet been attained. In Canada we are familiar with many of the defects of popular government. In the neighboring republic the defects in its adaptation are still more marked, and the political condition is consequently far from satisfactory. In Great Britain, the cradle of modern representative government, where the system should have attained the highest perfection, similar evils have been developed.

That the political evils which everywhere attract attention are attributable to imperfect methods of carrying out the representative system may justly be inferred. The fundamental principle of representative or popular government is, that the sovereign power of a State rests in and proceeds from the people, and that it is exercised by the representatives of the people assembled in Parliament. We have accepted this the democratic theory as our principle of government ; but an examination will show that the methods adopted in carrying it into practice, have failed in their object. We, in fact, follow a course which, in its results, operates in a manner diametrically opposed to the true theory of our political constitution. The theory is that the mass of the electors shall be present in the persons and heard in the voices of those who constitute the national assembly or Parliament. Such undoubtedly is the principle of government which we aim to carry into effect, but it has never in practice been even approximately attained ; moreover, it is impossible of attainment so long as members of Parliament continue to be chosen according to the present method of election. The obstacles to obtaining a true representation of the people in Parliament are due to the combined influence of two causes. The *first* is the expedient universally adopted in choosing members of the legislature by a majority of votes in each constituency. The *second* is the division of the people and the representatives into two great parties. The second, indeed, follows in a great measure from the first ; undoubtedly the primary radical error is in assuming that the aggregate numerical majorities in the several constituencies are representative of the whole community. On this assumption, all those who do not vote with the majorities are unrepresented in Parliament. The aggregate majorities represent only a portion, in place of the whole people ; the electors who voted for the defeated candidates, together with those who had no vote, or did not vote, remain unrepresented. Under these circumstances, even if the whole elected body gives its unanimous support to the administration, we do not obtain a true and perfect model of popular government, that is to say, a people self governed. We have but the government of a part over a part ; possibly, but not necessarily, the major over the minor part. It is proper, however, in considering the question, that we should deduct the members in opposition, and then we still less have the government we are told we possess ; that is the government of the people. We then have practically government by the minor over the major part. It can be conclusively shown that the minor and governing part is but a fraction of the whole, and that we are, as a matter of fact, usually governed by this fractional part. There cannot be a doubt that from this circumstance spring the unhappy forces which so much disturb the harmony of our political machinery.

It has elsewhere been made clear by actual statistics, that the electoral methods which we follow prevent a large portion of the community from being represented in Parliament, and exclude a still larger portion, generally the great majority of the people, from any share or participation, directly or indirectly, in the government. It has been likewise established that in place of the supreme power being exercised by the people's representatives, the whole power of the State is absolutely possessed by a minority, and practically by an exceedingly small minority. Thus we utterly fail in attaining what is understood to be representative government; in its place we have acquired a totally different and perverted system—a system of the character of an oligarchy, and, it is hardly too much to say, exhibiting some of its worst features. We have accepted the fallacy that a part is equal to the whole. We give supreme authority to a part, numerically in the minority, and we allow it to assume the power which should be exercised by the whole; at the same time we exclude a large part, generally the majority of the people from the rights and privileges which by theory they possess.

Is it surprising that this system should result in the constant recurrence of difficulty? Would it not rather be a matter of surprise if those excluded from participation in government, or from representation in Parliament, should quietly acquiesce in the injustice? It is only natural that they should resent the deprivation, and strive to regain their lost rights and privileges, by waging political warfare against the men who for the moment rule; hence it is that they employ every means, good and evil, to drive them from power. The dominant party for the time being, on their part strenuously defend the position they hold, and leave nothing undone to thwart the efforts of their adversaries to displace them. On the one side, there is a persistent and relentless attack upon the party controlling the government; on the other a life and death struggle for political existence. Thus we have the political peace of the community continuallly disturbed, and we witness, in and out of Parliament, a never-ending conflict with all its concomitant evils. Such to-day is the chronic condition of public life in Canada, whatever party be in power, and it seems to be much the same in all countries similarly circumstanced. In the work of Sir Henry Maine on popular government the condition of party government, is mildly described as "a system of government consisting in half the cleverest men in the country taking the utmost pains to prevent the other half from governing."

It is easy to be seen that the source to which we may trace our political difficulties is an incomplete, if not absolutely false, electoral system. The method of election which we follow, in its effect disfranchises half the population entitled to representation in Parliament, and, without any doubt whatever, it is this grave defect in our political system, which throws all our constitutional machinery out of gear. It is this defect which brings the organized parties of the present day into being, and which animates and intensifies party feeling. It is this defect which leads to party abuses and vices, and while this defect remains, improvement is not probable, indeed, unless humanity changes its nature, it may be affirmed that any marked improvement is not possible.

Glancing over the pages of history, it cannot be denied that a party had its good side as well as its bad in the early days of representative government. There were special objects to be attained, and questions of great importance to be settled. But great questions do not last forever, in some way they are disposed of, and one by one disappear from the political surface. If parties had depended on great questions to keep them alive, they would have long since perished, and would not to-day be known as permanent organizations. With truth it may be said that we stand upon the graves of great questions, and it is impossible to conceive that the ghosts of dead issues are of themselves sufficient to maintain the vitality of parties for any length of time. But every effect is associated with a cause, and the parties which flourish to-day have other and adequate cause for their continued activity. Until this cause be removed, parties will survive as living antagonistic forces to disturb the peace and political harmony of the nation. Until the day comes when Parliament shall be properly constituted, and we have representative government, *in fact*, we cannot look for a truce in political warfare; until the whole electorate be fairly represented in the national assembly—a cessation of hostilities is, in the nature of things, impossible.

In order clearly to understand a guiding principle of party government and gain an insight into the ideas of leading party men, let us endeavor to ascertain their aims and aspirations. Suppose we ask those in opposition to the ruling power what their views are with respect to the future. Will they not declare their determination to gain office, and that their hope and desire is to hold the reins of government permanently? If we make the same enquiry of the ruling party, will they not tell us that they have no intention of throwing up the power they hold, and that they will, if they can, retain power always.

Is not the cardinal idea of each party, that it shall exclusively rule? That is to say, the ideal government of each for itself is a class government, the class to consist of the men of the party. If this be the logical inference it seems to be indisputable, that party government is utterly at variance with free institutions.

All history goes to prove, and it is indeed a necessary result of our human nature that the end of government is primarily and essentially the welfare of the ruling class. If an oligarchy governs, the first and great aim is the benefit of the oligarchy. Similarly with respect to a party, and the consequences are the same whatever party may govern. This rule has always obtained, and we may rest satisfied that it will be the rule to the end of time. If, therefore, our object be the welfare and well being of the whole people, it is perfectly clear that the whole and not a part must govern. It becomes a fundamental necessity, therefore, that some way must be devised by which we shall obtain government by the whole people, or by representatives or deputies of the whole people, if we are to make any advance in the art of government.

It is quite true that in Canada we follow much the same methods as in Great Britain, where representative institutions took their origin, where the greatest experience has been obtained, and where we look for the highest perfection. It is undeniable that elections determined by the numerical majority of votes, and the division of the electors themselves into two great parties, are methods which have been practised in the mother country more or less since the latter end of the reign of Charles II. It must nevertheless be admitted that the numerical majority system is but a rough and ready means of choosing representatives, and that party government is found in the United Kingdom as elsewhere to be productive of serious political evils. Moreover, even if these traditional methods be held to be the only available means of carrying on government in a country which has emerged from feudalism, the circumstances of their application on this side of the Atlantic are not the same. Here the whole people are on equal footing. There is no privileged class, all are equal in the eye of the law, possessing identical rights and privileges. It is our pride to be in close alliance with Great Britain, and our boast to be an integral portion of the British Empire, but in local government we possess the fullest measure of independence, retaining control of our own affairs, untrammelled by the hereditary rights and practice which spring from past social and political conditions. In the mother country there are ways and usages which are historically intelligible, and among them may be classed the political methods we have named ; the circumstances on this side of the Atlantic are however different, and there will be less difficulty in discarding such ways and usages, if they are found seriously to impede progress or interfere with the essential principles of representative government, " the government of the whole by the whole."

In Canada we have been accorded full liberty to manage our own affairs substantially in our own way. There is no cast iron rule which we are bound to follow ; there are no theoretical impediments to constitutional changes which we may generally desire ; no reason can be adduced why we should rigidly adhere to usages of the past, if we have been made to feel that they are productive of evil.

Feeling clear on these points, two courses are open. First, we may adopt the *laisser-aller* policy, and allow matters to go on as now, with the prospect, nay, the certainty, that the evils we experience will become greater, and even more confirmed. Second, we may make an honest attempt to rectify Parliament, and obtain a government based on the true principles of popular representation.

If we are satisfied that some change in our political methods will be advantageous to us, we are not only free to make the amendment, but it is a duty which we owe to ourselves and to our posterity, to endeavour as much as we are able, to perfect the organization of representative government, so that in this Dominion it may attain the fullest development and most symmetrical form.

Following the second course, the problem which challenges our attention is : to devise a scheme of electoral representation, by which the whole electorate may be equally recognized in one deliberative body, and every elector may have an equitable share through Parliament in the general administration of public affairs. It is, in short, to perfect our constitutional system so that every interest within the Dominion shall be fairly represented in its government.

This problem may be difficult of solution, but considering its vast importance it ought not, in this inventive and constructive age, to be insoluble. What is a party but a portion of the people organized for political purposes ? If it be practicable to organize two political parties in the community, it should be quite possible to form one organization, the outcome of that one organization to be the Parliament we are in search of. We are led to think that political organizations are costly affairs. In the one case, each of the two parties obtains funds from private sources or secretly and improperly from public sources. In the other case the expenditure on a single organization would be purely in the public interests, it could be made openly under the highest authority and be a proper direct charge on the public exchequer.

The writer has elsewhere given expression to his views on this subject, and has submitted certain principles by means of which Parliament might be constituted so as to represent truly the whole electorate. While he does not attempt to furnish a scheme, complete in all its details, the maturing of which would indeed require much time, much consultation and much consideration, he ventures to think that such a scheme as the circumstances demand, could, without great difficulty, be arranged and made perfectly workable ; that while conserving all that is good in our present constitution, and without involving any radical or revolutionary change, we could have presented to us a plan by which we would realize in our parliamentary system the true idea of representative government.

In forming a new scheme of electoral representation, the central idea should be to constitute Parliament so that in reality it will be "the nation in essence." With this central idea constantly in view, it would be found that no good purpose could be secured by giving exaggerated importance, as is often done at present, to abstract political questions during the period of a general election. It would be in the interest of the whole community to choose men to sit in Parliament who are best qualified by common repute to represent the electoral mind, and to leave the settlement of all public questions to the assembled legislature. Representatives ought not to be considered mere delegates to echo conclusions, dictated perhaps by whim or passion, or formed on insufficient evidence and immature judgment. It is well known that often during general elections one question brought into prominence will decide which party shall rule ; while in Parliament many questions arise, some of which may involve far more important considerations than the one which receives special attention at the moment of the election. It is not sufficient that members should represent their constituents on the one question, or on several questions. The electorate should be well and thoroughly represented on all questions which may arise throughout the duration of Parliament. What is needed in a member is a man of rectitude, good ability and good sense, in direct touch with, and in full sympathy with those whom he is called upon to represent. The duty of the electors is to select the men who have the proper qualifications, and leave the final settlement of every public question to Parliament. When Parliament assembles, each representative should feel himself unpledged, and free to speak and vote on his own clear convictions, unbiassed by preconceived opinions, formed possibly upon incomplete information. In Parliament a member following a debate has the means of acquiring a more perfect knowledge of the subject under discussion than he previously had, or which the generality of those, who have selected him to represent them, could possibly have. The position of a member provides the best opportunity of obtaining familiarity with all sides of a public question. He will hear the most eminent men in public life, he will have access to the best evidence which can be obtained. For all these reasons, repre-

sentatives of the people in Parliament should be left free to act according to the dictates of their own judgment, after full examination, and full consideration of every subject. It is not possible for an electorate to determine in advance, the varied demands for legislation or the conclusions which should be reached on the many questions which will arise.*
The greater is the necessity, therefore, that they should select men of the proper calibre to represent them, men whose ability and reputation is well established. The representative on his part will owe his constituents the exercise of his best judgment and the maintenance of perfect rectitude in all matters.

This point has an important bearing on any new scheme of representation. While the electorate has the right, and should whenever necessary, exercise the right to discuss public questions, it is obviously infinitely more important for the constituencies to obtain as members, intelligent independent men, known to be generally sound on vital questions, in preference to those who are willing, in order to obtain a seat, to pledge their opinion on any given question.

Legislation is not so simple that it may be undertaken by any one. It is not a matter of indifference who undertakes it, or what character of legislation is obtained. We should have as legislators the wisest, the most clear-headed, the best informed, the most just and honest members of the community. The average elector may or may not be well grounded in matters of legislation, or in forming correct opinions on all subjects ; but he can, without any doubt or difficulty, exercise his judgment as to who he can trust, and it becomes him to choose some trustworthy man as his proxy to represent him and deliberate with other trustworthy men ; and having done so, he can leave the decision on all legislative questions with confidence to the Parliament which they would constitute.

A Parliament so constituted would be a miniature copy of the aggregate

---

* It would be absurd to throw on the people at large the actual work of legislation,—since the people only form general aims and wishes, for which it is the business of the legislative expert to supply appropriate particular rules fit to be enacted,—but that these general aims and wishes should be regarded as paramount by a representative legislature. And certainly it would be difficult for the citizens at large to perform effectively the complicated discussion that is often required to mould a legislative scheme into the most acceptable form. Nor would it be practicable for the constituents to direct the action of the representative in every detail during such discussions ; since it would sometimes happen that compromises and modifications were suggested at the last moment, rendering any previously expressed wishes of the constituents irrelevant to the issue finally put to the vote ; while to give time for a reference to the constituencies in all cases would involve intolerable delay.—*Sidgwick, Elements of Politics London, 1891, p. 529.*

electoral mind—a microcosmus of the world it would represent. The legislature of the country would become a focal center, where all the currents of national life would mingle unembittered by party feeling, where all aspirations and impulses would come into friendly contact, where the different rays of public opinion would meet under the most favorable conditions, to modify each other into a unity of expression.

Among the important consequences to which a rectification of Parliament as proposed, would lead, there would necessarily be a modification in the formation of the executive, and in the relation of the ministry to Parliament and the people.

In order to maintain the harmonious operation of every branch of government, the chief executive and administrative body ought to be in full unison with Parliament; that is to say, Ministers of the Crown should have the entire confidence of the representatives of the people. As in Great Britain, we retain in the Dominion the form of Monarchy in connection with democratic principles. In all forms of government there must be a central authority, from which the national power for the time emanates ; the same holds true in this respect in a Republic as in a constitutional monarchy; it is from this source appointments to office are made, including those constituting the supreme executive. Following this principle, ministers should continue to be appointed by the representative of the Sovereign ; public policy, however, would exact that the chief advisers of the Crown should be chosen from and supported by, if not actually nominated by, Parliament. We would thus secure harmonious action and obtain the needed guarantees that "the wishes and interests of the people would on all occasions be faithfully represented and guarded."

The intimate relations between the Executive, Parliament and the people, between the government and the governed, would give to the chief administrative body, the greatest possible stability. It would stand as a central unit to command universal respect. The government so formed would not be greater than Parliament, it would be the executive of Parliament to exercise all the power deputed to Parliament by the people. The executive would be supported by and be amenable to Parliament, and for the reason that Parliament would represent the whole people, the government would rest on the broad basis of the entire nation. Thus we would establish our constitutional structure in a manner and with material so good that it could not be easily shaken. Its foundation would consist of a great electoral body comprising the best of the mass of the community. Its superstructure, a representative body of the best of the whole body

2

of electors. Its summit, a ministerial body the choice of the representative body, and from the apex of this noble political pyramid would be
reflected the lustre of the Imperial Crown itself. What constitutional
fabric could be imagined which would give greater unity, greater solidity,
and greater dignity?

Many will agree with the writer that it is our duty to face the problem of
our political difficulties, and make representative government in practice,
what it professes to be in theory—Government of the whole by the
whole. He has elsewhere submitted his views and offered suggestions
as to the means of overcoming the evils of our present system. He
disclaims any pretence to regard the alternative he has submitted as the
only or the best solution. In recognizing the gravity of the situation,
which indeed is apparent to each of us, he feels that we must, in all
earnestness, try to supplement the shortcomings, and eradicate the
vices, of politics; with that view he has ventured to offer to the
public the opinions he has formed, simply as a humble contribution to the
consideration of a vital question in which we are all concerned. One
feature of the proposal may require a word of explanation. An electoral
system was suggested by which small groups of electors having identical
opinions would select deputies by whom and from whom the ultimate
representatives would be chosen, the design being to give every elector an
equal interest in the election, and through the members elected, an equal
voice in Parliament and an equal indirect share in the government. In
order peacefully to overcome every obstacle and remove all possibility of
friction in special cases the writer suggested falling back on the Apostolic method of settlement by Lot. It is not a new principle of settlement in matters where disputes might otherwise arise; it was favoured
by the old Greek philosophers; it is sanctioned by the Old and New
Testament; it is employed to-day under the Danish electoral law of
1867; and it has been employed for centuries by the Moravians, in selecting fit men for the ministerial office. If employed at all in any electoral
system, its use should be restricted to those cases in which no decisive
judgment could otherwise be formed, and invariably its use should be exercised with due solemnity, if held expedient, before a court of justice.

The writer has ventured to suggest, as a corollary to the proposed
rectification of Parliament, that the executive council should be nominated by the assembled representatives of the people. There are reasons
for limiting the term of office of ministers, while at the same time there
are important advantages to accrue from a continuity of administration.
Both objects might be attained by an arrangement which would necessitate the retirement of a certain proportion of ministers by rotation each

year. They might, however, be eligible for re-appointment. The principle of retirement by rotation may indeed be applied with advantage to Parliament itself. If one-fourth or one-fifth of the representatives retired annually for re-election or to be replaced by others, Parliament would be regularly renewed from year to year, and by this means the Government and Parliament would continually be brought into direct touch with the people, and thus enabled faithfully to interpret the national mind.

Bearing on the proposal to rectify Parliament, it may be confidently affirmed that the present method of electing members does not furnish a correct reflex of the national mind. If the two parties into which the country is politically divided be evenly balanced, and if at a general election one of the parties, by skilful tactics or other means, succeeds in many of the constituencies in gaining the upper hand, however slightly in each case, the opposite party may be almost excluded from representation in the assembly. How misleading, therefore, it is to assume that the majority in Parliament represents the aggregate public opinion of the nation! and yet many are apt to do so until undeceived at the next general election by the movement of the political pendulum to the other side. The consequence of these administrative revolutions is often extremely unfortunate for the country, as each party on accession to power endeavours generally to reverse as much as it can the policy of its predecessor. This condition of unstable equilibrium, inseparable from party government, would, it is believed, be obviated, while continuity of policy, subject only to desirable modifications from time to time, would be secured by the plan suggested.

Election by majorities, it is obvious, is the immediate cause of this instability. Experience everywhere goes to show that elections are often carried by exceedingly narrow majorities, so that a comparative handful of electors, distributed over the constituencies, could, by reversing their votes, transfer the majority in Parliament from one party to the other, and entirely change the character of the administration.

This phase of election by majorities has been examined by Mr. H. R. Droop, in a paper read before the Statistical Society in 1881, in connection with the general elections of the United Kingdom of 1868, 1874, and 1880. Mr. Droop points out that in 1868 it would have been possible by the change of only 1,447 votes to have transferred 66 seats to opposite sides. In 1874, if but 1,269 voters had reversed their votes, 64 seats might have been changed; and in 1880 if 1,929 electors had reversed their votes 91 seats would have been changed from opposite party sides.* Similar illustrations of the great uncertainty, and the condition of unstable political equilibrium which results from the system of election by majorities are common among ourselves, establishing how disturbing and unsatisfactory the system proves. We should aim to substitute for these constantly recurring violent changes a means of securing continuity of government by a more natural process. By the annual change of a proportion of the members as proposed, we would obtain a settled government, which would mould itself to the varying needs of the people; we would, in fact, substitute government by regular evolution for government by party revolution.

One of the strong arguments advanced by the advocates of party government is that by means of the party organizations an interest is stimulated among the electors in public affairs, and without this stimulant it would be difficult to get voters to go to the polls. If this argument be well founded, the difficulty might be easily overcome through the instrumentality of properly devised machinery which would carry the polls to the electors. Such a device need not be widely different from the

---

* While these pages are passing through the press, a general election has been held in the Province of Quebec, which affords a good illustration of the instability, inseparable from the system of election by majorities. The party until recently in power, under the leadership of Mr. Mercier, had a large majority in the assembly. The general election of March 8th, 1892, resulted as follows :—

Supporters of De Boucherville..	54
Supporters of Mercier	17
Independents	2
Total	73

An examination of all the majorities shows that it would have been possible for 804 electors distributed over twenty constituencies, by reversing their votes, to have made the returns as follows :—

Supporters of Mercier	37
Supporters of De Boucherville	34
Independents	2
Total	73

If in 32 constituencies 2,006 electors had changed their votes, the returns would have stood as follows :—

Supporters of Mercier	49
Supporters of De Boucherville	22
Independents	2
Total	73

On such slight contingencies as the change of a few votes under this system the complexion of the government of a Province has been completely revolutionized. *Respice, aspice, prospice.*

means employed for effecting assessment purposes, or for taking the census.

Since the views of the writer on this subject have been made public, he has had the advantage of examining other schemes which at different times have been proposed for improving the electoral system. It is recognized by many that the present unsatisfactory system cannot be viewed as permanent, and that it must in the end give place to some better method.

Among the various proposals the electoral scheme of Mr. Thomas Hare, propounded in England in 1857 for the representation of minorities, appears to have met with the greatest favor. The late Right Honorable Henry Fawcett thus speaks of it: "It can hardly be denied that the advantages of this scheme preponderate immensely over its disadvantages, and these last appear insignificant compared with the disadvantages of the present system." In the writings of Mr. Fawcett published in 1873, we find a short explanation of Mr. Hare's scheme of representation. The explanation is a clear and concise exposition of the plan, reduced to its simplest elements, and is referred to in connection with Mr. Hare's treatise, by John Stuart Mill, in the following terms: "The more these works are studied, the stronger, I venture to predict, will be the impression of the perfect feasibility of the scheme, and its transcendent advantages. Such, and so numerous are these, that in my conviction they place Mr. Hare's plan among the very greatest improvements yet made in the theory and practice of government."

It is not a little remarkable that a Danish statesman, Mr. Andrae, should have arrived at the same conclusions as Mr. Hare, by a different process and from an entirely different standpoint. That the scheme is capable of practical application, must be admitted from the fact that its main features were embraced in the electoral law of Denmark passed in 1855, for the election of representatives to the Rigsraad. Mr. Andrae's method was likewise applied in 1867 to the law for constituting the Landsthing, and it is still in successful operation.* It will be seen then, that the scheme of minority representation, for which we are indebted to Messrs. Hare and Andrae independently of each other, has had the advantage of an experience of over thirty years. Thus establishing beyond all question, that there is no inherent obstacle in the subject itself, to the securing of an improved system of electoral representation. Mr. Hare's scheme is so important, that a short explanation of it together with other papers on the subject, is appended. This reference to the

---

* His Excellency Count de Sponneck, Danish minister at Washington, writes March 26th, 1892, "the operation of the election law is generally thought to have been very successful."

scheme may be concluded in the author's words : " If by the means proposed, or by any which are better and wiser, an electoral system can be
established which in the work of forming a representative body, shall
succeed in calling into action all the thought and intellect of the nation,
the effect would be to create a new object of enquiry and study, extending
over a field of which we know not the bounds. All attempts to engage
society in political conflicts for abstract principles would be henceforth
vain, and statesmen would seek to build their fame on something more
solid and durable than party triumphs."

The great aim and desire of Messrs. Hare, Andrae, Fawcett, Mill, and
writers who share their opinions, have been to secure the representation of
minorities. Will it be held as a political heresy to say that there should
be no minorities to represent ? But such is the view of the writer who
inclines to the opinion that, outside the walls of Parliament, minorities
and majorities should practically be unknown ; and moreover that
unless the whole electorate, as a body, finds its representation in the
national assembly, we do not obtain a true representative Parliament.
It is natural that there should be differences of opinion. Such divergences of view are to be expected on every question brought forward for
decision, when considered on its merits; moreover to act with ordinary
prudence and wisdom there should be deliberation in public affairs ; but
deliberation to be of any use must precede decision. It may be asked is
the public mind in the heat of a general election in the best state to
deliberate on all important legislative questions, or on any question?
and can there be any effective deliberation without the electors coming
together? Both these queries can only be answered in the negative.
It is physically impossible for all the electors to meet in order to
deliberate, and in consequence, deliberation can only be effected by
deputies or substitutes who assembling in a recognized form will satisfactorily represent the electors, and by their deliberation and decisions
will effect substantially the same results as the electors themselves would
effect if they had deliberated and voted in one body. Thus it is that
Parliament properly constituted becomes the deliberative assembly of
the nation, and it is quite obvious, that deliberation and decision on all
questions ought to be the function of Parliament alone. This principle
being recognised, in Parliament majorities and minorities would be as
diversified as the questions discussed. Members in all cases would give
their votes according to their own clear, independent convictions, unfettered by pledges or party ties. A stereotyped majority and minority
are not possible in a true deliberative body ; there would, therefore, be
none in the free Parliament we have portrayed. If such a parliament

can be constituted, if it be possible to elect members on some better plan than that now followed, and on sounder principles than that of a numerical majority, the foundation of standing parties would disappear. Neither inside nor outside of Parliament would there be the same causes to develop the growth of the dualism which now exists. There would be an absence of purpose in any effort to inflame the passions or stimulate antagonism in the community. In place of these evils there would be scope and encouragement for the awakening of a calm patriotism, and the nobler instincts of all classes, and under such conditions, it is believed that men of capacity and wisdom, and of good conscience, with minds evenly balanced, would be preferred and generally would be chosen as representatives. A Parliament thus constituted would, as much as it could be possible, be free from a contentious spirit. Its members would be in a fit state to exercise their highest reason in the positions they had been selected to fill.

If the means be put in practice of constituting a Parliament of the whole people, by whatever plan may ultimately be found best, the great and permanent cause of political conflict would be removed, inasmuch as no interest would be excluded from the legislative body, and no individual elector would be deprived of his fair share in the general government through Parliament, in which he would be represented. Thus it would result that party organizations would lose support, their lines of cleavage would be obliterated, and the party divisions which now form a dualism in the State would disappear and practically become blended into one. No doubt occasions would from time to time arise, when members in Parliament would differ in opinion on important questions, and those of the same way of thinking would co-operate in order to carry their views to a successful issue. Under such circumstances it might, with truth, be said that the combinations formed would be of the nature of parties, but they would be merely special and temporary associations, to cease in each case as the questions would be disposed of. There would no longer be the same cause to induce the organization of permanent parties with their members arrayed as foemen one side against the other —voting on all questions identically. There would be no *raison d'être* for two such antagonistic forces, as now exist, with fixed antipathies, disputing under party banners every inch of ground, and mutually wasting their energies in ceaseless conflict.

It will be generally admitted among thoughtful men that one of the most pressing needs of the Canadian people at this moment is the satisactory solution of the problem set forth ; and the purpose of these brief remarks will have been attained if it be shown that a way may be opened by which the flames of political discord may be extinguished, and the *virus* of evil which taints our body politic be neutralized.

A Parliament, fairly representing the whole people, would realize the idea of a true deliberative and legislative unit. Devotion to country would be substituted for devotion to party, and the tendency would be, not to exhaust and neutralize the mental forces of the people's representatives in fruitless agitation and barren debates, but to bring the united energies of the wisest and ablest statesmen on both sides to act with purposes in common. They would no longer appear as political enemies to lead on the rank and file in successive faction fights, and interminable struggles; if ever contentions arose it would be in generous efforts to determine who could accomplish the greatest public good.

As already pointed out, we have happily in this new land no social complications or traditional impediments to encumber our political constitution, or clog the working of any improvement in our system of government. In Canada we are in a state of general and continuous development. Year by year we advance forward as our fathers did before us. If the methods of our fathers do not serve the purposes of the present generation, we must, as they would have done, abandon the methods of our fathers. When we find defects in our political condition, it is our duty to discover their origin and remove causes of friction by a re-adjustment of the legislative machinery. Now that the foundations of the Dominion are laid broad and deep, we should, by every means in our power, endeavour to prevent and obliterate divisions which tend to cleave us in two. We should have one aim, one aspiration in our political partnership. We should seek to remove the causes which have led to divergence in the past and be animated with one desire, the welfare of Canada as a whole: one determination, to promote her prosperity and maintain her honour.

If imbued with these sentiments, the sons of Canada approach the consideration of the subject which the writer has humbly endeavored to present—who can doubt that we shall witness the dawning of a new day in public life in this fair land of ours? Let us with confidence entertain the conviction, that before long there will be a new departure in politics; that for divisions and weakness and instability, with a long train of evils, there will be the unity, and strength, and security, which proceed from wisdom, and peace, and concord.

SUPPLEMENTARY NOTE.

The writer feels himself called upon to express his great satisfaction that the Canadian Institute has been pleased to entertain the appeal to public opinion, contained in his letter of the 1st of January last, and that the Council has been enabled to bring forward the subject in a form to invite the serious consideration of all interested in the well-being of our common country.

The appendix contains several pages of extracts, expressing the deliberate opinion of well known public writers, which are worthy of careful perusal. They indicate the tone of thought in minds differently constituted in our own country, in Great Britain, in the United States and in other countries. In order to make the information as complete as possible, the writer begs leave to add the following excerpts :

1. A new Plan of Minority Representation by Professor J. R. Commons from the Review of Reviews, November 1891.

2. Proportional Representation—the Gove System—with Bill before the commonwealth of Massachusetts, 1892.

3. *Résumé* of Hare's work on the Representation of Minorities—specially prepared for the present publication.

4. Translation and abridgement of the constitution and electoral law of Denmark—also specially prepared.

It is stated in the preceeding "Note" that the scheme of Messrs. Andrae and Hare in its main features was in 1855 included in the electoral law of Denmark constituting the Rigsraad or supreme Council* and that in 1867 it was extended to the Landsthing or upper house of the kingdom. As the new principles of election were first introduced into Denmark and have been in operation in that country for a number of years, it is a matter of the highest interest to ascertain full particulars concerning their application and working ; a point of great importance as there is always room for objection against any untried system. The writer accordingly addressed the Danish Minister at Washington on the subject ; the latter was pleased to respond by forwarding the constitution and electoral laws of Denmark ; and to add, that the original law of 1867 continues to be in force, and that it is generally thought to have been very successful in its operation.

---

* The Rigsraad belongs to the history of the past ; it was the Parliament of the Realm before 1867. The Danish Parliament is now known as the "Rigsdag" and is composed of the Landsthing and the Folkething.

In the "Note" which the undersigned has submitted to the Institute, he has dwelt upon the expediency of tracing to the source whence they spring the political evils which prevail, and upon the necessity of contending with the first cause to which the difficulty may be attributed. The writer has continually kept before himself this view, and he has established to his own conviction, that the evils with which we are beset are traceable mainly to defects in the electoral system which prevail, and especially to the method followed in selecting members of Parliament by majorities of votes. This opinion is not confined to the writer.

Mr. Seaman in his work "The American System of Government" thus expresses himself on the subject: "The system of popular elections which gives all representation and power to majorities, however small, and none to minorities, however large, tends to stimulate both personal and partisan ambition too highly; to excite rivalship and strife, partisan passions and prejudices; to divide a people into parties, cliques, and factions; and to increase and intensify the violence of party spirit. It offers too great temptations to resort to improper means to insure success, for poor, weak, and selfish human nature to resist; and hence it tends to stimulate secretiveness and duplicity, petty scheming and trickery, falsehood and fraud,—and to encourage social drinking and prodigality, as a means of popularity and of getting votes. It tends to stimulate and sharpen the intellect; but to paralize the conscience and the moral feelings; to foster demagogism and a despicable scramble for office, and to demoralize politicians, and great numbers of people."

Sir Thomas Erskine May, in his Constitutional History of England, points out that party has exercised the greatest influence for good or evil upon the political destinies of the country. "It has guided and controlled, and often dominated over the more ostensible authorities of the state; it has supported the crown and aristocracy against the people, it has dethroned and coerced kings, overthrown ministers and Parliament, humbled the nobles, and established popular rights." He takes the most favourable view of party, passes lightly over the meaner and more repellent features, which are attributable to it,—and gratefully acknowledges all that we owe to its influence. "The Annals of Party embrace a large portion of the history of England;—we owe to party most of our rights and liberties:—we recognise in the fierce contentions of our ancestors, the conflict of great principles, and the final triumph of freedom." While thus forcibly admitting all that can be said in its favour he is constrained to add: "In the history of parties, there is much to deplore and condemn,—we observe the evil passions of our natures aroused,—'envy, hatred, malice, and all uncharitableness.' We see the foremost of our fellowcountrymen contending with the bitterness of foreign enemies—reviling each other with cruel words,—misjudging the conduct of eminent statemen, and pursuing them with vindictive animosity. We see the whole nation stirred with sentiments of anger and hostility. We find factious violence overcoming patriotism ; and ambition and self-interest prevailing over the highest obligations of the state. We reflect that party rule excludes one half of our statesmen from the service of their country, and condemns them,—however wise and capable—to comparative obscurity and neglect. We grieve that the first minds of every age should have been occupied in collision and angry conflict, instead of labouring together for the common weal."

Men of both parties, and those who hold themselves apart from all party must assent to the truth as it is expressed in these forcible sentences : Those who so think may not all agree in attributing to the same cause the evils described, but they will acknowledge that our electoral system requires amendment, and that the constitution of parliament calls for rectification, before we can claim that we are in the enjoyment of that national representative body which our political condition demands. The great mass of the people should have perfect confidence in the character and constitution of the Parliament by which our laws are made ; and on the part of its members, there should be an earnest and deep sympathy with the people. Neither this confidence, nor this sympathy, is attainable so long as one half of the electors remains unrepresented. This necessary relationship was understood by William Pitt whose words spoken in England a century ago may fittingly be repeated in Canada to-day. "How truly important is it to the people of this country that the House of Commons should sympathize with themselves and that their interests should be indissoluble ! It is most material that people should have confidence in the legislature. The force of the constitution as well as its beauty depends on that confidence, and on the union and sympathy which exist between the constituent and the representative. The source of our glory and the muscles of our strength are the pure character of freedom which our constitution bears. * * * The purity of the representative is the only true and permanent source of such confidence. * * * Prudence must dictate that the certain way of securing their properties and freedom is to purify the source of representation and to establish that strict relation between themselves and the House of Commons which it is the original idea of the constitution to create."

The question before us to-day is not one of franchise. It is not a question involving any convulsion in our constitution. It is simply to determine a practicable plan by which the whole body of electors, can form a standing committee chosen from among themselves, to manage and direct the national affairs. The present system places these affairs in the hands of a committee of a party—not a committee of the nation ; and it is to this condition that we may trace the chronic political difficulties from which we are suffering, and which we would greatly lessen, if not entirely remove, by transferring the power of executive government to a committee, really and truly chosen, from a body of electors representing the whole people.

It must be only too plain to all, that however desirable a rectification of system may be, it will not be easily attained, for those interested in its non-attainment are many and powerful, holding under control almost the entire press of the country. Nevertheless we should not be deterred from effort by the thought of the obstacles, real, or unreal, before us, nor yield to apathetic indifference as if the remedy were hopelessly unattainable. Our ancestors succeeded in overthrowing many theories which were destructive of the liberty of the subject and the well-being of the nation. We will be unworthy of our ancestry, if on our part we hesitate to grapple with the theory of party supremacy and injustice, however strongly entrenched by prejudice and interest. No one, whose opinion has weight, will contend that some clumsy machine of primitive times, which served its day and generation, is for ever to be regarded with superstitious reverence. Equally, no one can insist that a rude political contrivance introduced before the reign of Queen Anne is the best that can be conceived for the needs of this Dominion in the second half century of the reign of Victoria.

Edmund Burke, the orator and philosophic statesman of the last century, has frequently been alluded to as an advocate of Party government, and his well known definition of Party has been reproduced by nearly every writer on the subject. It must be borne in mind that Burke spoke and wrote in defence of Party, at a period in history when political convulsions were impending, and the attention of the British Parliament was directed to questions of a kind to incite strong feelings ; at a time, when, if ever, Party was justifiable and useful. The circumstances of Canada and America to-day are entirely different from the circumstances of England and Europe in Burke's time ; moreover, we must allow that there is such a thing as progression in the views of thinking men. Burke himself did not remain stationary. In a very few years he considerably altered his opinions on several great questions. Before he passed from the political field he deliberately separated himself from his old political friends and completely dis-associated himself from the party in which he had long been prominent. Every rational human being, with freedom of opinion, makes progress, and who will affirm that the intelligence of Burke, would have refused to admit the possibility of some advance in political science, 120 years after his defence of Party government?

Burke defined Party to be "a body of men united for promoting by their joint endeavours the national interests upon some particular principle in which they are all agreed." While he approved of this basis of joint action, he did not at any time advocate the party spirit which in modern times has been developed. Burke held in respect the observance of morality in politics, and he could recognize no virtue in the indiscriminate support of Ministers, at all times and under all circumstances. He commended the member who acted according to his own judgment, who voted according to the merits of the several measures as they were presented, who felt himself bound to follow the dictates of his conscience, not that of others. He pointed out that the principle of "an indiscriminate support to Ministers is totally corrupt," that it "destroys the very end of Parliament as a controul, and is a general previous sanction to misgovernment." Again he says, "The virtue, spirit and essence of an House of Commons consists in its being the express image of the feelings of the nation." . . "It was not instituted to be a controul *upon* the people, as of late it has been taught by a doctrine of the most pernicious tendency. It was designed as a controul *for* the people."*

In his "History of the English Government and Constitution," Lord John Russell sustains Burke's view of Party, and this authority has likewise been often quoted. He admits that Party has bad effects, but he disclaims as evils the animosities and violent contentions which proceed from Party feeling. "It is," he says, "from the heat and hammering of the stithy that freedom receives its shape, its temper and its strength." Fallacies often hide under metaphors, and this is a case in point. Every one admits that heat and hammering are good for iron, but no one would say that divisions and animosities are good for men, especially if the men are engaged in a common cause. But accepting the metaphor, we may ask, has not political freedom long been with us an accomplished fact? Is there any need for the empty clangour of the anvil long after the work has received the last effective blow? Is it not time to re-fit the national workshop with new tools, and introduce modern machinery, to be employed in the process of elaborating productions of quite another character, to meet the requirements of quite another age?

* Burke's Thoughts on the Present Discontents, 1770.

It has been urged that the Hare scheme of representation has been before the British people since 1857, without being accepted, and therefore it is inferred, that a departure from the old system of electing members is not required. This is no conclusive argument against a change. Englishmen are especially conservative in their habits of thought, and dislike change even when change is desirable. As an illustration of the national obstinate resistance to change, the reform of the calendar may be instanced. The Gregorian calendar was adopted by the advanced nations of Europe in 1582. It came into force in Scotland in the year 1600, but it was resisted in England for a century and a half longer. Finally after great difficulty an act of parliament was passed and the "new style" of computing time took effect in 1752.

The advocates of the Party system are in the habit of speaking of those holding more advanced views in the matter of representation, as weak and amiable persons, as dreamers and visionaries. The papers appended establish the increasing tendency on the part of many able men who have seriously considered the subject, to regard improvement in the election system as being both necessary and possible. A society has been organized under the presidency of Sir John Lubbock to promote electoral reform, and nearly 200 members of the British House of Commons have enrolled themselves in its support. This fact is in itself sufficient to set aside the idea that those who aim at a beneficial change are to be regarded as dreamers and visionaries.

The question is of the utmost concern to this young and aspiring community. However great the obstacles to be overcome it is not for a moment to be said that they are insuperable ; we cannot doubt that they will be eventually set aside if the work be undertaken in a resolute spirit, temperately, wisely, and free from all passionate desire for mere innovation.

It has been already stated that we do not aim at any radical change · in the constitution. There is no thought of any appeal to violence or revolution ; the object is rather to avert any extreme convulsion and even to escape from those administrative revolutions which result on every occasion when the power passes from one party to the other. Instead of the periodical disturbing changes with the violent transitions of authority and the reversals of policy which follow, it is held possible to obtain continuity of government while at the same time carrying into full effect the political constitution we now possess. It must be obvious even to those who have given little reflection to the subject, that until we succeed in so doing, we shall remain in a condition of political immaturity, and be subject to the evils which are a necessary consequence of our present imperfectly developed representative system.

Whatever difficulties may stand in the way of electoral improvement, it is impossible to believe that, in this age of increased enlightenment and progression, we can leave unperformed the task which is imposed on us. The problem which the Canadian Institute submits to the world appeals with peculiar significance to the younger men of this Dominion who, in a few years, will be called upon to exercise their political duties and bear the responsibilities of legislation and government. The appeal is directly made to the sagacity of every true Canadian and British subject, to effect the removal of the hindrances which impede the establishment of the representative system, in accordance with its cardinal principle. The main object in view is to make Parliament an efficient scientific engine of order and progress, so that it may perform its important national work without the bitterness and the waste of power, talent, and time, which result from party warfare.

The appeal does not affect the Dominion alone. It takes a wider range and possesses a higher import than may at first be discerned. All free communities are closely inter-related in the practical application of sound principles of government. If in Canada we succeed, in attaining an effective development of parliamentary representation, and in eliminating the evil consequences of party strife, we shall achieve results which in their beneficial influences will be felt wherever constitutional government is known. The chief obstacle to be encountered is the spirit of war,—a survival of primitive times, which has come to us through centuries of conflict. The representative principle is based on the more excellent spirit of peace. It was entirely unknown in ancient political life; indeed its application to government is comparatively modern. It is pacific in its conception, and but for its still being associated with contestation and turmoil, through the Party system, its pacific tendencies would permeate society, wherever true representative governments are established.

It is natural to expect that Party leaders will be the strongest opponents of any scheme of government which would displace their prestige and influence. Such men would probably find it difficult to descend to the less prominent positions of peaceful co-workers in state affairs. But in pointing out this difficulty, a well known writer remarks : "If it be objected that we cannot get eminent men to take office together, without party compact, the answer is simply—let us try. If party leaders will not work together, it seems to me that their services can be dispensed with in favour of others less influenced by individual likings, and more by public zeal."

The utility of party in its earlier history depended on political conditions which have long since passed away. No one will contend that these conditions will again return. This at least is indisputable, that the system which we follow is inconsistent with complete representative government, and is productive of many and grave evils. The question arises : How long shall it be necessary to endure those evils?

A hopeful answer is suggested by a modern writer, Mr. Homersham Cox, in his work, "The British Commonwealth," and, in words which may fitly conclude these remarks : "If I understand aright anything of the teachings of modern history, they are gradually inculcating the lesson that Party is a rude and barbarous instrument of legislation, only less bad than that legislation by despotic power which it supplanted. We may fain hope that the era is coming—is at hand—when Party having done that great task will itself be at an end."

SANDFORD FLEMING.

OTTAWA, April 7th, 1892.

APPENDIX.

THE CAUSE AND EFFECT OF PARTY.

From " A Disquisition on Government," by John C. Calhoun, 1849.

"The first and leading error which naturally arises from overlooking the distinction referred to, is, to confound the numerical majority with the people; and this so completely as to regard them as identical. This is a consequence that necessarily results from considering the numerical as the only majority. All admit that a popular government, or democracy, is the government of the people, for the terms imply this; a perfect government of the kind would be one which would embrace the consent of every citizen or member of the community; but as this is impracticable, in the opinion of those who regard the numerical as the only majority, and who can perceive no other way by which the sense of the people can be taken,—they are compelled to adopt this as the only true basis of popular government, in contradistinction to governments of the aristocratical or monarchical form. Being thus constrained, they are, in the next place, forced to regard the numerical majority as, in effect, the entire people; that is, the greater part as the whole; and the government of the greater part as the government of the whole. . . This radical error, the consequence of confounding the two, and of regarding the numerical as the only majority, has contributed more than any other cause, to prevent the formation of popular constitutional governments,—and to destroy them even when they have been formed."

"The conflict between the parties, . . . tends necessarily to settle down into a struggle for the honors and emoluments of the Government; and each, in order to obtain an object so ardently desired, will, in the process of the struggle, resort to whatever measure may seem best calculated to effect this purpose. The adoption, by the one, of any measure, however objectionable, which might give it an advantage, would compel the other to follow its example. In such case, it would be indispensable to success to avoid division and keep united;—and hence, from a necessity inherent in the nature of such governments, each party must be alternately forced, in order to insure victory, to resort to measures to concentrate the control over its movements in fewer and fewer hands, as the struggle became more and more violent. This, in process of time, must lead to party organization, and party caucuses and discipline; and these, to the conversion of the honors and emoluments of the government into means of rewarding partisan services, in order to secure the fidelity and increase the zeal of the members of the party. The effect of the whole combined, even in the earlier stages of the process, when they exert the least pernicious influence, would be to place the control of the two parties in the hands of their respective majorities; and the government itself, virtually, under the control of the majority of the dominant party, for the time, instead of the majority of the whole community;—where the theory of this form of government vests it. Thus in the very first stages of the process, the government becomes the government of a minority instead of a majority;—a minority, usually, and under the most favourable circumstances, of not much more than one-fourth of the whole community.

"But the process, as regards the concentration of the power, would not stop at this stage. The government would gradually pass from the hands of the majority of the party into those of its leaders; as the struggle became more intense, and the honors and emoluments of the government the all-absorbing objects. At this stage, principles and policy would lose all influence in

3

the elections; and cunning, falsehood, deception, slander, fraud, and gross appeals to the appetites of the lowest and most worthless portion of the community, would take the place of sound reason and wise debate. After these have thoroughly debased and corrupted the community, and all the arts and devices of party have been exhausted, the government would vibrate between the two factions (for such will parties have become) at each successive election."

" Neither would be able to retain power beyond some fixed term ; for those seeking office and patronage would become too numerous to be rewarded by the offices and patronage at the disposal of the government ; and these being the sole objects of pursuit, the disappointed would, at the next succeeding election, throw their weight into the opposite scale, in the hope of better success at the next turn of the wheel."

"That the numerical majority will divide the community, let it be ever so homogeneous, into two great parties, which will be engaged in perpetual struggles to obtain the control of the government, has already been established. The great importance of the object at stake, must necessarily form strong party attachments and party antipathies ; attachments on the part of the members of each to their respective parties, through whose efforts they hope to accomplish an object dear to all : and antipathies to the opposite party, as presenting the only obstacle to success.

" In order to have a just conception of their force, it must be taken into consideration, that the object to be won or lost appeals to the strongest passions of the human heart,—avarice, ambition, and rivalry. It is not then wonderful, that a form of government, which periodically stakes all its honors and emoluments, as prizes to be contended for, should divide the community into two great hostile parties ; or that party attachment, in the progress of the strife, should become so strong among the members of each respectively, as to absorb almost every feeling of our nature, both social and individual ; or that their mutual antipathies should be carried to such an excess as to destroy, almost entirely, all sympathy between them, and to substitute in its place the strongest aversion. Nor is it surprising, that under their joint influence, the community should cease to be the common center of attachment, or that each party should find that center only in itself. It is thus, that, in such governments, devotion to party becomes stronger than devotion to country :—the promotion of the interests of party more important than the promotion of the common good of the whole, and its triumph and ascendency, objects of far greater solicitude, than the safety and prosperity of the community."

"Its effects would be as great in a moral, as, I have attempted to shew, they would be in a political point of view. Indeed, public and private morals are so nearly allied, that it would be difficult for it to be otherwise. That which corrupts and debases the community, politically, must also corrupt and debase it morally. The same cause, which, in governments of the numerical majority, gives to party attachments and antipathies such force, as to place party triumph and ascendancy above the safety and prosperity of the community, will just as certainly give them sufficient force to overpower all regard for truth, justice, sincerity, and moral obligations of every description. It is accordingly, found that, in the violent strifes between parties for the high and glittering prize of governmental honors and emoluments,—falsehood, injustice, fraud, artifice, slander, and breach of faith, are freely resorted to, as legitimate weapons :—followed by all their corrupting and debasing influences. . . . Neither religion nor education can counteract the strong tendency of the numerical majority to corrupt and debase the people."

PARTY GOVERNMENT ADVERSE TO GOOD GOVERNMENT.

From Fraser's Magazine, Vol. XLIX. 1854.

The very nature of party tactics is fundamentally adverse to good government; for party tactics are essentially unpatriotic. Their object is simply to gain or hold possession of the Treasury bench. And therefore the measures selected for attack on the one hand will always be the weakest, that is, the most unpopular, not the worst; and on the other hand, the measures brought forward will be the most popular rather than the best. That popularity and unpopularity often coincide with goodness and badness is most true; that they by no means invariably coincide is assumed by us, when we delegate the functions of legislation instead of exercising them ourselves.

On the other hand, it may be said party gives us emulation and criticism. The emulation is undoubtedly worth much; it is even difficult to see how its place can be supplied. It would be inestimable, if the prize proposed was not as it is, the popularity of the hour, but the calm approval of distant years. The criticism is defective in this, that it is, and must be, indiscriminate and unjust. Many important acts and measures of government have been seen to be good by most people at the time; and by all people a few years after. But very few important measures of government have ever received the approbation of the opposite benches. Any presumably fair tribunal—such, for example, as an assembly professedly neutral and impartial—would be really a higher moral restraint upon elevated natures (such as we hope our governors may be) than the censures of an opposition which does not profess to be candid; and which, therefore, it is always allowable to baffle, evade, or in the last resort, crush, with a vote extorted under a threat of resignation. And we must remember the necessity of keeping followers together in this 'generous emulation' and the price which that necessity entails.

"Again, party government has made politics a perfect religion of hate—hate which reaches its height in those who, if they are to command our respect, ought to be more free than ourselves from vulgar passions. It is the duty of every Whig or Tory, in proportion as he is active in politics, to see the character and actions of every member of the opposite faction in the worst possible light. If accident happen to throw a man into a different political combination from that which he has been in before, though his measures and sentiments may remain essentially the same, his whole conduct and every feature of his mind undergo a complete metamorphosis in the eyes of his quondam friends. Every blunder of the opposite side is detected with delight, and exposed with exultation; even blunders which imperil the country in a struggle with a foreign foe. The Tories cripple Marlborough, and throw away the fruits of his victories; the Whigs 'pine at the triumphs of Wellington;' the Peelites embarrass Palmerston; the Derbyites embarrass Aberdeen. English manliness and generosity come in to supply correctives which have not been supplied in other countries where the party system has been tried. But the system is distinctly one of organized enmity, very fatal to patriotism, and utterly destructive to loyalty. And yet after all, considering how little political wisdom is ever likely to reach the mass of the people, loyalty towards the rulers of men's choice is a principle in politics with which we can scarcely afford to dispense.

To this state of enmity is of course to be attributed the immense waste of time and energy in combative oratory, and the most undue value set on that accomplishment. What will a sane posterity think of debates in which nobody aims or pretends to aim at enlightening or convincing his neighbour, but only at inflaming the passions and confirming the prejudices of his own faction? What will it think of Parliamentary reputations won, and high places in the state obtained by mere dexterity in wounding the feelings of a rival, without the utterance of a single wise thing, or the performance of a single noble act?

Again, party government, as it leads to a constant change of persons and principles in the administration, is absolutely fatal to anything like forecast or a far sighted policy, etc., etc.

We return however to the point from which we started. We have hitherto gone, practically, on the theory of party government. But party principle fails us. As some think, it fails, owing to special accidents, for a time ; but as we think, it will soon fail us, if it is not already failing us, vitally and for ever. We commend the question to political philosophers as one which strongly affects the morality of public life at this moment, and which is big with the most momentous issues for the future.

CHECKS AND BALANCES.

By Earl Russell, 1854.

"Now it appears to us that many advantages would attend the enabling the minority to have a part in these returns. In the first place, there is apt to be a feeling of great soreness when a very considerable number of electors, such as I have mentioned, are completely shut out from a share in the representation of one place. . . . But, in the next place, I think that the more you have your representation confined to large population, the more ought you to take care that there should be some kind of balance, and that the large places sending members to the House should send those who represent the community at large. But when there is a very large body excluded, it cannot be said that the community at large is fairly represented.

"HARE ON REPRESENTATIVES," 1857.

A Résumé by John Francis Waters, M.A., 1892.

The three words heading this article form the short title of an excellent work, namely, " A Treatise on the Election of Representatives, Parliamentary and Municipal," by Thomas Hare, Esq., Barrister-at-Law, published in 1859, in London, by Longmans, Brown, Green, Longmans & Roberts.

This work has been reviewed by many persons of distinction, and an excellent synopsis of Mr. Hare's scheme of representation has been given by Millicent Garrett Fawcett, wife of Henry Fawcett, M.P., so well known as Professor of Political Economy in the University of Cambridge. Mr. Hare has for his great object to remove the anomalies, absurdities, and tyrannies of the present method of electing members of Parliament and municipal representatives by giving to each elector a direct, equal and personal representation in Parliament. Of course this does not mean that every elector is to represent himself in Parliament, for then Parliament would be but another name for the adult male population of the realm ; but it means that every elector should feel that his vote has done a real substantial good by placing in Parliament some man who shall be the honest exponent of the elector's honest views. In following in the footsteps of the distinguished persons who have written more or less exhaustively about Mr. Hare's scheme, and given compressed reports upon it, it is to be premised that in the limits at my disposal no more can be done than to give an outline of the main shape and symmetry of the plan. The writer cannot therefore enter as fully as he would wish into the analysis of the admirable statement by which Mr. Hare justifies the assumption that our present methods of parliamentary and municipal elections are faulty, unjust, and even ridiculous. It may be asked here, " Is not the direct, equal and personal representation of every elector guaranteed by the present system ? " The best reply to this is to state very briefly the substance of Mr. Hare's words on this point :—

He shows what must be apparent to any one who gives the matter five minutes' consideration, that a system like ours which permits the nation to be practically governed by a handful, to the total ostracism of the wishes and representation of practically half the community, cannot be other than radically wrong. Thus, to make matters plainer by an illustration at home, let us look at the result in Canada of our system of parliamentary elections. Successive contests have shewn that the Liberals in Canada form not far from half the population. But what share have they in the government of the country as long as the Conservatives, by a slight plurality, have entire control of the Treasury Benches ? Therefore, every elector who cast a vote for a Liberal candidate practically wasted it, and really has no representation in Parliament, since the Liberals in Parliament, with things as they are, have no voice effective in moulding the destinies of the nation. Again, there are thousands of persons interested in special subjects of legislation apart from the more or less well-defined issues separating Grit and Tory ; but those persons are perfectly well aware that, as things are, a vote given for any other than the regular party candidate is utterly wasted, since nobody refusing to ally himself with one or the other great political party has any chance of gaining a seat in the House of Commons. The votes, then, of a certain number of Liberal electors are not wasted in one sense since, according to the majority system which prevails, they do succeed in returning a certain number of members to serve in the Commons ; but their votes are really wasted in this sense, that these members, being in the minority in the Commons, have no power whatever to give effect to the wishes of their constituents One of the absurdities of the present system is perhaps best illustrated by an example. Let us suppose that ten candidates seek the suffrages of a constituency or pocket borough which has fifty voters ; every candidate except one would receive five votes, let us suppose, but one would receive six votes ; he would, therefore, be elected to represent the borough, that is to say, he represents really six voters, while forty-four are left out in the cold wholly unrepresented. This, of course, is an extreme case, but it shows as well as any other the state of affairs existing under our present system in which there is hardly any provision for the representation of minorities. Even the feeble attempt made by Mr. Mowat for minority representation in Toronto has been the subject of unending ridicule and unjust accusation. But really the Premier of Ontario, by preventing voters from marking a ballot for more than two of the three candidates for the Local Legislature has done no more than secure representation for the large Reform minority in the City of Toronto, which otherwise would be left without a voice in the conduct of public affairs. Mr. Hare's scheme is emphatic in providing that every elector shall have no more votes than one, because Parliament could not become what he wishes it to become, " the mirror of the nation," unless the voting power of every elector were equal. Under the present *régime* a man may vote in every constituency in which he has a property qualification. A radical difference between Mr. Hare's plan of voting and that in vogue is that, by an elaborate system which he claims, however, to be quite workable, a voter should have permission, if the candidates in his own constituency did not suit him, to vote for candidates according to his choice in another constituency. Candidates, therefore, of a kind to poll votes from constituencies in different parts of the realm, and who could not be correctly described as candidates for any particular constituency, might be classed as "all England" candidates. It is well-known that under our present system a candidate often receives an enormous plurality over an opponent less distinguished. Mr. Hare's idea is that a quota of votes necessary to secure the election of a member should be established, and that no candidate should receive more than the required number. It would be objected at once to this that the voter, not having the omniscience of Providence, cannot know whether the candidate of his choice will or will not receive the quota, but Mr. Hare meets this objection by providing a form of conditional ballot by which the voter records first his preference for his candidate and then directs that "in the event of such candidate being already elected, or not obtaining the quota," the vote should go to a second or third or fourth candidate of his choice in that constituency or in "all England," as the case may be. It is obvious, then, that if the proposed system were worked out to its logical conclusion every member of Parliament would represent an equal number of voters, and that no votes would have been thrown away, since, in the case of candidates either elected or who have failed to receive the required quota, the elector's ballot would be placed to the credit of another eligible candidate. It is claimed by those who favour this plan of representation that the House of Commons would then really be a representative assembly and an assembly of peers in the sense that every constituent member would represent an equal voting power. Of course, the enemies of Mr. Hare's idea claim that the House of Commons, by the adoption of this system of electing its members, would become little better than an assembly of men for ventilating eccentric and crotchety notions, an objection met, in a sort of way, by the counter-statement that the people who have no crotchety notions have it in their power to secure representation as well as the eccentric voters have. It is claimed by the advocates of the system that more public interest would be felt in the constituencies if it were possible to elect parliamentary and municipal representatives on the basis proposed; that voters would study by degrees questions of political economy and statecraft; that they would eagerly scan the list of candidates; and that bribery and corruption would gradually, but withal speedily, become unknown, because the temptation to bribe and to be bribed would be removed. It is provided that with the exception of a registration fee all expenses of election should be borne by the State, and since no candidate could receive more than the quota of votes, bribers would not be anxious to spend money in getting ballots marked in all likelihood for men other than the one in whose supposed interest the bribery was perpetrated. Mr. Hare's plan provides for territorial designations as at present, if that be preferred, so that an "all England" candidate receiving votes from every part of the kingdom would be designated as a member for that place in which he would have received a majority of his votes; this would obviate the difficulty of filling vacancies caused by death or resignation, and would seem to render the retaining of territorial designations necessary; for otherwise, if members were elected to the House of Commons without territorial designation, how would it be possible to issue a writ for an unnamed constituency! One writer says naively enough, " perhaps rather an Irish way of getting over the difficulty connected with filling up those accidental vacancies which occur between general elections, is not to fill them up at all; and in order to avoid constituencies remaining long unrepresented, to have triennial, or even annual Parliaments." A further objection to Mr. Hare's scheme is that the "all England" character of the representation would tend to destroy local representation and would prevent members of Parliament from taking that interest in forwarding and expediting the process of private bills dealing with local works, which now members of the different constituencies so zealously evince. The counter-statement is that these services could just as well be performed by members under Mr. Hare's scheme as at present, and that the great centres of shipping and commercial activity would for their own interests combine to send a sufficient number of local members to conserve local interests. Other objectors find great fault with Mr. Hare's plan on the ground that the working of it would be incompatible with voting by ballot. The objection is not well founded. But it should be said here that Mr. Hare himself did not favour voting by ballot, which in one part of his book he speaks of as " a degradation." Further, he maintains that it is a fruitful source of bribery. People will say, " How can the ballot encourage bribery when the person to be bribed votes in secret, so that the briber cannot know whether or not the bribed voter stuck to his bargain?" One answer is not far to seek, namely, that payment of bribes could be, and often has been, conditional upon the success of the candidate in whose interest the bribery is committed. The bribed voter would then have a guilty interest in sticking to his bargain, since he would not get the bribe unless his candidate were elected; and, on the other hand, the briber, if he were not elected, would at least have the satisfaction of saving his money.

I cannot now do better than quote Mrs. Fawcett's words regarding what she calls "the only really formidable obstacle to the practical application of Mr. Hare's scheme" :—

"No completely satisfactory solution," says Mrs. Fawcett, "of this difficulty has as yet appeared ; it is, therefore, desirable that the advocates of the scheme should not disguise the existence of a serious obstacle in the way of its application. Making the difficulty known, and provoking thought and discussion on the subject, are the surest means of arriving at the wished-for solution. It has already been stated that no candidate shall be allowed to record more votes than are sufficient for his return, and that when a candidate has obtained his quota of votes, the voting or balloting paper on which his name is the first mentioned shall be reckoned to the score of the second named candidate. The difficulty we have alluded to is this : suppose the necessary quota of votes to be a thousand, and that two thousand voting papers are sent in with Mr. Gladstone's name first, the second name on one thousand of these voting papers being that of Mr. Jacob Bright, and second name on the other thousand being that of Sir Wilfred Lawson. In this case Mr. Bright and Sir Wilfred Lawson would occupy exactly similar positions : each is the second choice of a thousand electors, and yet it is possible that the one may obtain his full quota of a thousand votes and be consequently returned, while the other is not able to record a single vote. For if all the voting papers with Mr. Bright's name second are used for Mr. Gladstone's return, the remaining thousand will be reckoned to Sir Wilfred Lawson. It is of course highly improbable that such a result would ever actually take place, as all the papers would be deposited in a balloting urn, to be opened by a responsible authority, and the votes would be recorded in the order in which they were drawn out of the urn. The appearance of all the papers would be exactly similar, and there would consequently be no opportunity for the display of any unjust partiality in the opening of the papers. Still, the suspicion of the possibility of an election resulting in a manner approximating to the imaginary case just described, would do much to destroy the moral effect which might be produced by the adoption of Mr. Hare's scheme."

I shall be glad indeed if giving this quotation in this place will result in some suggestions being offered with a view to overcome this difficulty.

A good deal of space is devoted in Mr. Hare's work on Representatives to "Representative Government in Municipalities," but the subject is too large to be entered on within my limits : suffice it to say that his general principles remain unaltered. He is emphatic on the question of safeguarding the suffrage, and he very properly considers that in a Christian Kingdom voting day should be hallowed by prayer and supplication of the Almighty, as is the case on the day of the greatest function under the English Constitutional system, namely, the coronation of the monarch.

Our author has strong objections to making the line of demarcation too strongly defined between the electors of boroughs and of counties. While he is strongly imbued with ideas of class distinction, he is quite democratic in insisting that working men should have their own representatives in the House of Commons, pointing out that while wise and good men belonging to other spheres in life may devote their time and means to the amelioration of the condition of the labouring classes, they cannot know the true state of affairs as well as men who have experienced the different hardships, trials, and discomforts of the poor man's lot. Mr. Hare indignantly puts aside a theory advanced by certain vulgar and insolent political economists, to the effect that labouring men would be apt to send to the House representatives so uncouth and boorish that the refined members of the House would shrink from contact with them, and he states what is true enough, that real gentlemen would never think of countenancing so base a doctrine.

A very interesting part of this book is that which treats of the geographical, local, and corporate divisions of electors ; but no abridgment, be it ever so carefully condensed, can do justice to this and other portions of the Treatise, as the author goes very much into detail, apparently forgetting nothing. His book contains all the forms, schedules, lists, etc., necessary to make it a complete hand-book of the subject. One thing very pleasing in the whole work is its Christian tone, and this in a manly, unaffected, downright sort of way, wholly removed from sanctimonious hypocrisy and cant, and broad enough to be accepted by Christians of every creed. In this he does no more than follow the illustrious publicist and statesman Edmund Burke, whom he frequently quotes, and with whom he entirely agrees in laying down the fundamental principle that all authority is of God, and that princes and peoples exercise it only as His vicegerents. In fact there has been no great statesman—no man of the highest order of merit in anything—without religion. This was true even before the Christian dispensation, and Cicero and Plato were no less emphatic in recognizing the authority of Heaven according to their lights, than are Mr. Gladstone and the greatest moderns in Church and State in bowing submissively to the authority of the true GOD. The infidel, the atheist, and the agnostic cannot, because of the fatal defect in them, be men of the highest power; and when they occasionally evince greatness it is because they are not able, with all their malice, to escape from the Christian influences which surrounded their earlier and better years. Therefore, we must most heartily endorse Mr. Hare's proposition as to individual responsibility in the State : " a soul," says he, " is not a corporate thing. There is no corporate conscience."

In common with the best minds in the United Kingdom and on the continent our author is opposed to the American system of paying legislators, claiming that this is to degrade politics and, what is still worse, patriotism, to the level of a mere hunt after dollars. This subject, or rather this part of the subject, is one on which there is room for much argument pro and con. Naturally in such a system as Mr. Hare's there would be great need of defining the duties and powers of returning officers, and he has not failed to attend to this with a patience and fullness of detail that must commend his work to the admiration of every student and lover of order and system, even though he may not be able to see "eye to eye " with our author on many points brought up and dealt with. The same remark applies to the very technical portion of the book dealing with the duties of registrars, which, from Mr. Hare's point of view, leaves nothing to be desired as regards fullness and boldness of statement ; for one of our author's most admirable traits is that he does not needlessly beat about the bush, but goes straight to the mark with simple directness and conscious strength. Another notable feature in the work is the excellent power of discrimination shewn by the author in making quotation from the works of men of light and leading, such as Guizot, Edmund Burke, Calhoun, Passow, and others. It may not be amiss in this connection to say a word or two about the excellence of his own diction ;—he has a style well suited to the exigencies of historical and political essay writing, a style remarkably clear and free, never heavy or ponderous, but also never light or frivolous. It is grave without being severe, and dignified without being bombastic : always interesting—a matter difficult of attainment when treating of a subject regarded by most people as dry and uninviting—he has a happy faculty of blending information with philosophical reflection and of clothing his facts with language not unworthy of the diction of historical romance. Perhaps one cannot take a better specimen of his style than his description of London :—

" Of what," he asks, " does the Metropolis consist? It contains the abode of the sovereign, and of the regal house and household, and of all who compose the court and council of the Queen. It contains the mansions of an ancient and powerful nobility, and their numerous connexions and dependents. In it are all the chief military and civil departments of the army, the navy, the ordnance, and the control of their vast equipments ; the public treasury, the mint, and the immense offices which are concerned with the receipt of the revenues of the kingdom from foreign and inland trade, and all the subjects of taxation, and for the appropriation and liquidation of the principal and interest of a public debt equal in amount to the value of the fee simple of the dominions of some not insignificant monarchs,—and with the collection and audit of the public accounts of the empire. In the metropolis are the chief stewardships of the great estates of the Crown and its palatinates.

In it reside all the functionaries connected with the Imperial Parliament,—the secretaries, councils, and officers, engaged in communication between the Government and its dependencies,—the Canadas, Australasia, Africa, and the Indies,—and with foreign nations. In it are the immense establishments of the General Post Office, the great triumph of civilization, —sowing daily and hourly, with its thousand hands, the seeds of public and private intelligence gathered from every part of the habitable globe. In the Metropolis are the seats of the Courts of Equity and Law, and to it are brought all appeals in the last resort, from every territory and colony. Here reside the Bar, and the other professors of legal science concerned in the supreme administration of justice, and in the settlement and transfer of most of the great properties in the kingdom. In this detail is comprehended but a few of the multitude of conditions and occupations engaged in the affairs of the Empire. There are classes almost beyond the possibility of recapitulation,—merchants, shipowners, brokers, manufacturers of an infinite variety of fabrics,—traders, capitalists composed of companies and individuals, having ramifications of business with every port, inland town, market, and village. Here are associations, academies, and museums, for the promotion of learning and science in all their developments. Ireland sends its brilliant imagination and its romantic bravery ; Scotland its keen intellect and its untiring perseverance. The metropolis attracts to itself much that the kingdom produces of high talent or superior energy, it gathers together the diversities of gifts with which nature endows her most favoured sons. Here the learning of Johnson, the erudition and wisdom of Burke, the genius of Reynolds, of Lawrence, of Flaxman, and Chantrey, found their home. Here the eloquence of Erskine, of Copley, and of Brougham, had their appropriate theatre. . . . From the metropolis flows that comprehensive literature, the seemingly ever-increasing and inexhaustible stores of which are daily poured forth in article and volume, to feed and guide the realm of thought.

Foreigners should behold in the representation of this mighty community a condensed picture of the greatness of our country, and be compelled to recognize in it a triumphant display of the dignity and virtue of its institutions."

These words of Mr. Hare, and not least his closing allusion to metropolitan representation, should stimulate us all in carrying on the great work of improving our system of electing parliamentary and municipal representatives, looking upon it as a veritable "labour of love," because a labour of patriotism. For patriotism is based on love ; for which we have the authority of the great Passow, who, speaking of it, says,:—"It must rest like every other kind of love on something unutterable and incomprehensible."

THE DANISH ELECTORAL LAW OF 1855.

By the late Lord Lytton, then Mr. Lytton, Secretary of Legation. 1863.

COPENHAGEN, July 1, 1863.

With the details of Mr. Hare's electoral theory the purpose of this report is not immediately concerned. That purpose is merely to make intelligible the main features of the Electoral Law established in Denmark in the year 1855 for the election of Representatives to the Rigsraad.

To do this, however, the speediest and simplest means will be to take Mr. Hare's scheme as a point of comparison and reference. It will, therefore, be necessary to state what is the substance of this scheme. I will endeavour to do so as briefly as I can.

It will then be possible to contrast this scheme, in its chief characteristics, with that which is now law in Denmark, and which I propose to describe, pointing out to what extent the two systems coincide and in what respect they differ. Rightly to appreciate either the one or the other, it is necessary to bear in mind the ends which, in both cases, it has been sought to attain, and the reasons for which these ends have, in each case, appeared desirable. I must, therefore, ask permission to refer in passing to this important part of the subject. I shall do so as rapidly as is compatible with the claim of such a subject to be seriously considered. It will also be necessary, in referring to the Electoral Law of 1855, to point out the peculiar circumstances which, unfortunately, by limiting the application of that law, diminish its value as a practical example. Finally, I shall endeavor to record what, so far as I can yet judge, from such conversations as I have been able to hold with persons of intelligence and impartiality, interested in the subject, is the general impression in this country, after eight years' experience, of the practical effects of the electoral system devised by Mr. Andrae, and how far the result of it may be considered as having satisfied the intentions of the author.

I. Notwithstanding the length of time during which Representative Government has existed under various forms, it is not surprising that the majority of questions concerning government by representation should still be open to debate ; for the conclusion to be formed upon any question of this kind must always be in relation to circumstances peculiar to the country in respect of which the question has to be solved. But in regard to the fundamental principle upon which all government by representation is based, and to the complete realization of which every form of Representative Government must approximate, in a greater or less degree according as the development of it is favoured or impeded by local circumstances, there would seem to be no reasonable ground for difference of opinion. It has been admitted on all sides that the completest form of Representative Government must be that in which the greatest number of interests and opinions are completely represented ; that form of government, in short, which most nearly approximates to the government of the whole by the whole. But by those who have arrived at the conclusions which have dictated, in the one case Mr. Hare's electoral scheme, in the other Mr. Andrae's electoral law, it is argued that such a result is incompatible with any system of representation which tends to assume the part as tantamount to the whole ; in other words, to confound the majority with the people.

If, it is argued, the representatives of the majority be suffered by a political fiction to represent more than the majority, not only an arithmetical misstatement, but also a great political injustice, takes place. For the minority is then not merely unrepresented, but it is actually misrepresented. It is compulsorily incorporated into the majority ; and this forced fellowship is, to use the words of Mr. Burke, "conquest and not compact." If it were possible to suppose (what is never the case) that the whole of a country were, indeed, divided into only two sections of opinion, of which one was more numerous than the other in the proportion of three to two, the minority in that case, adequately represented, would stand in the representation at a proportion of two to three ; but if it should occur, as it naturally would occur without some provision to the contrary, that the majority in each constituency were to dispose of the entire representation of that constituency to a member of the more numerous class, instead of there being in the Legislature two of the less numerous to every three of the more numerous sect, the minority would, in fact, have no means of meeting their adversaries in the Legislative Body at all. "They are," says Mr. Hare, "previously cut off in detail ; " and in qualifying such a result, he cites the authority of M. Guizot, "Si la minorité est d'avance hors de combat il y a oppression."

But the evil, it is further argued, does not stop here. For all customary majorities are, indeed, only an agglomeration of minorities, each of which, rather than remain altogether unrepresented, has preferred to secure a sort of partial and collateral representation as part of an aggregate, which coheres only, perhaps, upon a single and often secondary point. The majority is thus only a majority of a majority, "who may be," says Mr. Mill, "and often are, a minority of the whole." "Any Minority," he adds, "left out, either purposely or by the play of the machinery, gives the power, not to a majority, but to a minority in some other part of the scale."

And, although this inequality is, no doubt balanced to a great extent, in a system of representation such as that which obtains in England, by the fact that opinions, predominating in different places, find rough equivalents for the minority with which they are swept away in one place by the majority they secure in another; yet, if the suffrage were to be extended much further (and it cannot be considered as final at a point which leaves out of direct representation the most numerous class in the country), the danger which, under the present system, must then arise of government by a single (and that, on the whole, the least educated) class has long been apparent to statesmen of all parties. At the same time it would be palpably unjust and humiliating to advocate the permanent exclusion of this numerous and important class from all direct representation, on no better grounds than those which involve the admission that the whole representative machinery of the country is constructed upon a principle so erroneous that the motive power cannot be augmented without throwing the entire machine out of gear.

To these considerations is added that of the deterioration of political character to which voters may be exposed by any sort of compulsion, to select as their representatives, not those men whom they regard as the most enlightened and most honest exponents of their opinions or interests, but those who seem most likely to conciliate the local, and often ignoble, animosities by which majorities themselves are divided.

II. The above summary, although very imperfect, is sufficient to indicate the principal motives which, both in this country and in England, have suggested to eminent statesmen the necessity of devising, if possible, some modification of the Electoral system, calculated to secure a more adequate representation to the interests of minorities.

I will now enumerate, within the narrowest possible limits, the most prominent of those provisions by which Mr. Hare proposes to obviate a deficit, the existence of which is hardly disputed, and by which, in the Electoral Law of 1855, for the nomination of Representatives to the Supreme Council of Denmark, Mr. Andrae has sought to secure the same result, viz., the protection of minorities.

The essential character of the scheme proposed by Mr. Hare may be thus summed up :—

1. The number of votes to be divided by the number of members composing the legislative body. The quotient to form the electoral basis, that is to say, every candidate obtaining the quota of votes shall be returned.

2. No more than the quota strictly necessary for his return is to be counted in favour of any candidate. The surplusage of the votes given to any elected candidate is to be distributed in favour of other candidates, in conformity with the principle embodied in the following provisions :—

(a) The votes to be given locally ; but every elector to be entitled to vote for any candidate who may offer himself in any part of the country.

(b) Each elector to deliver a voting paper containing other names in addition to that which stands foremost in the order of his choice. His vote is to be counted for only one candidate. But if the candidate whose name stands first upon his list shall either fail to make up the quota, or shall have made it up without the assistance of his vote, the vote in question may then descend in the order of preference given to it by the elector to some other candidate who may stand more in need of it, and in whose favour it shall then count towards completing the necessary quota.

(c) The question which of the votes obtained by each candidate shall count for his own return, and which of them shall be released in favour of other candidates, shall be decided in such way as to secure the representation by the candidate in question of all those who would not otherwise be represented at all. The remaining votes, not needed for his return, to be disposed of by lot or otherwise.

(d) The voting papers to be conveyed to some central office and there counted; first votes being preferred to second votes, second to third and so on. The voting papers, after being verified, shall remain in public repositories accessible to all.

This is a very meagre exposition of Mr. Hare's scheme, which is as minute in its details as it is large in its scope.

It is, however, enough to serve the only purpose with which it is here alluded to. For the scheme of Mr. Hare is devised with a view to its adaptation to existing circumstances in England; and this report being only directly concerned with existing circumstances in Denmark, I may at once pass to the consideration of the law of 1855, merely noting by the way that, if the aims and aspirations of Mr. Hare and Mr. Mill be worth realizing, then the extent to which they have been realized by the law, and the general results of such experience of the working of the law as must have been acquired in Denmark during the course of eight years, are subjects well worthy of attention.

III. The constitutional history of Denmark, although comparatively short, is far from deficient in interesting phenomena. Nurseries of self-government were planted in this country in 1834 by Frederick VI., who then established Consultative States throughout the kingdom : so that when, after the revolutionary movement which convulsed Europe in 1848, it was deemed advisable to expand the basis of government in this country, the population was not wholly unprepared for increased participation in the management of public affairs. Those, indeed, who at that period were engaged in the work of political reconstruction appeared to have been disposed to give to the representative element a larger scope than was eventually accorded to it, and they justified their hesitation on the ground that the constituencies were, as yet, too inexperienced. An able writer, who has warmly engaged in the defence of Mr. Andrae's electoral system, has ridiculed this notion by pointing out that the greater the electioneering experience of the constituency (that is to say, the more *rusés* the electors) the more certainly must the majority (unless some provision exist to the contrary) succeed in crushing the minority, and monopolizing power. For if, as would have been the case under the system then contemplated, 65 members were to be chosen by 65,000 electors, no one elector being entitled to increase the value of his vote by voting for less than the full number of candidates, it is clear that the majority, consisting of 32,501 electors, would only have to hold firmly together, in order to carry the whole number of the 65 seats in accordance with their choice. And, in that case, no matter how prudently or sagaciously the minority, consisting of 32,499 electors, might exercise their franchise, those 32,499 electors would remain without any representative at all. How, then, should the real opinions of the electors be ascertained, in order that they may be represented in their just proportion? Suppose that of these 65,000 electors, a compact majority of 32,501 is opposed to various dispersed minorities, amounting altogether to 32,499. If the elections are distributed over 65 districts, it is possible that 32,064 of the majority might be found united in 64 districts against 31,936 of the minority. So that it would be only in the 65th district that the minority could make its voice heard. Nevertheless, the majority could only with strict justice claim 33 seats, and the remaining 32 should, in that case, it is clear, fall to the representation of various opinions, provided those opinions be not so dispersed as to be unable to come together in any place.

To attain this result, to secure the adequate representation of every tangible opinion and corporate interest, in such way, that, while the majority of the electors shall be able to name the majority of the Representatives, the minority of the electors shall be insured an equivalent minority in the representation, this is the great problem which, in 1855, Mr. Andrae undertook to solve.

Of all men in this country His Excellency was, in many respects, the most fitted by antecedent experience and natural qualifications to succeed in the difficult task which he thus spontaneously attempted.

Mr. Andrae is a man of original and speculative intellect, a keen investigator, a bold thinker, admitted by all his countrymen to be the first mathematician in Denmark, and, from his position as Minister of Finance, experienced in the art of bringing the fundamental principles of abstract calculation practically to bear upon complicated facts.

The scope of his experiment, however, was painfully limited by conditions over which he had no control ; and the law of which he is the sole author forms only the incidental part of an institution shaped rather by the force of uncongenial circumstances than by the deliberate option of the ostensible founders of it.

According to the Census of 1860 the entire population of the Kingdom and Duchies amounted to 2,604,024, so that it was only for the direct election of 30 members out of a population of upwards of 2,000,000 to an Assembly of 80 members, that the electoral system of Mr. Andrae was empowered to provide.[1] Holstein and Lauenburgh have always refused to send members to the Rigsraad. For these Duchies the Constitution of 1855 is suspended ; and, therefore, 20 members must be deducted from the total of 80 nominally composing the Rigsraad, and 8 members from the 30 originally contemplated as the quota of direct representation in the Rigsraad ; consequently, it is only the choice of 45 out of 60 members that is practically affected by the electoral system of Mr. Andrae.

This, no doubt, diminishes the value to be attached to the success or failure of the system as an example. It is somewhat like an experiment in a pond upon principles of navigation which, if good for anything, must be good for the ocean. Nevertheless, it is an example ; and, in questions of this sort, an example of any kind is most valuable. Eight years' practical experience of the working of an electoral system devised for the realization of an important principle applicable to all representative institutions is, no matter how " cabined, cribbed, confined " be the sphere of that experience, a great and noteworthy addition to the knowledge of mankind.

V. Within the comparatively narrow limits to which this report must be confined, it does not appear advisable to add any extracts to those already given from the Danish Electoral Law of 1855. Those extracts, indeed, comprise the essence of the law. The subject under consideration is so suggestive and demands for its thorough comprehension an examination so various and minute, that I cannot possibly hope to do more on the present occasion than indicate ground for further and fuller inquiry. No extensive comment, however, is needed to distinguish the aim and character of the clause above cited.

I shall now endeavour to state precisely what these clauses are designed to prevent, and what they are designed to secure. It appears to me that the marrow of the whole matter is concentrated in Sections 22 and 23.

There are two ways in which local majorities may, if unrestrained by law, exercise their power in questions of representation, to the detriment no less of minorities than of themselves. They may do so both in the selection and in the election of candidates. They may virtually dictate the vote of the elector by indirectly circumscribing the freedom of his choice. By this means, indeed, apparent unanimity may be obtained ; but the greater the unanimity the greater the mischief, if it be only a unanimous submission to " Hobson's choice this or none :" and when this is the case, it may be truly said of the majorities themselves,

[1] The indirect election of members to the Rigsraad by the local legislative bodies is, however, conducted upon the principle, and in conformity with the stipulations, of Mr. Andrae's Electoral law. This should be borne in mind.

"*dominationis in alios servitium suum mercedem dant*,"—"they are content to pay so great a price as their own servitude to purchase the domination over others."[1] For in order to secure unanimity in the choice of the majority, it is previously necessary for the majority itself to abdicate individual action on the part of its own members. Men are more likely to admit unanimity in their passions and prejudices than in their sober judgments: and the candidate thus selected may perhaps represent only a selfish compromise between narrow interests and petty animosities. When this happens majorities, indeed, may show their power by converting a bad candidate into a worse representative, but in doing so they will have also shown that their power is incompatible with their freedom; and that may be said of them which Socrates is supposed to say to Polus in the Gorgias, when speaking of other tyrannies, "They do not do what they wish, although they do what they please."

But, on the other hand, it is undoubtedly true that all political action necessitates a compromise between opinions in matters of minor import. The absence of this compromise is anarchy It is only when the compromise is compulsory, instead of spontaneous, that it can be called tyranny. For the foundation of all society is confidence in others. All human creeds must originate in faith of some sort, and men can do nothing without taking something on trust. In the public business of life, individual action will always be guided and controlled by collective opinion; and, practically, the opinion of the many is controlled and guided by the wisdom of the few. Every man has a right to think and choose for himself; but all men are not equally able to think and choose well, or equally disposed to think and choose at all; so that, as long as there exists in the world that discreet deference to the judgment and that wholesome confidence in the character of others without which political combination is impossible, no conceivable electoral system will prevent the choice of constituencies from being greatly influenced by the bias of those local notables who, by personal capacity or social position, are fitted to guide the conduct of their neighbours. The object of Mr. Andrae's Electoral Law is, not to annihilate this controlling power, but, on the contrary, to give the amplest scope to its natural operation, by relieving it from the crippling circumscription of arbitrary conditions. Thus, the constituent who demurs to "Hobson's choice," is ensured every reasonable facility for bringing forward the candidate he prefers without pecuniary sacrifice and without incurring that social martyrdom which, in such cases, sometimes seems to justify an assertion of Machiavelli's (whose experience of uncontrolled and triumphant majorities was certainly as great as it was bitter) that, "he who deviates from the common course and endeavors to act as duty dictates, insures his own destruction."

By enlarging the scope of the voter's choice, moreover, you elevate the quality of his judgment. When he is free to choose whom he will, not constrained to choose merely whom he must, it is probable that if he gives the preference to a person from his own immediate neighborhood, the person thus preferred will be, not simply the slavish nominee of a perhaps insignificant but petulant party, but a man whom the voter regards with affectionate confidence and respect. Surely it would be unwise to extinguish (even were it possible) those kindly influences which infuse into the public life and spirit of a nation the enthusiasm of local affections, whether they be embodied in a respect for noble names and illustrious houses, or in the grateful recognition of those good deeds which not seldom associate a particular family with a particular neighbourhood. But is it not rather the local demagogues than the real local *aristoi* who would have anything to fear from the most extended competition with intelligence and virtue? In any case, if the voter, by confining his vote to a single candidate, be exposed to the risk of diminishing its value without thereby benefiting the object of his special preference, it is to be presumed that he will extend the scope of his judgment and his sympathies, and provide for those contemplated contingencies in which his countrymen elsewhere may benefit by the exercise of his franchise. In doing so he will have to look further and think more carefully. It is probable that he will select the other objects

---

[1] Cowley, "Essay on Liberty."

of his choice from men of eminence and distinction ; because those who are neither eminent nor distinguished cannot then be arbitrarily thrust upon his notice. The voter who does this will elevate his own character and class ; and if the whole class of voters do this, the whole class of candidates will be improved.

In the next place, it is no doubt intended by the clauses above mentioned to withdraw from the voter every reasonable excuse for disregarding and neglecting the duty of exercising his franchise, as well as to provide for him every reasonable inducement to perform that duty with the most serious reflection, and to the fullest possible extent.

A further consideration here suggests itself in regard to the relations to be maintained between constituencies and Representatives. Representation has so strong a tendency to dwindle into delegation, that it can only be restrained from doing so, either by great moderation on the part of the masses, or else by great elevation of character on the part of the Representative class. These two restraining forces react, and depend upon each other. In proportion as the character of the Representative class is high-minded and scrupulous, it is presumed that the confidence reposed in it by the constituencies will be great ; but, in proportion as the freedom of the Representative is cramped and his responsibility impoverished by the exaction, on the part of his constituents, of exorbitant and vexatious pledges, the general character of the Representative class will be low and subservient, and the confidence it can command will be consequently small. In short, in this, as in all other matters of exchange, the quality and amount of the demand will regulate the quality and amount of the supply. When pledges are recklessly exacted, adventurers will always be found recklessly ready to accept them ; when the character of the compact is mistrustful, the character of those that undertake it will be untrustworthy. In America, the House of Representatives has long been, virtually, a House of Delegates, wherein the fate of almost every measure is decided before the opening of the Session, and the majority of speeches made are addressed not to the conviction of the House, but to the passions and prejudices of the constituencies who have sent its members to sit in political fetters. The solemn responsibility of legislation is thus remitted by those on whose part it is a public duty to those on whose part it is only a mischievous assumption. For the nation can impeach its representatives by the voice of its constituencies ; but to whom are the constituencies practically accountable ? The danger of this is in the fact that the intellect and conscience of the nation are not adequately represented in the national public life ; and the verdict of this intellect and conscience, which must ultimately be heard, not having been provided with any constitutional expression, can only find utterance in revolution. The Long Parliament could not have been swept away by a gesture of Cromwell's if the head and heart of the nation had been in that body. The temple which enshrines a constitution cannot long escape from destruction when it begins to be muttered about outside the walls of it, that "the gods are departing." In England the high moral and intellectual standard of the representative class is powerfully promoted and sustained by the unremunerated character of its service ; but under those continental systems of representation in which the representative body is paid by the State, the danger alluded to is not insignificant. Not only, however, is it the object, but I am satisfied that it is also the result of Mr. Andrae's electoral system (so far as that system has been applied) to facilitate the introduction into the National Legislature of the greatest amount of intelligence and high character, and to hinder the entrance of a great amount of ignorance and passion. I am disposed to think that, on the whole, this system in its practical result attains many of the objects of an educational franchise, without invalidating the salutary influence of property.

Two other results are involved in the arrangements of this law as concerning the question of personal canvass. It is undoubtedly to be desired that every facility should exist for free personal intercourse and interchange of opinion between candidates and voters, and it is not to be desired that the candidate should be to the voter not a man, but merely a name, an abstraction. Whether, however, it be not possible to provide for this reasonable and necessary intercourse without exposing it to the possible degradation of degenerating into one of barter and beggary, is a question worthy of consideration.

A writer, who was not the least distinguished of Milton's contemporaries, has exclaimed, "To what pitiful baseness did the noblest Romans submit themselves for the obtaining of a Praetorship, or the Consular dignity! They put on the habit of supplicants and ran about on foot, and in dirt, through all the tribes to beg voices; they flattered the poorest artizans, and carried a nomenclator with them to whisper in their ear every man's name, lest they should mistake it in their salutation; they shook the hand and kissed the cheek of every popular tradesman; they stood all day at every market in the public places to show and ingratiate themselves to the rout; they employed all their friends to solicit for them; they kept open tables in every street; they distributed wine, and bread, and money even to the vilest of the people. "En Romanos rerum dominos!—Behold the masters of the world begging from door to door!"

Might not these words receive with justice a more modern application?

Whether, however, the personal canvass be a good thing or a bad thing, according to this Electoral Law of Mr. Andrae it is quite out of the question.

And with the personal canvass also disappears a very influential personage intimately connected therewith, viz., the electioneering agent. How far the complete effacement from the electoral *dramatis personae* of this important but costly character is a result to be admired or condemned, involves a question which will be best answered by those who have had personal experience of the part he plays, both in connection with the pockets of candidates and the morals of voters.

Finally, it appears to be the intention of this law to increase the sense of individual responsibility in matters of public trust; to place the conscience of each voter in his own keeping and to take it out of the hands of those careless investors of other men's moral capital who flourish in all large communities and who appear to consider themselves a sort of joint-stock company for conscience, with limited liability. Moreover, it may be said that this law is, in its tendency, a civilizing law—for civilization is the parent of variety in opinions; and it is the intention of this law to provide, not only the amplest expression for all varieties of opinion, but also to utilize to the utmost all manner of ways and means provided by the kindly providence of civilization for the formation of these wholesome varieties.

That these intentions are wise and good will hardly be denied. The only practical questions that remain are, first, whether these intentions are fully realized by the mechanical operation of the law.

* * * * * *

Other and perhaps yet more important considerations, however, are involved in the questions of what are its political results in this country, and how far it may be applicable to other European communities.

These considerations are hardly within the province to which the present remarks must be confined; for they raise an infinite number of collateral and secondary inquiries, which cannot be followed out without bringing the inquirer into a disquisition upon the necessity and value of government by party, as well as upon the nature of the various answers which may be returned to the paramount practical question of, "How is the Queen's Government to be carried on?"

I may mention, however, that on lately referring to some of these topics in conversation with a Danish gentleman well acquainted with the political life of this country, I was assured that, in the discussion and settlement of great public questions by the Supreme Council of the realm, no disinclination is found to exist upon the part of representative minorities to combine and concur in the formation of a judicial majority for the decision of what is expedient.

I may also mention that I have been assured by Mr. Andrae that, in his opinion, the general standard of representative character supplied by this law is the best and highest in the country ; and that, although he does not consider that a sufficient time has elapsed whereby to test the effects of the law upon the constituencies themselves, he is nevertheless of opinion that, under its operation, the character of the voter as a class has improved and is improving. I have every reason to believe, moreover, that bribery is almost unknown to the constituencies for the Rigsraad. It appears to me, however, that the permission contained in clause 18 of Mr. Andrae's Law, and which equally appears in Mr. Hare's scheme—to fill up the voting paper in private—might, under very conceivable circumstances, facilitate intimidation.

A full and complete investigation into the character and operation of this law is a task which I should rejoice to see assumed by some person of known impartiality, capacity and experience. For, whatever may be the character or the consequence of the law, I venture to think that its existence is one of the most remarkable events in the history of representative institutions.

FAIR REPRESENTATION.

From a Speech, by Lord Sherbrooke 1867.

. . . There was nothing more worthy of the attention of statesmen in the new state of affairs than anything which would have the tendency to prevent that violent oscillation which they now witnessed. What happened in the United States? The minority of thousands might as well not exist at all. It is absolutely ignored. Was their country (England) in like manner to be formed into two hostile camps, debarred from each other in two solid and compact bodies? Or were they to have that shading-off of opinion, that modulation of extremes, and mellowing and ripening of right principles, which are among the surest characteristics of a free country, the true secrets of political dynamics, and the true preservatives of a great nation? He said, then, that what he proposed to the House was in itself just, equal, and fair, founded on no undue and unfair attempt to give a minority an advantage they were not entitled to exercise, and that it was peculiarly applicable to the state of things on which they were entering.

MISREPRESENTATION.

From the Fortnightly Review, Vol. VIII., 1870.

" It is evident that it is at least as important that a constituency be not misrepresented as that it be represented. A voter's *no*, therefore, is as important an element in determining his preference as his *yes*. Hitherto we have entirely ignored this negative element ; and no doubt our habitual indifference to principles will prompt us still to ignore it, and to be content with our old one-sided system, unless it be shown that serious evils must inevitably result from such a course. I propose to show that one of the most excellent reforms about to be made in our electoral procedure—that of keeping the progress of a contest secret during the polling will lead to the introduction of one of the worst features of American politics, unless special means of prevention be adopted.

" It is obvious that in all countries in which political feeling runs high, and different parties divide the suffrages of electors, there will always be a demand for organisation within each party for the purpose of advancing its interests. To a certain extent such organisations are necessary and beneficial ; but there is a point at which their activity becomes little else than a mischievous nuisance. The action of a committee is often necessary to promote unity, and to secure the victory even of the strongest party, and the election of the best or most favourite candidate. But when such functions become the sport of mere " wire-pullers" and " caucuses," and the suffrages of parties are demanded for inferior candidates, nominated for venal motives by venal men, and electors have no choice but to vote for such candidates or to see their party beaten altogether, then the organisation sinks from its original design and use, and becomes an intolerable evil. To such a height has this evil attained in the United States that "there is now absolutely no choice of representatives, strictly speaking, by the people. Nominations are either bought or obtained by personal or party influence. The whippers-in have full control, and intelligent public opinion has little to do with the result."

POLITICAL PARTIES AND POLITICIANS.

From " The American System of Government," by Ezra C. Seaman, 1870.

It is idle to talk about principles, without proper men, and men of principle, to carry them into effect. It is very unwise and dangerous, to elect selfish and corrupt men, to carry into effect good principles, and wise policies. The conclusion is obvious—that there is no good reason for maintaining permanent party organizations in our country, or in any country ; and that there is no propriety in doing so. All political parties should be temporary and changeable—based upon the questions and issues of the day, and upon the opinions of voters of the relative merits of the candidates for President of the United States, for Governors of States, and other high offices.

So far as political parties and the lines of division between them are produced by differences of opinion in relation to the principles, policies, and measures of government, they will be as permanent as the causes and issues upon which they are based ; and they should be no more so, and should pass away with the causes which produced them. Parties should not be based upon mere abstract principles, which have no direct practical bearing ; nor upon dead issues which have passed by, and are of no practical importance ; nor should they be sustained and made permanent by organization, party machinery, and party creeds, to promote the election and aggrandizement of party leaders,—regardless of the public good.

The mode of representation and the system of elections in the United States, are both very imperfect and defective. The former is defective, in giving the entire representation and power to majorities, and practically disfranchising minorities,—by allowing them no representation, and no voice in the government : and the latter is defective in omitting to provide any mode of selecting candidates for office, to be voted for by the electors at popular elections.

In theory, we have a popular government, in which the masses of the people select their own rulers ; but owing to the defects of its organization, system of representation and mode of electing officers, the practice is very different from the theory.

Officers to be elected by the people are not selected by any considerable number of the voters, but by the dominant faction or clique of the dominant party—by whom and their associates in nominating conventions, they are presented to the people, to be by them confirmed by formal vote—the masses of the voters having no choice, except between two sets of nominees, presented for their suffrages, by partisan conventions. In nine cases out of ten, a mere choice of evils is presented to a large portion of the voters,—the candidates of neither party being such as they would have preferred.

Though nominally a popular government, controlled by the voice of the people, practically our government has degenerated into an oligarchy of the leaders of the dominant clique or coterie, of the dominant party of the day ; and the people act a very subordinate part, even in the election of their own representatives—a majority of them merely ratifying and confirming the nominations made, and supporting the measures and policies prepared by the party oligarchy—while the minority look on and have no substantial voice or participation in the government. Party organizations and the party character of our government, have been in the process of development gradually, during a period of nearly fifty years—ever since the inauguration of the State and national, as well as local nominating conventions, the adoption of party creeds and platforms, and the election of Presidential electors by the people—by general ticket.

The theory of the government is, that it is a representative government—in which all the adult male citizens, (with few exceptions) are equally and fairly represented, by men of their own choice, and through their representatives have a voice in legislation, and in the government of the country—making it in some measure a self-government ; a government of the whole people, by the people themselves. But in practice, under our defective electoral system, the majority of the voters in each electoral district elect all the representatives, and the minority none—whereby the minority are unrepresented, and practically disfranchised, have no voice in the government, and no one to represent, advocate or defend, their special interests and rights.

It is the characteristic of zealous political partisans, to look at every measure presented, and at every political or national question, from the standpoint of their party ; and to see it and examine it on one side only. With the eyes of the understanding nearly closed, they listen to the arguments of their opponents—not for the purpose of learning what truth they may contain, and what weight should be given to them ; but for the purpose of finding defects in them, or what they may distort and make appear erroneous—in order to destroy their influence. Being accustomed to hear the merits of their own party extolled, and its principles, policies, and measures held up to view as tending to promote the best interests of the country, and the general welfare of the people ; and accustomed to hear the opposite party and its principles and policies reviled—as tending to evil, and to evil only,- political partisans usually take one-sided and partial views of all questions and measures of a political or public nature. They seldom view a question in all its aspects and bearings ; and hence they get only partial and imperfect views, and in their reasoning upon them, they necessarily arrive at conclusions more or less erroneous. They often become imbued with enthusiasm in relation to the merits of their own party and party creed, and inclined to attribute all the prosperity of the country to its principles, policies, and measures. They can see no good in the other party—either in its principles or its policies,- its leaders or its measures.

The first object of many partisan legislators, is to promote the success and secure the ascendency of their party. To promote the general good and welfare of the country, and of the whole people, is with them a secondary consideration—being regarded by them rather as a means of promoting the success of their party, than as the proposed end and object of their legislative action.

The tendency of party spirit is to tolerate no man as a leader, who is not blind to the faults of his own party, and to the merits of his opponents. Men of sound understandings, who look at both sides of political questions and judge fairly and impartially of their merits, soon lose the confidence of violent partisans, are distrusted by them, and no longer recognized as leaders. A fair-minded man, who looks at both sides of political questions, and considers them carefully, with a view to judge of their merits, is unfitted for a party leader, and must stand in the back-ground. Partisan enthusiasts, and men who have one blind side, and are accustomed to see and appreciate the merits of one side only, must occupy the front seats.

The violent party spirit and party organizations of the present day, tend to make sharp, one-sided, and narrow-minded men, and cunning politicians—but not statesmen. They tend to discourage freedom of inquiry, freedom of thought, and freedom of speech upon political questions ; to destroy freedom of action ; and to unfit men to become statesmen, however long they may be in public life. Party spirit is, in fact, so wedded to temporary partisan expedients, that it can hardly tolerate sound statesmanship.

The power of party organizations and the intensity and violence of party spirit, have greatly increased during the last fifty years.

Party organizations, such as we have in this country, exist in no other, and are not necessary in a well-organized government. They were invented long since the organization of our government, partly to supply the defects of our system of elections, and partly to promote the success of party, and party leaders (as is shown in the first chapter of this work) ; and they can be dispensed with when those defects are supplied by law. The principal evils of our system of government, grow out of these organizations, nominating conventions, and other party machinery, devised to stimulate party spirit, to secure success at elections— either by fair or foul means, and to control the destinies of the country.

By the caucus and convention system, everything is arranged in secret by a few leaders, without any public discussion in convention, of the resolutions presented, or of the merits or relative merits of the candidates named ; and when they come to vote, the silent vote is cast, without any reasons being assigned. Conventions come together simply to record the decisions of the leaders, when they are united ; and to determine by vote, which faction or section is the strongest, when they are divided.

Political partisans often justify themselves, and quiet their consciences, in practising deception and falsehood, and other corrupt means, to promote the success of their party, by alluding to the fact, that their opponents do likewise ; that to do so is sanctioned by custom, and necessary to success. Criminals of all grades reason in a very similar manner, to apologise to themselves, for their crimes.

The bad practices of each party tend to corrupt the other ; and unless some remedy can be devised, to correct the corrupt practices and evils which have grown up under our system of party organizations, nominating conventions and caucuses, and electing public officers, there is great danger of such widespread corruption and distrust of all public officers, and of legislation and the administration of law, that we shall sink into anarchy, and a chronic state of revolution and civil war—as Mexico has done.

Party organizations tend to foster party spirit, a spirit of exclusiveness and intolerance. By means of party creeds and platforms, adopted without debate or much consideration, to fan the flames of class interests, and the prejudices of race and party, and to catch votes, they tend to create and perpetuate artificial distinctions between parties, for mere party purposes. They furnish rules and tests of party faith, by which to determine the fidelity of the members, and to discipline or denounce as unfaithful, those that presume to think for themselves, contrary to the party creed.

Party organizations and machinery have become so complete, party spirit so intolerant, and party discipline so rigid and efficient, that if a party man, having any position or influence, presumes to express opinions differing from the creed or the policy of his party, the party leaders combine against him, charge him with deserting his friends and the principles of his party, and denounce him as a political heretic. Very few men have popularity and strength sufficient to withstand such attacks, and maintain their position. The result is, that most of the public officers of our country are the mere slaves of party and party leaders—without much freedom of action, or freedom of speech —being accustomed and required, to speak and act, in accordance with the creed and policy, and the supposed exigencies of their party ; and if they fail to do so, they are usually denounced as traitors.

What is the moral of all this, but that in American politics to-day, there is no place for middle men ? He who would achieve political success must ally himself with a party, abide by its fortunes, and endorse its policy, whether or not it commends itself to him. There can be no hope for promotion in any other line of action. The day for middle-men is past ; the field for those in this country or in England, who would win power without the sacrifice of independence, is closed. Henceforth, the successful men in our politics are to be the partisans who will stick at nothing which is avowed by the party to which they belong.

Party organizations and creeds, and party spirit, tend to magnify the importance of many questions of but little real consequence, and to encourage the formation of immaterial issues, in order to multiply the differences between parties,—to enable them to maintain party lines as distinctly as possible. They lead men to study the success of their party, and their own success connected with it, rather than the interests of the country ; to consider every question from a party standpoint ; and to regard principally, its bearing upon the future success of the party. In legislative bodies, they induce party leaders to oppose, as a matter of policy, the measures of their opponents,—even if good ; rather than lend their efforts to improve and perfect them—for fear they may inure the future success of their opponents.

Party organizations have become so strong, and their machinery so extensive, far-reaching and powerful, that they dictate interpretations of the constitution, the creeds and political faith of the people, and the leading measures and policies of the government ; and in a great measure control the action of the government. They have checked and restrained freedom of inquiry and freedom of thought, freedom of speech, and freedom of the press ; increased the intensity and violence of party spirit ; engendered political intolerance and tyranny ; and nearly destroyed all freedom and independence of official action.

The machinery and influence of party organizations, tend to form and mould the opinions of the people, in accordance with party creeds ; to form narrow-minded politicians ; and to prevent the development of enlarged views, and a high order of statesmanship—which can spring only from freedom of action, freedom of thought, and very mature deliberation. They are inconsistent with the formation of great statesmen, and noble-minded, self-sacrificing patriots. The great civil war, through which our country has passed, developed and formed some great commanders ; but very few statesmen have been produced in our country, during the last forty years. Under our advanced system of party organizations, and party discipline and intolerance, statesmanship is dying out.

By electing to office, through the agency of party organizations, and subjecting to the domination of such organizations, and to the temptations to bribery and corruption, great numbers of politicians of pliable consciences and easy virtue, and many of bad or doubtful character, the legislation of the country, all the departments of the national, State, and city governments, and nearly all branches of the public service, have been more or less corrupted. Even the judiciary have not always escaped the taint of party influences, and partisan prejudices and partialities ; nor even the suspicion of bribery, in some instances. The whole tendency of such a system is, to corrupt politicians and office-holders, and to demoralize the people. If the evil be not arrested, it will undermine and destroy the stability of our government.

It is very desirable, that our system of elections should be so amended and reconstructed, that party committees and nominating conventions, party machinery and political leagues and societies, may all be rendered unnecessary, and dispensed with as not consistent *with a free and unbiassed* exercise of the elective franchise; nor with the right of the people to choose their own rulers; nor with a fair and upright administration of the government. The people have more reason to repose confidence in responsible public officers, either elected or duly appointed, and acting publicly, under the sanction of an oath, than in irresponsible party committees and political societies, whose operations are carried on in secret, for party purposes.

POLITICAL CORRUPTION.

From the Canadian Monthly, Vol. II., 1872.

"Corruption grows by what it feeds upon. It will increase, and increase in an ever accelerating ratio, while the moral resistance will become continually weaker, till among us, as in other countries, bribery becomes a jest, and corruptionist a name hardly more odious than that of politician. The progress of electoral demoralization is as certain as the increasing volume and rapidity of the descending avalanche. We shall sink to the level of the States, and perhaps below it For corruption is deeper, more complete, and more hopeless in a small nation than in a great one . . Who doubts the unsatisfactory character of the present state of things? Who believes that the deliberations of a party cabinet have, for their paramount object, the welfare of the country, and not the retention of office? The Opposition orators and journals thunder indignantly against the questionable acts of the Government. . . Without entering into details, at once needless and disagreeable, we do not doubt the general fact to which these various accusations point. We do not doubt that the present Government of the Dominion subsists, like other governments of the same description, by means which are more or less corrupt. We do not doubt that, even in dealing with the greatest interests of the nation, even in dealing with such momentous undertakings as the Pacific Railway, it is influenced by a motive which renders its decisions more or less untrustworthy, and its action more or less injurious to national morality, as well as to the material prosperity of the nation.

" 'Then,' cry the opposition, 'the remedy is obvious. Vote for us. Turn out the Government; put us in power. Corruption will vanish, and a reign of purity will commence.' But is it so? The general system, and the mode in which the cabinet is formed—out of a special group of office-seekers—remaining the same, will a mere change of Ministers make much difference in the morality of the Government, or in its method of maintaining itself in place? . . When Parliament meets, or rather long before Parliament meets, will commence a political auction, at which the articles bid for will be the votes of the unattached members for the smaller provinces, and the bidders will be a 'corrupt' Government on one side, and a virtuous Opposition on the other. . . The bidding will be high, parties being so evenly balanced, and the stake, under the present circumstances, being so large; and the expenses, whatever they may be, will be defrayed by the public. . .

"We have great faith in the honourable intentions of the leaders of the Opposition; and we are at the same time perfectly convinced that, as soon as they became the heads of a party Government, struggling for its life against a hungry and vindictive enemy, nearly a match for it in force, their intentions would give way to the exigencies of their position, and that they would do first things for which they would be sorry, and then things of which they would be ashamed. At last shame itself would cease.

"Electoral corruption has its source in Parliamentary corruption, which affords inducements to candidates and Ministers to purchase seats; and the source of parliamentary corruption is the system of making the offices of State, with the patronage annexed to them, the prize of a perpetual conflict between two organized factions, euphemistically styled party government.

" This question has been more than once presented to our readers within the last half-year ; but we wish to keep it before their minds for a time, on account of its transcendent importance to the country, and because it is more likely to command attention while the memory of the elections, and the evil influences revealed by them, is fresh. Moreover, as we have said before, this is the accepted season ; soon the malady may be beyond control, and the last chance may be lost of saving the country from the gulf into which it is too manifestly sinking.

" Already the sinister forms of American corruption have made their appearance among us. Already some of the most unprincipled members of the community have taken to politics as their congenial trade. The Wire-puller is here. The Log-roller is here. The Ward Politician is here. The Working Man's Friend is here. And at Ottawa, since the recent development of public works, we have seen plainly enough the sinister face of a Canadian Lobby.

" Party government, in England, dates as a regular institution from the reign of William III., who, after vainly attempting to form a cabinet without distinction of party, was compelled, by the factiousness and selfishness of the men about him, and his position as the occupant of a disputed throne, to form a cabinet on the party principle. And with party government at once came organized corruption. ' From the day,' says Macaulay, ' on which Caermarthen was called a second time to the chief direction of affairs, Parliamentary corruption continued to be practised, with scarcely any intermission, by a long succession of statesmen, till the close of the American war. . . . . It at length became as notorious that there was a market for votes at the Treasury as that there was a market for cattle in Smithfield. Numerous demagogues out of power declaimed against this vile traffic ; but every one of these demagogues, as soon as he was in power, found himself driven by a kind of fatality to engage in that traffic, or at least to connive at it. Now and then, perhaps, a man who had romantic notions of public virtue refused to be himself the paymaster of the corrupt crew, and averted his eyes while his less scrupulous colleagues did that which he knew to be indispensable and yet felt to be degrading. But the instances of this prudery were rare indeed. The doctrine generally received, even among upright and honourable politicians was, that it was shameful to receive bribes, but that it was necessary to distribute them. It is a remarkable fact that the evil reached the greatest height during the administration of Henry Pelham, a statesman of good intentions, of spotless morals in private life, and of exemplary disinterestedness. It is not difficult to guess by what arguments he, and other well-meaning men, who like him followed the fashion of their age, quieted their consciences. No casuist, however severe, has denied that it may be a duty to give what it is a crime to take. . . . And might not the same plea be urged in defence of a Minister who, when no other expedient would avail, paid greedy and low minded men not to ruin their country.'

" The only intermission of corruption, during the period mentioned by Macaulay, was when Chatham for a few years put party under his feet, and ruled as the Minister of the nation.

" But the mutual hatred, the mutual slander, and the reckless sacrifice of patriotism to factious passions, which party government brought with it, were worse if possible, than the corruption. Chatham himself conspired from merely factious motives—motives which were afterwards admitted to have been merely factious by the conspirators themselves—to drive Walpole into the iniquitous and disastrous war with Spain, which, as its natural consequence, brought on the attempt of the Pretender, and a renewal of civil war in England. In the recent controversy respecting the Treaty of Washington, Lord Cairns, a man who had held one of the highest offices in the State, supported with the utmost violence and with all the resources of legal casuistry at his command, the most outrageous pretensions of the American Government, simply for the purpose of embarrassing the Government of his own country. The same man had done his utmost, at the time of the American war, to impede the efforts of Lord Palmerston's Ministry to prevent the escape of cruisers and preserve the neutrality which was so essential to us as a commercial nation. Can it be doubted that Lord Cairns had been taught by the party system to hate Englishmen of the opposite party more than he loved England ? Did not Lord Derby, when he took his tremendous 'leap in the dark,' by carrying an extension of the suffrage, which, whether expedient or not in itself, was contrary to all the avowed principles of his party, and which he must have believed to be fraught with the utmost peril to his country, find comfort in the reflection that he had 'dished the Whigs?' And would not the Whigs have sacrificed the public good with equal facility for the satisfaction of dishing Lord Derby?

"In France party government was introduced with constitutional monarchy, on the restoration of the Bourbons, and reintroduced with the constitutional dynasty of Louis Philippe. There again it bred corruption, (the Government multiplying offices for corrupt purposes, till, under Louis Philippe, the number of officers actually exceeded the number of electors,) and not only corruption, but, as the fury of the factions increased, civil war and political ruin. Transported with hatred of his rival Guizot, Thiers, himself an adherent of constitutional monarchy, headed the movement which overthrew the constitutional throne.

"It is needless to show how corruption has attended party government in the United States. But it is equally certain that the spirit engendered by the struggle of the two factions for place contributed in no small degree to prepare the way for the civil war : and if any one feels assured that the possibilities of such calamities in the United States are exhausted, he reads the situation with different eyes from ours. . . .

"As we have said before, in England party has at least an intelligible basis, and one which may determine the allegiance of a reasonable man and a lover of his country, inasmuch as the great conflict between aristocratic and democratic principles of government, carried on for so many years and with so many vicissitudes, is not yet closed. But in Canada, since the establishment of Responsible Government and religious equality, party has had no intelligible basis ; it has been faction and nothing else. In all the speeches and manifestoes of the party leaders during the late contest, it was impossible to discover any principle which could form a permanent line of demarcation. There were reminiscences of a political past, before the concession of responsible government, when principles were really at stake ; but as regards the present, there were only administrative questions, such as that of the Pacific Railway, which, however important at the time, cannot furnish permanent articles of party faith. Saving such questions, we had nothing but vague though vehement assertions of the necessity of party government, and of the impracticable and visionary character of all who looked beyond it. British institutions, we were told, could not be carried on without party. If by British institutions is meant party government, the proposition is indisputable, though not profound ; but if it is meant that we cannot possibly have representative assemblies, self-taxation and trial by jury, without putting up the government periodically as the prize of a faction fight, the proposition agrees neither with reason nor with facts. Again, it was laid down that party was necessary because God had so constituted us as to think differently on most subjects. We imagined that God had so constituted us as to think alike on all subjects, truth being one, and our faculties being the same ; and that difference of opinion arose from error on one side, or both, which further investigation and discussion would in the end remove. Such has been the case in science and in all rational inquiry. But it seems that in politics Providence has made half the community incapable of ever arriving at truth, in order that there may always be a Parliamentary Opposition. A Ministerial orator avowed his theoretical belief in party, and in the necessity of having a body of 'astute and able men' as an Opposition, to criticize and control the Government ; but afterwards, coming to parties in Canada, he laid it down that there ought to be only two—one, that of patriots like himself, at once in the best sense Conservative and Reforming, carrying on the government in the highest interest of the whole nation ; the other that of 'Independents,' 'Annexationists,' and other infamous and disloyal persons, making it their business to 'paralyse' the government and prevent it from promoting the union and prosperity of the country. So that half, or nearly half, of the community are to be always disloyal, enemies of the nation, and devoted to the malignant work of paralysing the efforts of a Government which is labouring successfully for the public good. This is to be the basis of our political system for ever !

"On no subject but politics are such absurdities now current. But in former days the scientific world was divided into factions which throttled each other as the political factions do now. Perhaps, if lucrative offices had been the prize of the conflict, we should still have the parties of Nominalists and Realists wrestling over a psychological question which has long since been settled by mental science, and consigned to the grave of the Middle Ages. . . .

"In the old country, which we affectionately but somewhat unreflectingly imitate in spite of the great difference of our circumstances, party government, we repeat, has at least a rational and moral basis. It has also, to temper its evils, antidotes which are wanting here. In England there is a strong and settled public opinion which restrains the excesses of the party chiefs ; there is a great body of independent wealth and intelligence which, though it may to a certain extent belong to the parties, belongs more to the country ; there is a corps of public men whose tenure of their places in Parliament is practically assured to them for life, and who are deeply imbued with traditions of government, which amidst all their rivalries, they continue to respect ; there are the grave experiences and heavy burdens of an old country, which impose, even on the most unscrupulous, a prudence unknown to political adventurers gambling with the virgin resources of a young nation ; there is a great Civil Service, which fortunate accident has combined with wisdom to place outside party, and which carries on the ordinary administration of the country almost independently of the party chiefs who form the Cabinet ; there is a press in which, though there are plenty of organists and Bohemians ; there are also a great many independent writers on politics of the best kind, furnished in many instances by the numerous fellow-ships of the great universities, which thus exercise, in their way, a critical and corrective power. And yet, even in the old country, how superior to all mere party governments was the government of Sir Robert Peel during that brief hour for which faction permitted him to rule, in some measure, as the Minister of the nation ! How mournfully did the hearts of the people follow the retirement, how anxiously did they expect the return, of the one statesman who aspired to rule, not for a faction, but for the country !

"A party government is essentially a weak government. It cannot venture to offend or estrange any one who commands votes. It is unable to grapple with the selfishness of local interests, sections, rings—the perpetual enemies of the common weal. It cannot even give its attention steadily to its proper work. The greater part of its energies is devoted to the maintenance of its own existence against the attacks of the Opposition—the smaller part to the public service. It can contain only half the leading statesmen of the country, while the faculties of the other half are devoted to obstructing and paralyzing the conduct of affairs. Probably it will not contain the greatest administrators of all ; since the temper of the great administrator is peculiarly alien to the narrowness of faction. . . .

"But the system of government by organized factions is a process by which the most unprincipled members of the community are almost infallibly selected as the holders of power, and as cynosures for the imitation of the community at large. It may safely be said, that no rational being would have thought of instituting such a system if he had not been misled by false examples and blind adherence to tradition.

"It would probably be a further improvement if the election of members for the Dominion Parliament were vested in the Provincial Parliaments, as that of the American Senate is in the State Legislatures. This would at once settle the relations between the local and central Assemblies, and bind them together in a united whole. It would spare the country one set of popular elections without derogating from the electoral supremacy of the people. It would, probably, act in some measure as an antidote to localism in the choice of representatives, the prevalence of which has ruined the character of the representation in the United States, and to which there is a marked tendency here. The standard of English statesmanship has been hitherto maintained by keeping the representation national, and freely electing eminent men to seats for constituencies with which they have no local connection, as in the case of the present Premier, and in those of Lord Palmerston and Canning before him. Of late the House of Commons has been invaded to a formidable extent by 'locals,' and the consequence has been such a falling off in ability that, when the present leaders go, it is difficult to say who will take their places. I might fairly be hoped that in elections to the Dominion Parliament, conducted in the manner here suggested, by the members of the Provincial Parliaments, exercising their electoral power as a trust in presence of the people of the province, while mere wealth would generally prevail, room might sometimes be found for capacity, and that a sufficient succession of statesmen might be provided for the government of the nation. It may perhaps be thought by some that statesmanship has become unnecessary, and that we can get along very well with a Parliament of opulent gentlemen, who subscribe liberally to local objects, and give picnics to their constituents. Those who have studied with attention the critical changes which are now going on in the whole tissue of society, religious, moral, social and industrial, will probably be of a different opinion.

" There is nothing cloudy or chimerical in the proposal to substitute legal elections for faction, as the mode of selecting the Executive Council out of the Legislature. It is a definite remedy for a specific disease, a remedy for which is urgently needed, and being perfectly feasible in itself, it is a fit subject for practical consideration. That which is cloudy is the theory that Nature or Providence has divided the community into two sections, which are destined to be for ever waging political war against each other without a possibility of agreement. That which is chimerical is the notion that faction, when recognized as the instrument of government, and called by a soft name, will cease to be faction, and, at the height of a furious struggle for power and pelf, curb its own frenzy, and keep its selfish ends in subordination to the paramount claims of the public good."

PARTY POLITICS.

From the Canadian Monthly, Vol. II., 1872.

" A friend of ours was once a good deal puzzled in attempting to explain to a young lady of an enquiring turn of mind the nature of a Parliamentary Opposition. Government she understood and Parliament, as a deliberative and legislative assembly, she understood ; but the idea of a party of men, whose sole function was to *op*-pose what others *pro*-posed, seemed to be beyond her grasp. If it could have been explained to her that the so-called Opposition was a mere temporary organization for a temporary purpose—the government of the country having fallen into bad hands and it being very desirable to harass them into an abandonment of their position—the thing would have been more easily intelligible ; but no, the truth had to be told, that this ' Opposition ' was as permanent an institution as Government itself, and that the eagerness and bitterness with which it pursued its ends, bore no assignable relation to the merits or demerits of the holders of authority. However faultless an Administration might be, there must still be an Opposition, or the British Constitution would fall to pieces. ' Why don't they content themselves with opposing what is wrong?' was asked, with simplicity. ' Well, of course, that is what they professs to do,' was the answer. ' Then there is no particular reason for calling them Opposition, for everybody professes the same thing. I am Opposition, and you are Opposition—we are all Opposition together, if that is what it means.'

" The difficulty in which our young friend was involved was one which, in some shape or other, presents itself to everybody. Even grown men, tolerably familiar both with the theory and the working of the Constitution, find themselves wondering how the thoroughly artificial distinctions which prevail in the political arena, came to acquire such force and persistence ; wondering, too, whether no new page of political history will ever be turned, and the monotonous see-saw of party strife—Oppositions becoming Governments, and Governments becoming Oppositions, and each with every change of fortune, displaying most, if not all of the faults of those whose places they take—be succeeded by something more in accordance with reason, and more favourable to true progress. The subject is one which a little honest thought will do a great deal to clear up ; for, to tell the truth, the difficulties that seem to surround it are mainly the creation of those who think they have an interest in the perpetuity of the present state of things. It is commonly assumed, for example, by the defenders of party, that those who are disposed to regard it as out of place in this advanced stage of human culture and reason, are bound to devise a complete new set of institutions for the government of nations ; and having devised them, to demonstrate their practicability. This assumption we entirely repudiate, for reasons which will sufficiently appear in the course of our argument. What we have to do, is to try and render a true account of party to ourselves, to ascertain what it is and what the conditions are that call it into existence. As we pursue the investigation, we shall see that the conditions which give it its greatest vitality have passed away, and are little likely to return ; and that party, if limited to its natural and legitimate development in these days, would be a very different thing indeed from what we now witness.

"We cannot do better than take our departure from Burke's well-known definition. 'Party,' says the great philosophic statesman, ' is a body of men united for promoting, by their joint endeavours, the national interest, upon some principle n which they are all agreed.' Party, in this sense of the word, is something every one can understand : it calls for no justification, any more than any other form of association for a worthy object. It will be observed, however, that according to Burke's definition, party is but a means towards an end, and a means which is only available in certain defined circumstances. The end is the national interest, and the condition necessary to give vitality to party, is the agreement of all its members in ' some particular principle' which they wish to see applied in the government of the country, and to which of course, another party in the State is opposed. Burke says not a word to justify the opinion that parties are essential to the well-being of the State, under all circumstances : for that would be simply tantamount to saying that no country could be prosperous in which there were not those radical differences of opinion upon political subjects, which alone afford a rational basis for party organization. Nearly all the talk we hear in the present day on the subject of parties, really involves the absurd proposition that, *unless* a country is divided against itself, it cannot stand. Because parties were once a necessity of the times—the natural expression in Parliament of real and lamentable antagonisms that existed throughout the country, therefore parties must exist for ever ; and if we have not real antagonisms to support them, we must get up sham ones ! The Chinaman, in Charles Lamb's charming apologue, set his house on fire, in order to have, indirectly, some roast pork. Our roast pork is the party system ; and, in order that we may taste the savour again and again, we set the State on fire with all kinds of false and factitious issues.

" In Burke's time, and almost down to the present day, in England, there have never been wanting more or less serious causes of division among parties ; moreover, in a country like England—the continuity of whose political history has never been broken by revolution, and where, consequently, many institutions exist, simply because they *have existed*, and not because they are peculiarly adapted to the present time—there will always be a certain opposition between those who wish to preserve what time has handed down, and those who, imbued with the spirit of the present, aim at bringing everything as much into harmony with that spirit as possible. Even in England, however, there are unmistakable signs that the palmy days of the party system have passed away for ever. It is in politics, in these days, very much as it is in war : men see the inevitable much sooner than they used to do ; and, when they see the inevitable, they yield to it. This arises simply from the greater sway that reason has over the minds of men, and, particularly, over the minds of those fitted by nature to lead. . . .

"The political circumstances of Canada are very different from those of the Mother Country. *There*, where so much exists which it interests one class to maintain, and which it seems to interest a much larger class to destroy, there will, for a long time to come, probably, be some real significance in the terms ' Conservative ' and ' Liberal,' or ' Tory ' and ' Radical ;' though there is every reason to hope that the political struggles of the future will be mitigated by the influences to which we have just referred. In Canada, however, when the same terms are employed, nothing can exceed the sense of mockery they bring to the mind. In olden times, when a knot of infatuated men, thought they could govern the country for their own private interest, the political designations that had been borrowed from the parent State, were not so entirely out of place. But in the present day, you who call yourselves Conservatives, do tell us, for heaven's sake, what it is you wish to conserve that anybody else wishes to destroy? And you also, who call yourselves Liberals, where are we to find proofs of your liberalism or liberality, or whatever it is you pride yourselves upon? Or, if you prefer to call yourselves Reformers, what is it that you wish to reform? Your political creed, if we credit your own professions, is one of the intensest conservatism, regarding all the established principles of the constitution. You find fault with nothing, so you say, in the political frame-work of the State, and only complain of a few abuses of executive authority on the part of a set of men whom you hope soon to consign to perpetual oblivion ; and yet you dub yourselves Reformers, just as if there was work to be done for a generation or a century, in the redressing of abuses, the removal of anomalies, and the general reconstitution of a disordered commonwealth. When you have acceded to power and have wrought such improvements as you are able or disposed to do in the management of public affairs, what will there be to hinder you from adopting the title of 'Conservatives,' now appropriated by and to your opponents? Nothing in this wide world. And what will there be to hinder them, after you have committed a few blunders, as you are sure to do within a short time, from seizing, if they choose to do it, for political effect, upon your special name of 'Reformers,' on the plea that they are going to put to rights all the things that you have put wrong? Surely you are both to be congratulated on the peculiar felicity of party designations so chosen that you might make an impromptu 'swap,' and look neither wiser nor more foolish in your new colours than you do at present. . . .

  " It is not the *bitterness* of political discussion that seems to us the worst result of the party system ; it is its amazing *hollowness*. A reasonable man is simply lost in wonder as he reads day after day, in ably-edited journals, whole columns of writing in which there is hardly the faintest gleam of sincere conviction to be discerned. Day after day the same miserable evasions, the same varnishing up of unsightly facts, the same reiteration of unproved charges against opponents, the same taking for granted of things requiring proof, and proving things that nobody questioned ; the same hypocritical appeals to the good sense of the electors whom every effort is being used to misinform and confuse ; the same dreary, unmeaning platitudes : in a word the same utter abuse of man's reasoning powers, and of the privileges and functions of a free press. Of course so long as both sides indulge in this kind of thing, each can make out at least a partial case against the other ; and so a constant cross-fire is kept up in the exposure of misrepresentations, and the rectification of all that has been set down in malice on one side or the other. To-day a good point perhaps is made by the Opposition ; to-morrow it will be returned to them, if possible, with interest. Such is the party system of political warfare—a system which ought to have won the admiration of Archdeacon Paley, since it possesses the attribute that was wanting to that celebrated watch of his—the power, namely, of perpetually reproducing itself. Looking simply at the wordy strife between two such organs say as the *Globe* and the *Mail*, what is ever to bring it to an end? There is no termination to their arguments, any more than to a repeating decimal, which, truth to tell, they very much resemble.

  " ' Like everything good,' says the former of the two journals we have just mentioned, ' party may be abused.' We should like very much to know where the proper use of party ends and its abuse begins. The abuse, we suppose, is when men do things in the interest of their party that are not for the interest of the state ; when, for example, the supporters of a Government convicted of some reprehensible act rally around it to save it from just condemnation ; or when an Opposition, knowing that the Government is dealing with a very difficult and dangerous question, walking, to use Horace's metaphor, on hot cinders lightly covered over with ashes, seek to hamper and distress it by every means in their power, even at the risk of fanning the smouldering fires into open conflagration. But if this is abuse, it is of the very essence of party politics. Either the interest of the country or the fortunes of their party are to dominate in men's thoughts : if the former, then all party tactics are at an end : if the latter, then it is simply absurd to talk of party being 'abused.' It is all abuse from first to last. You might as well talk of selfishness being abused, or dishonesty being abused, or of hypocrisy being abused.

" Let us, however, hear a little more about party from that thorough believer in it whom we have just quoted :—'All the essential characteristics of party,' he proceeds to say, ' enter into the very idea of free popular government, and when they are eliminated, such a government is not only impossible but inconceivable. Who is to say what is really for the good of the nation ? All may be equally patriotic, all equally anxious to lay aside self-seeking and everything mean and unworthy, but they may have different ideas how this greatest national good is to be secured : nay they will have if they think freely and intelligently. And with what result ? Why, with the formation of more or less distinctly opposing parties, with more or less keenness in their discussions, and more or less divergence in their eventual courses of action. The whole history of the past tells of this : while the ' national principle ' would at best but give us something like the slumberous stillness of a sultry summer noon—quiet and peaceful, but at the same time stagnant and the fruitful parent of injurious miasmata.'

" Here let us draw breath. Who would have imagined, had we not let out the secret, whence this charming picture of party politics was taken? There is a touch of idyllic tenderness and sweetness about it which the great Sicilian poet himself could scarcely have surpassed. ' More or less keenness in their discussions '—of course ; but then each side is so ' anxious to lay aside everything mean and unworthy '—among other things, all mean and unworthy suspicions of their opponents—that really their divergences of opinion serve only to procure for those who take part in politics a reasonable and healthful amount of intellectual exercise. Under the ' national' system we should all stagnate and be choked by noxious miasmata ; while under the party system we are braced and vivified by the pure powers of free discussion. What a happy, golden dream, one cannot but exclaim, for the writer to have who was penning an article for the same columns that contained ' Wha wants me ? ' Not more fancy-free was Colonel Lovelace in his prison than is this editor in his sanctum. He cannot for a moment assume the patriotism of his particular political opponents—*they* are tricksters, corruptionists, deceivers—everything in fact that is morally execrable ; but when he wants to draw a picture of the party system at work, why, all at once the political atmosphere becomes pure if not altogether calm : there is equal patriotism on both sides, and men are only divided by theoretic differences which do not in the least impair the profound respect they entertain for one another.

" Now the truth of the matter is that what this enthusiastic advocate of party has been here describing is not party at all ; but that very ' national ' system, the application of which to popular institutions he pronounces to be sheerly ' inconceivable ' (though not *too* inconceivable to allow its miasmatic results to be clearly foreseen). No one pretends that if men could be induced to give up the conscious imposture and rant and gibberish that are now dignified with the name of party controversy, they would forthwith all be of one mind. The great difference would be that men would endeavour to make their opinions triumph by legitimate means ; and further, the expression of all opinions would be very much freer than at present. As things are now a man is not at liberty at all times to utter the thought that is in him : he has to consider how his party will be affected by what he may say. In this way truths that would be eminently seasonable, so far as the country's interests are concerned, are suppressed as being unseasonable from a party point of view. The credit that a man would, personally, feel inclined to give his opponents for something he knows them to have done well, he withholds out of consideration for his party who would be seriously compromised by any admission in favour of those whom they are steadily trying to undermine in popular favour. It is the rarest thing in the world at present to see a man get up in Parliament and seem to utter his real and innermost conviction on any important question. You note his place in the chamber, and before he speaks you know almost all he has to say. Such is the party system. Instead of stimulating thought and teaching intellectual honesty, it does just the reverse—puts a ban on the free exercise of a man's mind, and leads people to conceal or misrepresent their real opinions. . .

" The great difficulty in arguing the thesis that the public interest is not promoted by an arbitrary division of the legislature and of all those who take an interest in politics, into two opposing camps, is to avoid saying things that are self-evident. It is perfectly clear that a party would not be a party, as the word is commonly understood, if it were actuated only by a desire for the public good, and if it followed out a strictly honourable line of action towards its adversaries. Such a body would not and could not display what is called party spirit ; and as to party discipline, it would be lost in the higher and nobler discipline of duty. The agreement that existed amongst its members at any moment, however perfect it might be, could not be held to guarantee their agreement on any new issue ; for *ex hypothesi* every man, as often as a new question came up, would shape his course upon it, not with a view to improving the position of his party, but to promoting the advantage of the State. It is understood now that those who act together to-day will act together to-morrow and next day. Why ? Simply because *they mean to do so ;* that is all about it : they have determined that their opinions shall not differ. For how could they ever hope to gain party triumphs without party organization and party orthodoxy ? If the country does not thrive under such a system ; if the vices of government are not cured ; if the people are not educated to disinterestedness and high-mindedness : in other words, if patriotism and public spirit are not encouraged—so much the worse for all the interests, moral and material, involved. The British Constitution of which party government (we are told) is the noblest tradition, cannot be allowed to fall through merely because a nation threatens to go to ruin.

" When we are told that party is absolutely essential to free, popular government, we cannot help thinking what a vast amount of government is done, and what vast interests are successfully managed, without any help from the party principle. Look at our municipalities ; look at our banks, our railways and other public enterprises ; look at our churches. Would it really be well to see our city corporations, and our county and township councils divided between two parties, each trying to hamper the other to the utmost of its ability? Who would care to hold stock in a bank or railway, whose affairs were made the sport of party struggles? Whenever party spirit has shown itself in connection with the latter class of corporations, it has been the product of, as it has in turn ministered to, the very grossest and most shameless forms of corruption and robbery. We see party here assume its final and perfect development as the *ring* —an association of robbers who have agreed to aid in filling one another's pockets. When however, (as fortunately is most often the case) this horrible disease has not fastened upon a great public company, its administration is a fair type of what the administration of a country's affairs might be, if the organized selfishness of party were to pass away. Every shareholder knows that the value of his property depends on the successful administration of the company's affairs, and the maintenance of its credit before the world. His great anxiety, therefore, is to have the right kind of men as directors, and, when the right men have been found, it generally rests with them to say how long they will remain in the responsible positions assigned to them. Men get thanks for conducting the affairs of a company or association prudently and successfully ; they get none for doing their duty by the State : they get interested and formal praise from their supporters, and unvarying depreciation and abuse from their opponents. The praise affords them no satisfaction, and the abuse, in the long run, hardens them and takes the edge off all finer feelings. The great difference between a member of a joint-stock company and a member of Parliament is, that while the former would lose more than he would gain by pursuing an obstructive course, or in any way trifling with the interests of the society, the latter may pursue a similar line of conduct, and profit by it. His interest as a private citizen in sound legislation, and effective administration may easily be overcome by those special inducements which party leaders can offer. That is precisely the position, and hence it is that party is possible in the Legislature and *hardly any where else.* Party may therefore be defined with absolute correctness as a body of men whose interest in supporting one another is greater than the interest they have in giving a right direction at all times to public policy. We should scarcely call this, however, a good thing *per se.*

" What becomes then of Burke's definition of party as ' a body of men united for promoting by their joint endeavours the national interest upon some principle in which they are all agreed ? ' Is it of no application at all in our day? Certainly ; as often as a body of men honestly agree in a particular principle, let them unite their efforts to make that principle triumph, and if they choose to call themselves a party, why let them do so. No harm will result from that. Harm results when men take a license to themselves to do, as a party, things that are not for the national interest at all, and that, in their own consciences, they know are not for the national interest. It is certainly a strange thing that, because a number of men have got hold of one sound principle through which they hope to triumph, they should feel themselves excused in giving their sanction, if not their active support, to a number of evil ones. Yet this is precisely what our parties do ; they have one end in view which perhaps they sincerely think a good one, and this end they allow to justify or sanctify the most scandalous means. Such is the party system ; and if any one hints that a system, which not only permits but erects into a code the loosest moral practice, may not be worth perpetuating, he is pronounced at once an enthusiast, a dreamer, a doctrinaire, a person whom all sensible, practical men may complacently laugh at, without troubling themselves in the least to enquire into the value of his ideas. . . .

" We hold that a great portion of the evils from which we suffer are due to a defective political system, and to that confusion of mind on political subjects which the current language in regard to party is so well calculated to produce. The heart of the people is not so unsound as some would have us believe ; and if the people make up their minds to it, they can have honest men to serve them—men who will prefer honour to office, and the sense of duty performed to personal triumphs however flattering. To preach the cessation of party strife is no doubt, at present, like crying in the wilderness, but our hope is that, like other preaching that has begun in the wilderness, it will end by converting the multitude. Stripped of all verbiage and of all subtleties, the question is simply one between good and evil ; and the good must either gain on the evil, or the evil on the good."

EXPLANATION OF HARE'S SCHEME OF REPRESENTATION.

By M. G. Fawcett, 1872.

The end and object of Mr. Hare's scheme is the direct, equal and personal representation in Parliament of every elector. If this end were accomplished, Parliament would become the mirror of the nation, and, in proportion to the extension of the suffrage, all opinions would have in Parliament a strength corresponding to their strength in the country. To attain this end it would be necessary that each voter should have an equal amount of electoral power. At present there is nothing to prevent an elector from having a score of votes in different constituencies. Non-residence not being a disqualification for the county franchise, a man may have a vote for every county in the kingdom, if he can possess himself of the requisite property qualifications. To remedy this inequality Mr. Hare's plan provides that each elector shall have but one vote ; and in order to enable the elector to obtain real representation, he would be permitted to give this vote to any candidate, irrespective of the restrictions of local representation. For instance, a voter living in Hampshire could vote, if he chose, for a candidate standing in Yorkshire, or in any other part of the kingdom. Under this system, those who are willing to serve in Parliament might be described as " All England " Candidates, because they could poll votes in every constituency in the kingdom. If this plan of choosing members of Parliament were adopted, those candidates would of course be elected who obtained the largest number of votes : but in order to prevent inequality of electoral power through one candidate receiving an immensely large number of votes, Mr. Hare's scheme provides that no candidate shall receive more votes than are sufficient to secure his return. For this purpose the following arrangement is proposed. It is obvious that if all electors were allowed to vote for any candidate, well known and popular men, such as Mr. Gladstone and Mr. Bright, would receive a large proportion of the entire number of votes polled. Equality of electoral power, which is one of the main objects of the scheme, would be destroyed if Mr. Gladstone received six times as many votes as any other candidate ; for his constituents would then not be sufficiently represented in proportion to their numbers. It has therefore been proposed to find, by dividing the total number of votes polled by the number of vacancies to be filled, the quota of votes necessary for the return of each member. If 658 members are to be elected, and the total number of votes recorded is 2,632,000, four thousand votes would be the quota necessary for the return of a member. Each elector would vote by a voting paper, which would be drawn up in the following form :—

Name (of voter) _____

Address _____

Vote, No. _____

Parish of _____

Borough of _____

    The above-named elector hereby records his vote for the candidate named first in the subjoined list ; or, in the event of such candidate being already elected, or not obtaining the quota, the above-named elector votes for the second-named candidate, and so on, in their numerical order, viz.:

1. (Name of candidate)_____ _____

2. (Ditto of another)_____

3. (Ditto of another)_____

4. (Ditto of another)_____

(and so on, adding as many as the elector chooses).

The foregoing form, filled up with the names proposed by the voter, expresses in substance this :—I desire to be represented by the candidate whose name I have placed No. 1. If he should obtain his quota of votes before mine comes to be counted, or if he should fail to obtain a sufficient number, and therefore cannot be elected, I direct that my vote be transferred to the Candidate I have placed sa No. 2, and under the same conditions, to candidate No. 3, and so on.*

The above comprises the whole of the so-called complexity of Mr. Hare's system of representation. The main principles of the scheme might be tabulated as follows :—

1. All voters to be represented in Parliament.

2. Each Member of Parliament to represent an equal number of voters.

3. Each elector to have one vote.

4. Electors to be allowed to vote for any candidate.

5. Electors to be allowed to transfer their votes from one candidate to another, so that no votes are thrown away for candidates already elected, or for those who have no chance of obtaining the quota.

The most striking effects of such a deviation from the traditional method of conducting elections would first be seen in Parliament itself. The House of Commons would then no longer be filled with local magnates, whose names are unknown outside their own boroughs, and whose only recommendation to serve in Parliament consists in their employing a large number of workmen, and being able consequently to command a considerable number of votes. On the contrary, the House of Commons would be filled by really representative men, who would be sent to Parliament not solely on account of their wealth and local influence, but on account of their

---

* Pamphlet on Representation Reform, issued by a Committee appointed by the Reform League, p. 9.

opinions. A common charge brought against this plan of proportional representation is that it would bring into the House of Commons nobody but the representatives of crotchets. In reply to this it may be stated that it will be their own fault if people without crotchets are unrepresented ; if, indeed, they are so few as not to be able to secure a quota of votes for their candidates, then the House of Commons will justly be composed of crotchety members ; it would not be representative if it were not.

The effect of Mr. Hare's scheme upon constituencies would be more gradual, but not less beneficial, than its effect on the House of Commons. The present system of selecting candidates leaves little or no choice to the mass of the electors ; they must either support the candidate started by the wire-pullers of their own party or not vote at all. Hence the franchise is too often exercised merely mechanically ; little study is given to political questions. Men vote with their party as a matter of course, and the minimum of political intelligence is evoked. If, on the other hand, electors were free to vote for whom they pleased, they would probably be induced to examine into the respective merits of a considerable number of candidates. Instead of voting blindly, and for no assignable reason, for the local candidate, they would be obliged to make a selection between many different candidates, and would feel that they were acting foolishly if they could not justify their choice. An elector is now seldom asked, " Why did you vote for Mr. A ? " If such a question were asked, the reply would probably be, " Mr. A was brought out by the party ; we didn't like him particularly, but we voted for him, because, if we had split, the other side would have got in their man." If electors were free to vote for any candidate, the question, " Why did you vote for Mr. A ? " would receive a very different answer. It would probably be something like this, " I read through his address, and his views on the political questions of the day are those that I hold ; and, as far as one can judge of his character, I believe him to be an honest and independent man." In this way the selection of a candidate would produce an educational and moral influence on each elector, especially as he would be required to name a succession of candidates, and to place them in the order in which he esteemed their merit. The educational effect produced by inducing electors carefully to weigh the respective claims of a large number of candidates would be very considerable, and would probably stimulate a great increase of the mental activity brought to bear on political questions. The moral effect produced by giving a free and independent choice of a representative to each elector would be invaluable. At present a candidate, no matter how bad his personal character may be, is thrust upon a constituency by half-a-dozen active wire-pullers, and the electors frequently have no choice between not voting at all, voting for a man of notoriously bad character, or voting against their political convictions. Few electors would deliberately declare that their free and unfettered choice as a representative, the man whom they desired above all others to see in Parliament, was a well-known *roué*, a fraudulent director of companies, or one who had been convicted of personal bribery..... ....

The great advantage which Mr. Hare's plan possesses over all other schemes of proportional representation is, that it would give to each elector one vote, and would allow him to give this vote to any candidate he pleased. The choice of an elector would not be restricted to the candidates who might happen to present themselves for election in any particular constituency. By this means a minority, however locally insignificant, could join its votes with those of other electors in other localities, and thus secure the return of a representative. If, for instance, 600 members had to be returned at a general election, and the voters in all the constituencies amounted to 600,000, any thousand electors, no matter where they resided—they might be scattered in twos or threes all over the country—could secure the return of a representative. The present restricted choice of constituencies seems to act as a process of natural selection to weed out from Parliament, and from political activity in constituencies, men whose opinions are characterized by special loftiness or originality. Even ordinary uprightness and intelligence sometimes deter electors from joining actively in political life. An honest, intelligent and cultivated man is apt to turn in disgust from taking any part in an election, when he finds that he has to choose between voting for a promoter of false and fraudulent companies, a religious bigot, or a

5

man who has never read a book or had an idea in his life. If such an elector could feel that he was not compelled to submit to the farce of being represented by such candidates, but could choose from among all public men, who were willing to undertake the duties and responsibilities of a member of Parliament, he would no longer feel himself shut out from real representation, and a stimulus of the very best kind would thus be given to political activity. In all contests there is enough and to spare of the worst kind of activity and enthusiasm, springing from the meanest and most contemptible of passions ; if political life is to be improved, it is not by crushing out activity and enthusiasm, but by changing the source from which they too often spring. A strong influence would be brought to bear in this direction by affording the means of real representation to all voters, instead of leaving them to the tender mercies of local candidates.

THE DECLINE OF PARTY GOVERNMENT.

By Goldwin Smith. Extract from Macmillan's Magazine, Vol. XXXVI., 1877.

It is curious with what implicit faith we have all reposed upon party, as the normal, permanent and only possible mode of carrying on a free constitution, disregarding not only the objections which reason obviously suggests to the system and the general evidences of its bad effects on politics and political character, but the facts which showed plainly enough that its foundations were giving way, and that if this was the only basis of government, government was likely to be soon left without a basis.

. . . In normal times the occupations of legislatures and governments will be matters of current administration, not one of which is likely to form an issue of sufficient importance to swallow up all the rest and form a rational ground for the division of the nation into two organized parties struggling each to place its leaders in exclusive possession of the powers of the state.

In the second place, questions of expediency, however important, do not last for ever ; in one way or other they are settled and disappear from the political scene. Slavery dies and is buried. Parliamentary Reform is carried out with all its corollaries, and becomes a thing of the past. What is to follow? Another question of sufficient importance to warrant a division of the nation into parties must be found. But suppose no such question exists, are we to manufacture one? That is the work to which the wire-pullers devote themselves in democracies governed by party.

. . . In Canada, for example, while New World society was struggling to repel the intrusive elements of the old *régime* forced upon it by the Imperial country, and to extort self-government, the parties, though not altogether edifying in their behaviour or salutary in their influence upon popular character, were at least formed upon real lines. But the struggle ended with the abolition of the State Church and the secularization of the Clergy Reserves. Since that time there has been no real dividing line between the parties ; they have ceased to be truly directed to public objects of any kind ; their very names have become unintelligible. Politics under such a party system must inevitably sink at last into an " interested contest for place and emolument " carried on by "impostors who delude the ignorant with professions incompatible with human practice, and afterwards incense them by practices below the level of vulgar rectitude." It is needless to say what effects an incessant war of intrigue, calumny and corruption carried on by such party leaders, with the aid of the sort of journalists who are willing to take their pay, must produce on the political character of a community, however naturally good, and well adapted for self-government. Nobody is to blame. The blame rests entirely on the system.

It is needless to dilate upon the relations of party, its machinery, its strategy, the press which serves it and expresses its passions, to public morality and the general interests of the state ; the facts are always before our eyes.   But experience of a colony or of some new country is needed to make one thoroughly sensible of the effects of this warfare upon the political character of the people, and of the extent to which it threatens to sap the very foundations of patriotism and of respect for lawful authority in their minds.

Party is no doubt indispensable to selfish interests, which by taking advantage of the balance of factions are enabled, to an almost indefinite extent to compass their special objects at the expense of the community.   It is indispensable to political sharpers who, without legislative powers or any sort of ability or inclination to serve the public in any honorable way, find subsistence in an element of passion and intrigue.   To whom or to what else it is indispensable, no one has been able definitely to say.

The tendency inherent in party government to supersede the national legislature by the party caucus has long been completely developed in the United States, where it may be said that in ordinary times the only real debates are those held in caucus, congressional legislation being simply a registration of the caucus decision, for which all members of the party, whether they agreed or dissented in the caucus, feel bound by party allegiance to record their votes in the House ; just as the only real election is the nomination by the caucus of the party which has the majority, and which then collectively imposes its will on the constituency ; so that measures and elections may be and often are carried by a majority but little exceeding one-fourth of the house or the constituency, as the case may be.   The same tendency is rapidly developing itself in England ; and it is evidently fatal to the genuine existence of Parliamentary institutions.

So far as England is concerned, the institution of an executive regularly elected by the legislature at large in place of a cabinet formed of the leaders of a party majority would be substantially a return to the old form of government—the Privy Council.   Parliament is now the sovereign power, and election by it would be equivalent to the ancient nomination by the crown.   The mode of electing and confirming a Speaker shows how the forms of monarchy may be reconciled with the action of an elective institution.

THE REPRESENTATION OF MINORITIES.

By Leonard Courtney.   Extracts from Nineteenth Century, Vol. VI. 1879,

. . . . The idea of the representation of minorities is this : that if you have got one thousand electors to elect ten representatives, any hundred of the thousand might combine together to vote for one of the ten, and if they combined you might get the whole thousand electors represented in your ten, each hundred getting a representative.   So throughout the whole kingdom the forces might be so distributed that each group will be collected together, and vote for a particular man, sending him to represent them.   If that could be realized, you would secure the first object of the representative principle : you would get the representation of the whole.   The elected body would have the flexibility and the life of the electing body.   It would be the electing body itself in miniature.   As the people in the country would combine, so the elected representatives would combine, representing every determination of the original body.   You have, therefore, under this principle of the representation of minorities, an assured result—namely, the security that in the body elected there will be an accurate reflection of the persons who elected them.

This is only the first reason, though it is one of great importance, why this system should be preferred.   What is the effect of the present system on the character of the representatives chosen? And again what is the effect on the electors themselves? How are the men chosen under the present majority system? It is a very great difficulty to get a candidate; you have some experience of that here. How shall you get hold of a proper candidate? Under the old plan, now becoming discredited, there was usually some select committee, who had interviews with certain people, tested them, and then came to a conclusion to run for the constituency. Under the new plan you have election-committees of hundreds by which you intend to make a selection. We don't know what will be the principle of action of these committees. Under the old plan the primary object was generally this: 'We must have a man to keep the party together. We want a man who will not lose the support of any section of the party.' This last was the great point held in view. You must keep the party together; therefore your candidate must have in him nothing that will drive away any members of the party from adhering to the choice of the few. In order to do that you must have a man who will offend nobody—who will be free from all tendency to kick over the traces: whether in thought or in action, he must keep well within the party lines. If he will vote steadily and pledge himself to support the leader for the time being, he has the best chance of success. That is the way in which the mass of members have been chosen, and candidates have always been obliged to bear this in mind. The first duty of a candidate is to be prudent—not to offend anybody—to subdue his mind as far as possible to the lowest level compatible with any life at all, and to be careful not to disturb the prejudices of any section at all. That is the necessity of getting a majority of any constituency. The result is to produce a candidate with the gift of mediocrity. You would not find a majority of your constituency to go together for a man who is pronounced in his opinions, or in his character, or in the force of his thought; and the result is, that the strongest man has to be put aside in order that the moderate man may be run, because the moderate man has the best chance of winning. If this is anything like an accurate representation of the facts, the result must be a degradation of the character of your candidates, and of your electoral body. If you get indifferent materials to work with, you cannot do good work; and if you send into the Legislature such men as I have described, you will not make a brilliant assembly out of them.

But the evil goes further than that. Having brought down in this way the temper and mind of candidates, you produce a feeling throughout the country that the thing to be regarded is the movement of the mass of the people. You will find that from the candidates the sense of dependence upon the cohesion of unknown masses passes on until the leaders themselves are affected with the same dependence upon the words and thoughts of the mass of the people. Instead of having leaders inspiring and instructing their followers, you will have leaders waiting on the swaying hither and thither of the people, waiting for the movement of the masses.

Now as to one other merit of this system. If you could get it into operation, you would at once get all the persons in the electorate represented in the elected body, because there would be none outside who would not have a representative inside. Under the present system many of those outside, have no representative inside, having no living connection with the governing body of their country. If a person outside has a living connection with those inside—if he can always say, 'I voted for that man'—he will keep his eye on what is going on inside; he feels he has an interest in what is going on. Every one can understand what an astonishing effect it has on the interest we take in the House of Commons if we have a relation inside. If this interest was extended to all—if, as I have said, every man could feel that he had some one there for whom he voted, who was his man—then, to use expressive words, every one would feel he was 'built in' to the State. The House of Commons would be vivified, and the nation with it, and all would make up one living existence of which the House of Commons was simply the consummation. Instead of having a half-dead-alive country, you would have a living, growing country—you would have fresh and vigorous life bursting forth on all sides throughout the country. Bear in mind also that a Chamber thus representative would be a Chamber of larger information, of broader sympathies, and of wider range of aim than any we can now possess; that being truly representative, all classes would find their representation in it.

One great result that would arise from the reform I advocate would be disintegration of party. Parties would not cling together so closely as Conservatives and Liberals do now. Amongst Conservatives you would find differences of opinion as also amongst Liberals, and you would more freely detach men, one by one, from any majority. At present scarcely any member of a party ever dares desert it; but if a man had not to depend for his seat on mere party cohesion within a limited area—if he knew that his independence would bring support from a wider range—you would have more freedom of thought, and there would be more room for conversion than you now have. Not that men are not converted now. Many are converted in their minds, but they do not change their votes.

PARTY RULE IN THE UNITED STATES

From "A True Republic." By Albert Stickney.

In the minds of the men of 1787 who framed the Constitution of the United States, one idea stood out more strongly than any other.

The intention was that this Government should be, as the phrase is, a government by the people, that—

1. The people should choose their own rulers.

2. The people's offices should be used only in the people's service.

The result has been a government by party.

1. Party has chosen the people's rulers.

2. The people's offices have been used in the service of party.

As it seems to me, few men are in the habit of thinking how far these two statements are true, how thoroughly the interests of the people have been sacrificed by our public servants to the needs of the party. It is a point worthy our careful consideration.

Party did not at once get its full growth. Nor did the system of party rule at once bring its full fruits. Able men wished to serve the people under the Government; and the people wished and had their services. It took many years for party politics to drive our best men from public life, where they wished to be.

But the system began its work early. The abuses began as soon as parties got their existence. In the earliest days of party history, party men acted on true party principles. They used the people's offices to pay for party services. They used official power for party ends.

In theory and in law, the people elect their rulers. In fact, these rulers are not elected by the people, but are appointed by the party leaders. The real working of the Government is controlled, not by the officials whom the people nominally elect, but by the party managers who really appoint those officials. These party managers hold, as such, no position known to the law; they have no duties or responsibilities under the law. Usually they hold some official position for the purpose of drawing a salary from the people. But the real power they have, not from their official position, but because they control the party policy, and, above all, the party nominations. And they hold their real power in the State, not for any short term of years, but without any limit whatever as to time, simply until tyranny becomes unbearable, and we have a peaceful revolution at the polls.

When our Constitution of 1787 was formed, the American people intended to use wisely the lessons they had from English history, and from all history. They had learned that

irresponsible power in a hereditary monarch certainly made a tyranny. They said, therefore, we will have no hereditary king, and no tyranny by any man or set of men. They
established, as they thought, a true republic—a government, of the people, by the people,
for the people. They established, as a matter of fact, a powerful oligarchy, a tyranny, of the
people, by party, for party. They kept, as they thought, the real control of the Government.
They kept, as a matter of fact, nothing but a right of peaceful revolution. Elsewhere
tyranny and revolution both violate the law ; with us they both follow it. Often, before
our time, revolution has resulted only in a change of tyrants; with us it is still the same. We
rebel against the tyranny of one party ; we simply place ourselves under the rule of the other
party ; and then again go through the same cycle of tyranny and revolt.

The Constitution of the United States had been formed "to secure the blessings of
liberty" to the people of the United States in the year 1787, and their posterity after them.
. . . We have had the election of our rulers taken from us by party oligarchies. We
have had the money of the people stolen and their lives wasted by the officers who should
have guarded us from harm. We have had our courts of justice used, not to protect the
life, liberty, and property, but to rob honest men, and open prison doors for convicted
thieves.

But, it is sometimes said, the real cause of the present condition of our public affairs is
the fact that we no longer have the same class of men in public life as in years gone by.
Where are the Websters, the Calhouns, the Clays, in our national Government of to-day, it
may be asked ? It is said we suffer from our own apathy ; we have in our hands the remedy
against these wrongs—we must choose a better class of men for our public officers.

But why is it that we no longer have the same class of men as of old in public place ?
How does it happen that our public men are no longer as able or upright as they were in
former years ? For, without imagining all the glory to have passed from the earth, it will
be generally admitted that there has been a falling off in the character of the men in our
public service.

This is only another effect of party rule.

No man can now hold office under our Government for any long time unless he will
sacrifice the interests of the people to the interests of party. The party leaders wish pliant
men who will serve party, and not honest men who will serve only the people. They will
not have in official position men whom they cannot control and use. The men they cannot
control and use they drive from public life.

The men who stay in public life are compelled to yield and submit to party. They cannot resist the immense party pressure which surrounds them. We have notably three
Presidents—Mr. Lincoln, General Grant, and Mr. Hayes—each of whom, as most men will
agree, took office with the purpose of always serving the people without regard to the
interests of party. They all at last gave themselves more or less completely to the control
of the party men. So long as they tried to do their simple duty to the people, they found
themselves in the midst of enemies, without friends. They had to surrender. To resist
would take strength more than human.

But is there any way out of this party tyranny ? May it not be that this party tyranny
is a necessary incident of republican institutions in any form, that it is an evil which we must
submit to, and bear as well as we can ? May it not be, even that party has its good points,
its advantages ?

To answer these questions, we must consider what are the causes which bring party into
existence, the nature of party, and its uses.

All men will admit that party rule, as we have had it in this country, has been attended
with great evils and abuses. But most men think that these evils are merely accidents o

the time, that in some way party government can be kept and these evils can be removed, that these evils are far outweighed by the good results which party brings, and that party, with all its evils, is a machinery without which free government cannot exist.

I believe this to be a mistake ; that these evils which we have had are not mere accidents, but that they are of the very essence of party ; that we cannot rid ourselves of these evils unless we rid ourselves of party ; that what men call the good results of party we should still get if we had no parties : that party, instead of being a machinery necessary to the existence of free government, is its most dangerous foe ; and that in order to get anything which really deserves the name of republican government, we must destroy party altogether.

Our public servants, who depended for keeping their offices on carrying elections, in the same way gave their best efforts to carrying elections. Whether they wished it or not, our public servants were driven by this point in our system of government to make this work of carrying elections their regular profession. In that profession they gained great skill. In that work they were sure to have more skill than the ordinary citizens, who gave their time and thought to other things. The professional must always beat the amateur. These party organizations became vast and powerful. The leaders of these parties controlled party action. It came to be the fact (almost without exception), that no man could be chosen to an office without a party nomination, and no man could have a party nomination against the will of the party leaders. And the party leaders would give party nominations to no man who did not do party service. The natural and certain result was, that party leaders, for party purposes, controlled the elections of public servants, and the action of public servants after they were elected.

So it has always been in English Parliamentary history. Each party has been, at one time or another, on both sides of every important question of government policy. Principles and measures have had little to do with the action of parties in England, except there, as here, the party leaders have used the great questions of the day as battle-cries in the struggle for place. Many great men and honest men in England have been party men. They have, too, done great service to the English people. But they have done that good service always in spite of party and party influences.

We have in this country developed not only parties, but enormous party machinery for the mere purpose of carrying elections—a machinery that is intricate, costly, powerful, and tyrannical. The man in public place in these days in this country must be, not a statesman, but a man of skill and capacity in manipulating this election machinery.

It is said that parties are combinations of citizens for the purpose of carrying measures. I maintain, on the contrary, that these combinations, which we call parties, never can be anything but combinations of office-holders, or office-seekers, to carry elections.

And with the men who manage these parties, however upright may be their intentions, the end which is first, in point of time, is to get office for themselves ; to this end they must have the support of other party men ; to this end they must give their support to other party men. The party organization naturally and certainly becomes an organization of men who combine and work together to secure their own election to the different places under government. It becomes, try to disguise it as we may, a system of trading in office.

In the affairs, too, of great nations, or even of a single city, there are, not one or two, but very many, weighty questions of public policy. As a matter of fact, the men composing these large parties cannot all agree on more than one or two of those main questions. Nor do they profess to. And as to those one or two main questions, they agree, not on actual measures to be carried, but only on what they are pleased to term general principles.

There is, however, one point on which the party leaders can agree—their candidates for office. And here they do agree. On all other points they must differ, and they do differ.

They do indeed, before each election, say something about "principles;" they make a "platform," as they term it—a collection of "sounding and glittering generalities," so vague as to mean nothing, by which they think they can catch votes. This word "platform" truly describes the thing for which it is the name. It is something to be put under foot.

Whatever may be the theory of political parties as they should be, wherever there are many offices and many elections, the natural and certain result is that these party organizations, as a fact, are used for the purpose of carrying elections and not measures. Parties do not elect men to put into action certain principles; they use principles as battle-cries to elect certain men.

That is not only the working of party rule, it is the theory of party rule as it actually exists. Any other statement is only the theory of party rule as men wish it might be.

We have seen so much of parties and party contests that we have almost come to look on them as an end in themselves. But what is always the real end to be reached in public affairs? As we should all agree, it is *action* of some kind. In order to have that action wise, we need calm thought and discussion before we decide what that action shall be, and united effort after our action is decided. We need at every stage, not strife between two factions, but harmony of all men. We must have the *working together*, of all men's minds, to get the wisest thought, of all men's wills, to get the strongest action.

And how does this machinery of party tend to help or hinder us in getting these results, wise thought and strong action, from both the people and their public servants?

Parties and party contests make it an impossible thing to get from the people their calm wise thought and action. One party seizes one side of the question, the other party takes the other side, or, oftener, each party takes different sides in different sections of the country. What the party men labor for is not to find out the best thing to be done by the men of all parties, but to catch votes for their own party. And their whole effort is to make men follow party and work for party success, instead of using their minds and their judgments. In party contests men do not think over measures; they fight for candidates. We have always strife, not deliberation.

So it is as to the action and thought of the people themselves. But how is it as to the action of our public servants? It is our right to have our Senators and Representatives sit down together and give us the best possible results of their combined wisdom. When once they enter our legislative halls they have no right to know that there is such a thing as party in existence. They are bound to think only what are the best measures for the people's interest, and to give us those measures. That is not what they do. Every measure is made a "party question." If the administration party, as it is called, brings forward a wise measure, the opposition party, if it dare, opposes it, for fear their enemies may gain votes through having done the people good service. These party men may be able men; they may be men of honest intentions. They are driven by the pressure of this vast party machinery to serve party and not the people, whether they wish it or not; for on party they depend for their future.

So much as to whether party and party machinery helps or hinders us in getting from the people and their servants wise action. But when measures are once decided and taken, surely no one can claim that party strife as to those measures should go on unceasingly. But it never ends. No question is ever at rest.

In private affairs, when men have once made a decision, they act. The decision may or may not be wise. Of that they cannot be certain. But when the decision is once made, they do something—they put their decision to a trial; and if, upon trial, they find they have made a mistake, then they try something else. In public affairs we should do the same. When a course of action is once determined on, then all men should agree, in putting it to the test of experience If the course of action is not wise, time will so prove ; and then we can try other measures. And so we should do, were it not for party.

But it is in time of war, when a people should be united, when they must show an unbroken front to their enemies, that the greatest evils from party have ever come. In every time of danger that the people of the United States have yet had, party has nearly ruined us. Party men, whatever may have been their intentions, have in practice not heeded the needs of the people, have looked at party ends, have brought war on us when it suited their purposes, and, when war has come, have done much to bring on us defeat and destruction.

In the only two important wars we have had, the war of 1812 and the war of the rebellion, when all men should have united against the common enemy, we have been nearly ruined by party strife.

The calm opinion of to-day is that the war of 1812 was entirely needless, that it was begun on no sufficient reason, that it was carried on with disgraceful inefficiency, and that it brought no substantial results. That the war ever came, or that it was carried on as it was, was due to the violence of party contest. One party dragged us into war for party reasons. The other party, after war had come, did its utmost to cripple the administration and make the war a ruinous failure, for party reasons.

The war of the rebellion came. As to whether it would have come had it not been for party strife, many men differ. But after the war once came, as to the disastrous effects of party strife men cannot differ.

Again, as in the war of 1812, when the nation was in the greatest danger, when we needed, of all things, that all loyal men should sink their differences of opinion on other matters, and fight together for mere existence, we had nearly half the men at the North arrayed in opposition to the Government, doing all they could, whatever may have been their purpose, to aid the public enemy and destroy the nation.

In short, at all times, in war and peace, the need of the people is agreement—on something to be done. The need of parties and party men is always strife over what they call " principles."

We have in this country every four years a convulsion of the whole nation. The entire business of the community stands still at an immense money loss. If the men of a new party come into power, they may adopt a totally new system of levying revenue ; they may bring in a new tariff ; they may overthrow the existing currency, or issue a quantity of irredeemable paper money. The commercial and banking operations of the whole country may be thrown into utter confusion. Prosperity may be changed to ruin, for large numbers of our citizens, according to the particular measures that demagogues think will carry them into office. The mere machinery and labor of a Presidential election cost immense sums of money. This money is paid, in one shape or another, by the people, and out of the people's purse. Why should the people pay this immense tax every four years, have their public servants at all times doing duty to the party instead of the State, and be subjected to this immense business loss and this enormous upheaval of the whole social fabric ? We may, indeed, live through it. The people's liberties may not be permanently destroyed by it. We may be prosperous in spite of it. But why should we have it ?

The English system of government and our own system are both bad. We have a revolution once in four years. They have one whenever the ministry are beaten in the House of Commons. I do not yet feel certain which system is the worse.

We come, then, to the next point. Is it a necessary thing to have this party strife, in order to keep alive the interest of the people in public affairs?

One of most frequent complaints of the day is that our people, and especially the educated men, do not take an interest in public affairs. And the complaint is in a measure well founded. Men do not take a healthy interest in the affairs of our Government. And why is it so? Simply this: the ordinary citizen knows that he has no power, that the party men can and will manage our government affairs very nearly as they choose. But before party machinery and party power became so fully developed, men did take the deepest interest in all the affairs of the nation.

All men in the country, but the educated men more than any others, think and read and talk of public affairs more now than ever before. As a class, the educated men are more eager than any others to go into public life. Nothing else has for them such fascinations. But they cannot get there. They are kept out by the party leaders. They try again and again, and they fail. What has at times seemed the indifference of elegant leisure is in fact the despair of repeated defeat.

Is it a possible thing that men of any class should lose their interest in the public affairs of their own country, of their own time? This government and these laws, we live under them. They make or mar men's fortunes and the fortunes of their children. Men who read and think at all, read and think of the affairs of every people and of every age. Wherever we go, in a railway train or in the farm-houses, we hear all men discussing matters of European politics. Are we suddenly to lose all interest in the affairs only of our own country, and in the making of our own laws? On the contrary, remove these party oligarchies, and the best men in the country would again come into public life. Remove these party contests, and we should have instead of this feverish upheaval once in four years over a mere struggle for office, a steady, healthy interest in questions of public policy. When men found that they really had some power in the affairs of State, they would try to use it. Men in any country have never, under any circumstances, been able to lose their interest in the affairs of their own Government. We are not now to have such a miracle for the first time in the world's history.

To say that we must have these party contests in order to keep up the interest of the people in public affairs, is to say that a man must have a fever once in four years to keep warm.

Are these party combinations, then, necessary to preserve free government?

All the republics in history have been destroyed by party—by these organizations of men who have made a profession of carrying elections. The tyranny of kings has been often overthrown by one people or another in the history of nations. The tyranny of party is the most dangerous enemy freedom can have. No people has ever yet conquered it. These single royal tyrants, with only one life, are puny things; but this immense monster party, which is immortal, has the people's own strength.

But if these were the only evils resulting from party combinations we might be comparatively at ease. We have not yet the worst point. It is this necessity of carrying elections, under which we put all our public servants, which is the root of all the corruption of our public men. We bind them hand and foot, in the chains of party slavery. And we do more: we compel them to serve the powerful interests in the land which control votes. Our public servants, on questions of revenue, on all matters of legislation, where we have a right to their honest judgment and honest action, do not give us their honest judgment and honest action. They are driven to look at the next election. They say they work for their party. They give it too good a name. They shape their official action in such a way as to gain the support at the next election of the rich and powerful men and corporations. Disguise it as we may, they sell their official action for votes; and the next step downward, the selling of official action for money, is one that is easily and often taken. But that is not often the first step.

Some men have been in the habit of thinking that the corruption which we have had among members of Congress and of State Legislatures was some special fruit of some special feature of republican institutions. This is a mistake. Whenever, under any system of government, it is necessary for public officers to catch votes for elections, they will catch the votes. The votes will be bought and paid for in money, or office, or official action, as the case may be, whether it be under a monarchy or a republic.

This thing that we call party is the poison which makes a healthy national life an impossible thing. These great party combinations, instead of being combinations of citizens to carry wise measures in the interest of the people, are only combinations of politicians to carry elections in their own interest. Parties, so far from being necessary to carry measures, to keep alive the interest of the people in public affairs, and thus to preserve free government, are the most powerful hindrances to efficient action, keep alive endless and needless strife. are hot-beds of corruption, and are the most dangerous enemies that free government can have.

This party oligarchy under which we now suffer is not the creation of any one set of men. The present party leaders are not responsible for its existence ; they are not to be blamed for it. It is the natural legitimate fruit of our government system. It is not from choice that our public men sacrifice the interests of the people for those of party. They form these immense and powerful combinations only because our system of government drives them to it. They must carry these elections, or they will lose their places.

The people of the United States have a new and great problem to solve. That they will solve it I make no doubt.

The immense growth of party which we have had in this country is something new in history. I do not think its evils have been duly weighed ; nor do I think its causes have been carefully studied.

Party and party rule, as they now exist with us, are, as I believe, great evils—evils which naturally and certainly result from certain features in our political system.

In private life we find in every profession and employment many men who do their work as well as they know how. We have at times such men in public life ; but, as a rule. our public men do their work, not as well as they know how, but only as well as the interests of party will allow them. Many of those men have good intentions, but they are bound in the chains of party. Party controls the selection of our public servants ; it controls their actions.

I believe all this can be changed. There is somewhere a remedy for this state of things. That remedy can be found. And if the remedy can be found it will be used. I have unbounded faith in the honesty and sound sense of the people.

REPRESENTATIVE GOVERNMENT IN ENGLAND.

By David Syme, 1881.

In carrying out such a system as this it is evident that the good of the country is likely to be sacrificed for the benefit of party. If the government be carried on purely in the interests of party, it is very certain this cannot be to the advantage of the country. The motives and aims in the one case are distinct from, if not incompatible with, the motives and aims in the other, unless we are to assume that the interests of party and of the country are identical, which would be as correct as to assert that an individual in following his own selfish interests was acting disinterestedly or that a pickpocket was a useful and patriotic member of society.

. . . Once the policy of a party has been carried there is no longer a reason for the existence of the party, which should therefore be dissolved. There is a wide distinction between a party which exists solely as the advocate of certain principles, and a party which subordinates all principles to office. Unfortunately the two great political parties in the English Parliament belong to the latter category. Neither of them has ever been distinguished for honesty of purpose, or for strict adherence to any principles. Both of them, on the contrary, have made themselves notorious by their fickleness, by their greed of office, and by their unscrupulous use of means to attain it. They have been trimmers and time-servers; they have been everything by turns and nothing long. If they have supported a good cause it has generally been from a bad motive. They are ready to advocate one set of principles to-day and another to-morrow, if by so doing they may hope to trip up their opponents. . . . The conduct of neither of the two great parties in the State appears to have been regulated by any principle whatever. Their politics changed with the hour and the opportunity. What one party approved of the other opposed; whatever action one party took the other condemned. If the Whigs were in office and brought in a measure, the Tories would oppose it as a matter of course; if the Tories succeeded to office and brought in a similar measure on the same subject, the Whigs would pronounce it to be utterly worthless. And their successors follow precisely the same course. With Liberals and Conservatives alike everything is fair in party warfare. Truth, honour, and fair dealing are alike sacrificed to the exigencies of party. The end justifies the means, according to the ethics of either party, and the supreme end of both parties is to secure or maintain possession of the treasury benches. Government by Party is of a comparatively recent date. It was the outcome of a long series of corrupt Parliaments dating back from the Restoration. There is no trace of its existence till after the Revolution, and it was not till long after that event that it was organized as it now is. Macaulay tells us that political parties had their origin in the Long Parliament. It is true that there were two political parties in the Long Parliament, and that is all that can be said on the matter. They were not parties in the sense understood by the term at the present day. They were not organizations for the mere purpose of securing or holding office. The parties of that day had not become mere place-hunters. Previous to the Revolution the sovereigns of England chose their ministers on personal grounds alone, and often in defiance of Parliament. The king's ministers were the king's friends. William III. was the first sovereign who formed a ministry on a purely political basis, and his example was generally followed during the subsequent reigns. But this was not always the case, and it was not till the present reign that ministers were regularly chosen from the majority in Parliament. The last memorable instance of a sovereign dismissing a ministry which had a majority in Parliament was during the short reign of William IV. Taking advantage of the accession of the premier, Lord Althorp, to the peerage, the king suddenly dismissed his Whig ministers, and entrusted the Duke of Wellington with the formation of a government from the Tory party, who were in a minority in the House of Commons. The defeat of the ministry at the general election which followed showed that they were in a minority in the country as well as in Parliament, and from that time forth the premier, on whom now devolved the task of forming a cabinet, has invariably been chosen from the party which for the time being had a majority in Parliament.

Government by Party is usually spoken of as if it were the same thing as government by the majority. This is a great mistake. It is true, as I have said, that the government of the day is now chosen from the majority in Parliament, but it by no means follows from this that the government is carried on by a parliamentary majority; on the contrary, we know that Government by Party is not government by the majority, but government by the majority of the majority; that is to say, the majority of the party which has a majority in the House. And this majority of a majority may be, and often is, really a minority of Parliament. Let me explain what I mean by an illustration. Suppose a party in the House brings about a ministerial crisis which results in the leader of the party forming a cabinet. Suppose also the new cabinet has a large majority in the House, and that in attempting to carry out the policy of their party, they introduce a measure which is based on that policy. But the measure may not be acceptable to all the members of the party; indeed, it would be strange if it were, for there is almost invariably a dissentient minority in every party on some question or other. Party organization however, we shall suppose, triumphs over the dissentients, who vote, if they do not believe, with the majority on their own side of the House, and the bill is carried. Now what I wish to point out is that it is quite possible that the minority among the government supporters who were secretly opposed to the bill together with the whole of the opposition might make a majority of the House. In such a case the majority of the majority would be a minority of Parliament. Take another case. The government introduce a bill, some of the details of which are not acceptable to more than a bare majority of their supporters. The ministerial minority wish to amend it, and the amendments which they desire would also be acceptable to the whole of the opposition. But ministers refuse to give way, and the bill is eventually carried, the whole of the ministerial following voting for it rather than break up the ministry. In this case the majority of the majority would be a very small minority of whole House.

Government by Party and government by the majority are therefore two very different things.

. . . If Government by Party is not government by majority, on what ground can it rest its claims? It cannot be that party government is necessary to the progress of legislation, as we have seen six Reform Bills rejected in succession because they were made party questions, and the seventh only carried because both sides of the House agreed to withdraw it from the sphere of party politics. Nor can it be that party government is necessary for the support of the government of the day, for it is in order to get at the government of the day that ministerial measures are rejected, the opposition preferring to sacrifice even good measures rather than allow ministers to remain in office. Nor can it be said that party government is an essential part of the representative system, because it is evident that representative institutions would work far better without it. Representative institutions flourished in England for centuries before party government was ever heard of. Indeed, party government is a positive hindrance to the effective working of the representative system. The fundamental idea of the representative system is responsibility to the constituent body; the leading principle of party government is loyalty to party organization. The representative owes allegiance to his constituents and to them only; the party man sinks the representative in the partisan and votes and acts as his leader directs him.

The advocates of party government do not indeed deny that their system is at variance with the principle of representation. Nay more, they frankly admit the fact, though, strangely enough, they nevertheless cling tenaciously to their theory. "Parliamentary government," says Earl Grey, "is essentially a government by means of party. . . . The House of Commons owes its success as an active part of the supreme authority, and its peculiar excellencies, to what are regarded as defects and departures from the principle in our representative system . . . and it is chiefly through these defects that the ministers of the Crown have been enabled to obtain the authority they have exercised in the House of Commons." Parliamentary Government and party government are represented as synonymous, a mistake which runs throughout Earl Grey's book on the subject. But what we have here more particularly to note is, first, the admission that party government owes its success to "defects and departures" from the principle of representation; and, secondly, the statement that it is owing to these very defects and departures that "the ministers of the Crown have been enabled to obtain the authority they have exercised in the House of Commons." According to Earl Grey, therefore, party government has had the happy effect of enabling ministers to obtain "authority" in the House, and it is carried on for the benefit of ministers, and in order to enable them to coerce Parliament. And no doubt, in this respect, the system has succeeded admirably. Party Government has placed Parliament at the feet of the ministry of the day. We have already seen how a ministry, by means of a party vote, may coerce a majority; we may also see how a ministry may exercise authority and openly set the House at defiance.

. . . As a rule, ministers profess great consideration for the opinions of Parliament. It is only the opposition minority that they treat with contempt. Where an important vote is pending they first try to make sure of their majority. If there are any signs of disaffection in the ministerial rank and file, they rally their party, an appeal is made to party feeling, the disaffected have to stand out, all the influence at the command of ministers is employed to conciliate them, and when all else fails, a threat of resignation or of a dissolution of Parliament will generally bring them to terms. The ministerial ranks are then closed, and the re-united majority behind the treasury benches are used to crush the opposition minority. To the outside public all seems fair and square, but none the less effectively have ministers exercised their influence and authority to silence the voice of the majority.

But it is really desirable that ministers of the Crown should exercise authority over Parliament? Is it not desirable rather that Parliament should exercise authority over ministers? Is it not an essential principle of parliamentary government that ministers should be held responsible to Parliament, instead of Parliament being held responsible to ministers?...........

But, say the advocates of Party government, the business of the country cannot be carried on without a strong ministry. It is necessary, we are assured, that a government should have a large and pliant majority behind them to enable them to retain their position and to carry their measures through Parliament. We are left in no manner of doubt as to how this majority was got together in the pre-reform era. "The adherents of the ministry," says Todd, "were obtainable from the first by means of various small boroughs which were under the direct control of the Treasury, and of other boroughs which were subject to the influence of certain great families or wealthy proprietors, who were willing to dispose of the same in support of an existing administration." And this majority was, according to the candid admission of another friend and advocate of party government, retained in a still more objectionable manner. "Parliamentary government," says Earl Grey, "derives its whole force and power from the exercise of an influence akin to corruption."

. . . When there is no great question agitating the country, parties in the House are, as a rule, evenly balanced, and ministers are continually changing. A succession of weak administrations is the inevitable result of such a state of things. A notable illustration of this we have in the condition of political parties in the Italian Parliament for some time past. The Parliament of Italy is modelled on the English system of Government by Party, and there have been no less than twenty-five new administrations in that country in eighteen years, or an average of one every eight or nine months. In New Zealand, also, where the worst features of the parliamentary system of the mother country have been adopted, there were in 1872 no less than nine changes of government within seven months. A general election, and a good cry to go to the country with, would have put an end to this state of things. Party government in England has only been saved from merited contempt by the party leaders on either side adroitly seizing on every question of public interest, and turning it to account for party purposes. . . .

Like the dogma of the divine rights of kings and passive obedience, party government came to the front during the stormy period of the Revolution. The system is indeed so monstrous, that it could only have found acceptance at a time when national animosities ran high, and the people were in an abnormal state of excitement. Under no ordinary circumstances is it conceivable that the English people would have tolerated a political system so entirely different from that to which they had been so long accustomed, and so opposed to their practice in the affairs of everyday life. To the mass of the people it was, and always will be, a matter of utter indifference as to who were in office or who out of it, so long as the country is well governed. They had been accustomed to send their representatives to Parliament to confer togethe rand co-operate for the common good of the whole community. It must therefore have shocked their moral sensibilities when they discovered that their representatives, instead of attending to the business of the country for which they had been elected, were devoting themselves to far other purposes ; that no sooner did they come together than they immediately ranged themselves on opposite sides of the House ; that they openly avowed hostile intentions towards one another ; that they at once proceeded to open acts of hostility ; that they spent their time and energies in vilifying one another, in misrepresenting one another's motives, opinions and actions, and in attempting to ruin one another's reputations, to defeat one another's plans, and to delay and mutilate, when they could not reject, one another's measures. And that men eminent for their talents, their eloquence and even their uprightness in other relations of life, should do all this without any sense of its impropriety and its injustice, was a sight not calculated to raise parliamentary institutions in the estimation of right thinking men. Had it been the design of its authors to demoralize the public mind, to impede the public business, to create natural animosities and general anarchy, they could not have better accomplished their end than by the introduction of such a system as this. Nothing can be more obvious to common sense than that the representatives of a great nation could be bound together by the same interests, aims and aspirations as the people themselves, and that they should co-operate with them for the common good of the whole country ; and nothing can be more absurd than to suppose that the common good could be achieved by a system that tends to create and perpetuate party strife and national animosities. We might as well create discord in order to produce harmony, or provoke quarrels for the purpose of promoting friendship and cordiality. The most extraordinary part of the matter is that there are still men to be found who believe such a vicious system is essential to parliamentary government.

This species of party warfare, too, is peculiar to parliamentary life, I had almost said to English parliamentary life, for it has not fairly established itself in any non-English speaking races, and even in England itself it has found no place in any other departments of public or private service. It is unknown in the Church. Ecclesiastical assemblies, whether established or dissident, have not adopted it, and I am not aware that these assemblies are more disorderly, or that their business is worse conducted on that account. It is also unknown in municipal life, where the representative system is in full vigour. The local representatives do not range themselves in hostile camps and spend their time and energies in faction fights. On the contrary, they meet, discuss and vote on civic matters, and absolutely ignore parliamentary precedent in their mode of conducting business. Party organization is equally unknown in commercial life, where the representative system also exists. The board of directors is a minature parliament elected by the shareholders to manage their business for them. But no one ever heard of party organizations in the board-room of a joint stock company. A commercial undertaking conducted on the improved parliamentary model would be doomed to certain ruin. Had Government by Party not come into existence under exceptional circumstances : had it not been the slow growth of generations ; had it not been associated with the names of our most eminent men and with some of the proudest events of our history and had almost become a part of our natural life, it would find few defenders amongst us at the present day. The system is tolerated because of old associations, and because we have come to think that it is in some way an essential part of our time-honoured Constitution ; but if it were now, for the first time, proposed for our acceptance, I venture to say that it would not recommend itself either to the intelligence or to the moral sense of the community.

ELECTING REPRESENTATIVES.

By H. R. Droop. From the Journal of the Statistical Society, June 1881.

The election of representatives has become, in modern times, a most important part of all political and social machinery. Whenever a number of persons cannot conveniently meet together to determine how their common affairs should be managed ; whether because they are too numerous, or for want of leisure, or for any other reason, they elect representatives to act for them. Thus, not only national assemblies like the House of Commons, and municipal bodies, such as town councils, school boards, and boards of guardians, but also boards of directors for joint stock companies, and committees of voluntary societies, consist either altogether or to a great extent of elected representatives. It is assumed that the electors have it in their power to elect such representatives as will be satisfactory substitutes for themselves, and will, by their deliberations and votes, yield substantially the same results as if all the electors met and deliberated and voted as a single body. But whether and how far this assumption may be realised, will depend to a great extent upon the mode in which these representatives are elected. Until within the last few years it was almost universally taken for granted that there was only one possible mode of electing representatives, viz., that now known as majority voting, according to which each elector may vote for as many candidates as there are representatives to be elected, but may only give one of his votes to the same candidate. It is called "majority voting" because whenever a sufficient number of electors to constitute a majority of the constituency agree to vote for the same set of candidates, they can secure the election of their whole set of candidates.

Of late years, several other methods of electing representatives have been devised as substitutes for majority voting, and some of them have been not merely discussed theoretically, but brought into practical operation. Of these methods, those best known in England are, (1) the limited vote, applied by the Reform Act of 1867 to three-cornered constituencies and the city of London, and since introduced on a much more extensive scale in Brazil, (2) cumulative voting, applied in 1870 to school board elections, and also in use in the Cape Colony (since 1853), and in Illinois and Pennsylvania ; and, (3) the preferential vote of Mr. Hare's scheme, and of M. Andræ's Danish constitution. . . .

Obviously these different methods of electing representatives are all practical applications of the science of statistics. They all consist in collecting certain statistical data as to whom the electors wish to have as representatives, and putting together these data so as to construct these into a representative assembly.

Majority Voting.

The method of majority voting cannot claim to have originated in any scientific consideration of the problem how a representative assembly might best be formed. It has manifestly been developed gradually out of the mode in which an assembly decides upon any proposal that may be submitted to it. Until the abolition of the show of hands by the Ballot Act of 1872, the first stage in an English parliamentary election consisted in asking the electors, as to each candidate separately, whether he should be their representative. In the second stage, at the poll, when the votes of the electors were recorded systematically it was convenient to receive the votes for all the candidates at once, and then the majority vote rule was adopted, being no doubt recommended by the consideration that it would lead to the same practical result as if the electors had voted separately for or against each candidate. According to either process a majority of one more than half the voters in favour of any candidate or candidates secures his or their election. . . .

At the present day, at any rate in electing representatives for parliamentary or municipal assemblies, electors do not seek exclusively or mainly to select the most honest, intelligent, and competent of the candidates. On the contrary, with but few exceptions, the electors pay very little attention to the personal qualifications of the candidates, and look only at the views they hold and the measures they promise to support. What they aim at securing is that their views and their measures should prevail in and be carried out by the assembly.

Majority Voting may completely Exclude Minority.

It may happen that the same party has the upper hand in every constituency, and that the other party has no representative whatever in the assembly. Thus in Geneva, according to a report presented to the Grand Council in 1870, by three of its members, Messrs. Roget,

Morin, and Bellamy, "the opposition has always numbered more than one-third of the electors, and we have seen it successively represented by 0, 7 deputies, and 1 deputy." This refers to the grand council, which consisted of 102 deputies, for the election of which the canton was divided into three constituencies. The same happened in Maryland in 1868, according to Mr. Simon Sterne's "Personal Representation" (Lippincott, Philadelphia, 1870), p. 71. In this election 62,356 votes were cast for democratic candidates, and 30,442 for republican, and yet this republican minority of nearly one-third of the whole body of voters, did not obtain a single representative in either the senate or the house of representatives.

Majority Voting may give Minority Control of Assembly.

But as a rule the representatives are divided more or less unequally between the two parties, the proportions depending however not upon the comparative strength of the two parties in the constituencies, but on the number of constituencies in which each party happens to have the majority, and the number of representatives returned by these constituencies. This will usually exaggerate the difference between the two parties, and give the stronger party a much larger majority in the assembly than it has in the constituencies ; but sometimes on the contrary it assigns the majority in the assembly to the party which is really in a minority in the constituencies. To make my meaning clearer, I will assume that each constituency has a number of representatives in exact proportion to the number of electors it comprises, an assumption which will be very nearly correct in countries where representation is in proportion to population, e. g., in the United States and in France, and which is being more nearly realized in the United Kingdom by every successive Reform Bill. I will further assume that there are 1,990,000 electors who have to elect 199 representatives, or one representative for each 10,000 electors. Suppose now that 100 of these representatives are elected by the A party by narrow majorities of 5,100 to 4,900 in constituencies returning only one member, of 10,200 to 9,800 in constituencies returning two members and of numbers in the same proportion of 51 to 49 for constituencies returning three or more members, while the other 99 members are elected by the B party, by unanimous constituencies of in all 990,000. Then the A party which has elected 100 representatives, and therefore has a majority in the assembly, will have only received the votes of 510,000 electors, while the B party, which has only 99 representatives, will have received the votes of 490,000+990,000=1,480,000 electors, or more than 74 per cent. i. e., very nearly three-fourths of the 1,990,000 electors.

This is, of course, an extreme and improbable case, imagined to illustrate what majority voting may possibly do in the way of putting the minority in the place of the majority, but many very much more probable distributions of votes might be suggested, which would produce substantially the same result, i. e., that the majority of representatives would correspond to the minority among the electors. Moreover, such cases are known to have repeatedly occurred in practice. In the United States the President is not elected by a direct vote of all citizens entitled by the franchise, but by a body of electors in a representative assembly, of whom a certain number, from 35 in New York to 1 in Nevada, are elected by each State, all the citizens of a State voting as a single constituency. At three of the four presidential elections next preceding the civil war of 1871, the successful candidate only received a minority of the popular vote. Thus General Taylor had only 1,362,242 votes, when Cass and Van Buren had between them 1,515,173 votes. Mr. Buchanan, again, had only 1,838,229 votes, while Fremont and Fillmore had between them 2,215,789 votes. So Lincoln had only 1,866,152 votes, while Douglas, Bell, and Breckenridge, who were all opposed to him on the slavery question, obtained between them 2,813,741 votes, or nearly a million more.

The following additional instances are taken from an article, by Mr. Dudley Field, in "Putnam's Magazine" for June, 1870, p. 712: "In New York, in the Assembly, 76 republican members were elected in 1868 by 397,899 votes, while only 52 democratic members were elected by 431,510 votes." Proportionally there ought to have been 67 democrats, and 61 republicans. In the same year, "In California the republicans elected 23 members by 54,592 votes, while the democrats elected 97 members by a less number, that is by 54,078."

In Belgium, according to M. Leon Pety de Thozée, "Réforme Electorale," p. 8, Bruxelles. 1874, "In the elections of 14th June, 1870, 18,737 electors voted for the liberals, and only 14,096 for the catholics, and yet only 31 liberal members were elected, against 30 catholics, and if a very small number of votes had been changed at Charleroi, there would have been only 29 liberal members to represent 57 per cent. of the electors, and 32 catholics to represent the minority of 43 per cent.

These instances show that majority voting is not always able to ensure that the majority of representatives is on the same side with the majority among the electors.

Instability under Majority Voting.

Moreover, when an assembly is elected by majority voting the relative strength of the different parties is much more unstable and fluctuating than it would be under such a system of proportional representation as I have just referred to. Then the fluctuations would only be in proportion to the changes of opinion which time and circumstances might produce among the electors. Under majority voting it often happens (indeed much more frequently than would be anticipated à priori) that elections are decided by very narrow majorities, so that if only a very few votes changed sides the representation would be transferred to the other party.

Narrow Majorities under Majority Voting.

To illustrate this, I have prepared tables showing for the last three general elections for the United Kingdom, those of 1868, 1874, and 1880, (1) how many seats were won by majorities not exceeding 100, and (2) how many seats were won by majorities not exceeding 10 per cent. of the votes polled for the successful candidate.

From Tables I and II it appears that in 1868 34 conservatives and 33 liberals owed their success to majorities of less than 100, while 48 conservatives and 48 liberals gained their seats by majorities less in each case than 10 per cent. of the votes polled for the successful candidate. I have further calculated how many voters must change sides in order to transfer these seats to the other party. I find from Table I (of majorities under 100) that the 34 conservative seats would be transferred to the liberals if 790 voters changed sides, and that the 32 liberal seats would be transferred to the conservatives if 657 voters changed sides.

Instability Resulting from Narrow Majorities.

It is easy to understand how a slight change in political opinion among the electors may produce a very considerable change in the balance of parties among their representatives. The political system is in fact always in a state of unstable equilibrium, liable to be turned upside down by anything that may make the one party popular or the other unpopular at the time of a general election. This makes the leaders of parties extremely sensitive to fluctuations of public opinion, and unwilling to risk even a slight amount of temporary unpopularity ; while on the other hand it makes popular agitators much more influential than they would be if the elections did not so often depend upon small majorities, and thus come to be decided by that class among the electors whose votes are most readily affected by temporary fluctuations of opinion.

Corruption Due to Narrow Majorities.

The tables of narrow majorities (Nos. I to VI) will also explain why electors under majority voting are so liable to be influenced by bribery, treating, intimidation, and other undue influences. The bulk of the electors in a constituency may be too honest to be bribed or corrupted, and too independent to be intimidated, but there will always be some few who are accessible to such influences, and whenever the honest and independent electors are divided into two nearly equal parties, supporting two rival candidates, or sets of candidates, the election is really left in the hands of the corrupt or dependent residue. . . .

It occasionally happens, as election investigations have shown, that not only a small residue, but a considerable fraction, perhaps a majority, of a constituency has become corrupt. But in these cases it will usually be found that the corruption has gradually increased from small beginnings. A few voters having been bribed to turn an election, gradually more and more insist on being paid. If the election managers had not been tempted at first to bribe a few, the constituency would have remained pure.

Majority voting is also responsible for a great part of the expenditure incurred by candidates in retaining election agents, having committee rooms, advertising, and bringing voters to the poll. Within certain limits, expenditure for these purposes is legitimate, as contributing to make the views and claims of the candidates known to the electors; but, unquestionably, a very large portion of this expenditure is only incurred because elections depend upon narrow majorities, and it is, therefore, worth while to incur a very considerable expenditure for the chance of securing a few additional votes.

Gerrymandering.

There is another mode in which the circumstance that under majority voting elections frequently depend upon a small balance of votes, may be used to transfer seats from one party to the other. This is by altering the constituency, and either adding or taking away some class of electors which is supposed to be much more favourable to the party than to the other. This may be done either by altering the boundaries of the electoral districts or by enfranchising or disfranchising a particular set of electors. The alteration of boundaries for this purpose is extensively practised in the United States, under the name of gerrymandering.

Division into Two Parties.

Thus far I have reasoned on the assumption that the division into two, and only two parties, which is found almost everywhere under majority voting, will not be affected by the change to another mode of voting. But in fact, as I believe, this limitation of electoral contests to only two parties is due mainly to majority voting, and would be more or less broken in upon if any method of voting were substituted which enabled smaller sections of the electors to obtain separately their respective shares of the representation without being compelled to combine together to form a majority party. That majority voting by thus compelling smaller sections to combine together, on pain of being left unrepresented, tends to limit to only two the number of parties competing at an election, I have shown in a previous part of this paper. It may be thought, however, that this, though an adequate cause, may not be the only possible cause. It is a prevailing opinion among those who confine their attention to English party divisions, that though the creeds of the liberal and conservative parties may vary from time to time in their details, they correspond substantially to two opposite tendencies of thought, which produce naturally two opposite sets of opinions and two opposing parties. But even without going outside English politics, anyone who examines carefully the opinions from time to time advocated by these two parties on those questions of domestic and foreign policy which from time to time prominently occupy public attention, will, I think, come to the conclusion that not unfrequently the members of each party are kept in agreement with each other far more by reluctance to separate from their common organization (which under majority voting is the condition of their exercising any political influence) than by any of the principles which they hold in common. And when we look beyond the United Kingdom to other countries where representative government with majority voting has been for a long time in operation, to the United States, to Switzerland, or to Belgium, we shall find everywhere the same division into two and only two parties, but the character of the party division varying in different countries. In the United States the distinguishing characteristics of the rival parties have nothing whatever in common with those of our Liberals and Conservatives, and this is also true of the Independents and Radicals of Geneva. We find, moreover, that the same party divisions usually run through all elections, whether federal, State, or municipal, or, as the case may be, national or municipal, though there is no connection between the questions to be dealt with by the different sets of representatives. These phenomena I cannot explain by any theory of a natural division between opposing tendencies of thought, and the only explanation which seems to me to account for them is that the two opposing parties into which we find politicians divided in each of these countries have been formed and are kept together by majority voting.

PARTIZAN GOVERNMENT.

By Wm. D. LeSueur. From the North American Review; Vol. CXXXII. (1881).

In an article already referred to as written some years ago, we expressed ourselves as follows, on the subject of party journalism: "It is not the bitterness of political discussion that seems to us the worse result of the party system; it is its amazing hollowness. A reasonable man is simply lost in amazement as he reads, day after day, in ably edited journals, whole columns of writing in which there is hardly the faintest gleam of sincere conviction to be discerned. Day after day the same miserable evasions, the same varnishing over of unsightly facts, the same reiterations of unproved charges against opponents, the same taking for granted of things requiring proof, the same proving of things that nobody questions, the same hypocritical appeals to the good sense of electors whom every effort is being used to misinform and confuse, the same dreary, unmeaning platitudes,—in a word, the same utter abuse of the reasoning faculty and of the functions and privileges of a free press. Of course, so long as both sides indulge in this kind of thing, each can make out at least a partial case against the other; and so a constant crossfire is kept up in the exposure of misrepresentations and the rectification of all that has been set down in malice or unduly extenuated on one side or the other. To-day, a good point is made by the opposition; to-morrow, it will be returned to them, if possible, with interest. Such is the party system of political warfare—a system which ought to have won the admiration of Archdeacon Paley, since it possesses the crowning attribute which was lacking to that celebrated watch of his, the power, namely, of perpetually reproducing itself."

Now, in so far as this language is applicable to the political controversies of to-day,—and few will deny it a certain applicability,—it becomes the duty of all who have it in their power to influence public opinion independently of party, to call attention in season and out of season to the utter insincerity of the whole performance. If people answer that they do not look for sincerity in political journals, and that for their own part all they want is to hear all possible good of their own side and all possible evil of the other, nothing more can be said; they must die, if they are determined to do so, in their sins. Some, it must be allowed, though they are not likely to make such an avowal, might do so with truth; for there are misguided individuals in the community who outdo in party bigotry the most violent of their leaders, just as there are lay devotees who far outdo their priests in superstition. On the other hand, there are many who have a tincture of fair-mindedness, and some respect for their own understandings, and who would be inclined to resent any deliberate attempts to befog and befool them. To these an appeal on behalf of rational and decent methods in political discussion may hopefully be made; not in the expectation, as we have before said, of doing away with parties and caucuses, with managers and wire-pullers, but of leading these to recognize some limit to their powers.

That party controversy, is in general the merest parody of anything like legitimate and serious political argument, is easily shown to any one who is not himself a hopeless thrall to party; and not less demonstrable is it that the systematic depreciation and abuse of public men tends to poison the whole political atmosphere and to educate the rising generation in a sickly cynicism by robbing them of all opportunity of recognizing and admiring public virtue in their own land and time. Let genuine, unmistakable corruption be exposed and lashed; and, if possible, let the operation be performed by some one who hates corruption in a friend even more than in a foe; but let not errors of judgment receive the denunciation due only to deliberate misdoing. Where public services have been rendered, let them be cheerfully and unstintedly acknowledged; and where a man has won a general character for uprightness, let his character be reckoned the property of the nation, and not a foot-ball for faction. Is not our country's richest inheritance, to-day, the *character* of the men who laid the foundations of her national greatness? And shall it be said that the United States have ceased in the beginning of the second century of their independence to lay up this particular form of wealth? It is sad to think to what a trade calumny has been reduced, and that instead of a growing faith in those who are called to the service of the republic, there should be an established conventional tone of mockery and distrust. Yet who is there, practically conversant with public affairs, who does not know, that, many as are the evils that fasten themselves on government, the general state of things is not as bad, or nearly as bad, as is conventionally represented, that public men in general are far more honest than they get the credit of being, and that we are really, to a large extent, walking in a vain show of political wickedness, produced wholly and solely by the persistent falsifications of unscrupulous party journals? A vain show in one sense, for wickedness in the measure alleged does not exist; but a most serious reality in another, for this constant talk about evil *begets evil by begetting despair of good.*

PROPORTIONATE REPRESENTATION.

By Frederick Seebohm. The Contemporary Review, Vol. XLIV., 1883.

In the first place, it must be recognized that a Parliament is only a device for conveniently arriving at the will of the nation after proper discussion.

If a nation were one vast constituency, and could declare its will like a vestry, by a majority of direct votes on every question submitted to it, no system of representation would be needed. The process might be clumsy, and the proper discussion of each question imperfect, but the result would be simple, and in theory it would be a true government by the majority.

But in practice such a mode of government by *plébiscite* would be full of evils. A nation cannot deliberate and act *en masse*, and hence arises the necessity for a system of representation.

Now it is obvious that if instead of deciding each question by the direct vote of the whole nation, a certain number of members of Parliament were chosen by the majority of votes of the whole nation acting as one great constituency, Parliament would consist of members representing only the majority—*i.e.*, the larger half of the people—whilst the smaller half of the people would be unrepresented. The discussion in Parliament might be thus all on one side, and it would be possible that the conclusion arrived at by a majority of votes in such a Parliament might express the opinion of little more than a *fourth* of the *people*.

This, in a country pretty evenly divided in its political interests, would be recognized by every one as an altogether pernicious result—a complete failure of fair popular representation. For supposing, for instance, that there happened to be a contention of interests between trade and land, and that voters representing land had for the time the majority over those interested in trade. Parliament might find itself composed solely of landowners of various shades of opinion. The majority of these landowners might be the more bigoted half of their class; and thus a Parliament of bigots as regards land, representing little more than a fourth of the nation, might adopt a policy of Protection and cripple trade in the supposed interests of land, even against the will of the better though smaller half of their own class.

This is an extreme case, no doubt, but it is useful to put it, so that it may be seen clearly that government by the majority of a majority is no true popular representation. And further because it brings out the fact that the division of the nation into a multitude of separate constituencies is, after all, a device for securing that fair representation, which dealing with the nation as one great constituency would fail to secure. In old times, when only certain privileged classes had votes, it was the *only* device thought needful to obtain true representation. And it remained so till the introduction of the rough attempt, contained in the last Reform Bill, to provide for the representation of minorities in three-cornered constituencies.

PROPORTIONAL REPRESENTATION.

By Robert B. Haywood. From The Nineteenth Century, Vol. XV. (1884).

Mr. Cowen, in his fresh and vigorous speech at Newcastle, has seized this aspect of the question of reform, and well expressed it in the following words :—

" What is it we want ? Is it not government of the people by the people for the people ? Parliament should mirror the spirit, wisdom, and interest not of a section only, but of the entire nation. The elected should be an epitome of the electors. The majority must govern, but the minority should be heard. That is scarcely the case now, and every year it gets less so."

This then is real representation—that Parliament should be an epitome of the nation in all its variety. And does not this imply, when expressed in more formal, though less picturesque, language, that every group of electors who have common interests and common political sympathies and sentiments, should be represented in Parliament in due *proportion* to its numerical strength in the country ?

This is what is intended by the phrase " Proportional Representation." Strictly speaking the word *proportional* is superfluous, for representation, so far as it is real and fair, must be *proportional*, and if it deviates very widely from proportionality, it ceases to be in any true sense *representation* at all. But this word having been extended, or rather appropriated to the existing system, which I shall take the liberty of distinguishing in this paper as *majority representation*, and the phrase *minority representation* having been misunderstood or misrepresented, by those who are the slaves of phrases and catchwords, as implying that the minority should rule and not merely that it should be heard, the phrase " proportional representation " may be accepted as expressing the ideal representation which has been above described.

THE PROPORTIONAL REPRESENTATION SOCIETY.

By Sir John Lubbock. From The Nineteenth Century, Vol. XV. (1884).

Is there any way by which we can reconcile these views,—by which we can secure for the majority the power which is their right, and at the same time preserve for the minority that fair hearing to which they are justly entitled?

The present system, then, renders the result of a general election uncertain, and to a large extent a matter of chance; it leads to violent fluctuations in the balance of political power, and consequently in the policy of the country. In fact the present system may be good or may be bad, but it is not representation; and the question is whether we wish for representation in fact or in name only.

The adoption of proportional representation moreover would raise and purify the whole tone of political contests. What do we see now when there is a contest in any of our great northern cities? The majority of the Irish electors, instructed by the honourable member for Cork, withhold their votes. They do not consider the prosperity of the Empire as a whole, but what they regard as the advantage of Ireland. I do not blame them. They do not seem to me wise: yet I can sympathise with their devotion, mistaken though I think it is, to their own island. Then some deputy in the confidence of the Home Rule party has more or less clandestine and secret interviews with the candidates or their leading supporters. We hear the most opposite accounts of what has occurred. Each side accuses the other of truckling to the Home Rule Party, and selfishly imperilling the integrity of the Empire. It must be very unsatisfactory to all concerned; and it would be far better if Liverpool had eight votes, and the Home Rulers there are sufficiently strong to return a Home Rule member, than that they should extract doubtful pledges from reluctant candidates.

Moreover, the geographical differentiation of political views tends to become more and more accentuated, and might, I think, constitute a real danger. At present Scotland is overpoweringly Liberal, while the south-eastern counties of England, with scarcely an exception, are represented by honourable members sitting on the opposite side of the House. It is but a small consolation to the unrepresented Liberal of Kent to be told that the Conservatives of Scotland share the same grievances, and are as badly off as they are.

But further than this, it will be a great misfortune to the country if one part becomes and continues overwhelmingly Liberal and another Conservative—if their distinctive differences become questions of geography and locality rather than of opinion. The different portions of our Empire are not yet so closely fused that we can afford to despise this danger. In my own county we look upon the shires as distinctly lower and less civilised than we are.

America might have been spared a terrible civil war if the principle of proportional representation had been recognized in the composition of the House of Representatives. This was forcibly pointed out in the report unanimously adopted by the Committee of the United States Senate appointed in 1869 to consider the question of representative reform.

"The absence (they say) of any provision for the representation of minorities in the States of the south when rebellion was plotted, and when open steps were taken to break the Union, was unfortunate, for it would have held the Union men of those States together, and would have given them a voice in the electoral colleges and in Congress. But they were fearfully overborne by the plurality rule of elections, and were swept forward by the course of events into impotency or open hostility to our cause. By this rule they were shut out of the electoral colleges. Dispersed, unorganized, unrepresented, without due voice and power, they could oppose no effectual resistance to secession and to civil war."

We shall ourselves make the same mistake and run the same risk of civil war if we neglect all warning, and allow the loyal minority in Ireland to be altogether silenced and excluded. This is in my humble judgment perhaps the greatest danger with which England is now threatened.

The Proportional Representation Society has indeed hitherto confined itself to the adoption as the basis of its constitution of the following resolution : " That without prejudging how far the principle may be subsequently carried out, it is indispensible, as a first step towards securing the true representation of the electors, that whenever a constituency returns more than two members some form of proportional representation should be adopted."

I regret that this question has been so often argued as if the great or even the main reason for it was to admit representatives of small minorities. Indeed, it is often said that any such system would merely admit members who are in favour of crotchets. It is no doubt difficult to say what is really a crotchet. When Mr. Grote brought up the question of the Ballot was that a crotchet ? When Mr. Villiers brought forward Free Trade was that a crotchet ? Many and many of the opinions now generally entertained were regarded as crotchets when things first made their appearance. Everything must have a beginning, and almost everything, even proportional representation itself, has been regarded as a fad and a crotchet.

But in my humble judgment the representation of small sections is a very small part of the question. Whether small minorities represent the temporary delusion of the moment, or a great, although as yet unrecognized truth, the House of Commons is scarcely the proper sphere for their exertions. What I am much more anxious about is that the great parties in the State should be adequately represented in the different districts of the Empire.

Those who object to the fair representation of minorities do not seem to realize the difference between an executive government and a representative assembly. A government of course must be as far as possible homogeneous and of one mind, but a representative assembly should be a mirror of the nation. The exclusion of the minority, which is a necessity in the one case, would be tyranny and injustice in the other. We are told by those who have not studied the question that we wish to give the minorities the power which rightly belongs to the majorities. The very reverse is the case. An untrammelled system of proportional representation is, as Mr. Mill has truly said, " not only the most complete application of the democratic principle that has yet been made, but its greatest safeguard." I trust that under the new Bill we may secure for the new voters, as well as those already on the register, the right not merely of recording their vote, but of doing so in such a manner as may give to it all just and reasonable effect. If this be done, the Parliament of 1880 will have given effect to a great principle, and we shall have for the first time a really representative assembly. I venture to recommend the system of proportional representation to the House of Commons and to the country because it would give its just political weight to the vote of every elector ; it would elevate and purify the whole tone of electoral contests ; would obtain for the minority a fair hearing ; and last, not least, because it is the only mode of securing for the majority that preponderance to which of course they are justly entitled.

The following Members of Parliament have already joined the Proportional Representation Society :—

C. T. Dyke Acland	Rowland P. Blennerhassett	Francis Wm. Buxton
Henry G. Allen	Thomas William Boord	James A. Campbell
R. L. Allman	Charles Bradlaugh	William C. Cartwright
Ellis Ashmead-Bartlett	Henry A. Brassey	Lord E. Cecil
John E. F. Aylmer	J. Brinton	Sir Thomas Chambers, M.P.
Arthur James Balfour	Hon. St. John Brodrick	W. L. Christie
Thomas C. Baring	Alexander Brogden	Edward Clarke
Col. Barne	M. Brooks	Arthur Cohen
The Earl of Bective	Sir H. Harvey Bruce	Sir E. Colebroke
Michael Biddulph	James R. Bulwer	Eugene Collins

Thomas Collins
Colonel Colhurst
James Porter Corry
Alderman Cotton
George Courtauld
Leonard Henry Courtney
Joseph Cowen
Hon. H. F. Cowper
Ralph Creyke
Viscount Crichton
James Cropper
C. Dalrymple
David Davis
James Dickson
Thomas A. Dickson
Hon. John Charles Dundas
Viscount Ebrington
Henry Edwards
Lord Elcho
Hon. A. D. Elliott
George Errington
T. W. Evans
Wm. Ewart
Archibald Orr Ewing
Rt. Hon. Henry Fawcett
William Findlater
Sir W. H. B. Ffolkes
Viscount Folkestone
R. N. Fowler (Lord Mayor)
D. F. Gabbett
Rt. Hon. Edward Gibson
Sir A. Gordon
Daniel Grant
William Grantham
T. Greer
G. B. Gregory
Albert H. G Grey
Montague John Guest
Robert Thornhagh Gurdon
Lord George Hamilton
Mitchell Henry
The Hon Sydney Herbert
J. M. Maxwell Heron
‾ord A. Hill
Sir H. T. Holland
Lt.-Col. D. Milne Home
William H. Houldsworth
‛. Stafford Howard
William Lawies Jackson

Sir J. J. Jenkins
Hubert E. H. Jerningham
Coleridge J. Kennard
Colonel Kennard
Sir John Kennaway
Edward R. King-Harman
Colouel Kingscote
Dr. Kinnear
F. Winn Knight
Sir Rainald Knightley
Samuel Laing
Hon. F. W. Lambton
Sir J. Clarke Lawrence
Thomas Lea
Sir E. A. H. Lechmere
Hon. G. Leigh
Sir Baldwin Leighton
Stanley Leighton
Lord H. Lennox
Lord Lewisham
Sir Robert Lloyd Lindsay
Morgan Lloyd
Robert Loder
Rt. Hon. J. Lowther
Hon. W. Lowther
J. W. Lowther
Sir John Lubbock
Sir Andrew Lusk
Sir W. McArthur
Sir Thomas McClure
James Carlile M'Coan
Sir J. McGarel-Hogg
David MacIver
Colonel Makins
R. B. Martin
T. W. Master
Charles Henry Meldon
Sir Charles Henry Mills
Sir. F. G. Milner.
F. Monckton
Samuel Morley, M.P.
Arthur Moore
J. Mulholland
P. H. Muntz
E. Noel
J. S. North
Charles Morgan Norwood
Colonel O'Beirne
R. H. Paget

Robert William C. Patrick
Arthur Pease
Sir Henry Peek
E. L. Pemberton
John Pender
Frederick Pennington
Earl Percy
Lord Algernon Percy
Rt. Hon. Sir Lyon Playfair
Rt. Hon. David R. Plunket
Hon. W. Henry B. Portman
G. E. Price
John Henry Puleston
Pandeli Ralli
Sir John Ramsden
James Rankin
William Rathbone
Sir E. J. Reed
Sir Matthew W. Ridley
Chas. Campbell Ross
J. Round
Lord Arthur Russell
Thomas Salt
Bernhard Samuelson
Chas. Seeley
William Shaw
Henry B. Sheridan
Sir J. G. T. Sinclair
Rt. Hon. Wm. H. Smith
P. J. Smyth
Marquis of Stafford
C. H. Strutt
Henry Villiers Stuart
Charles Beilby Stuart-Wortley
Christopher Sykes
John Gilbert Talbot
John Pennington Thomasson
W. E. Murray Tomlinson
W. T. M. Torrens
Colonel Tottenham
Sir Richard Wallace
Sir S. H. Waterlow
Sir E. Watkin
Benjamin Whitworth
E. W. Brydges Willyams
Chas. H. Wilson
Henry de Worms
J. R. Yorke

REPRESENTATION AND MISREPRESENTATION.

Westminster Review, Vol. LXV., 1884.

A Society has recently been established under the presidency of Sir John Lubbock, with offices at Palace Chambers, Westminster, for the purpose of securing, as far as possible, the recognition of the principle of proportional representation in Parliamentary elections, and other representative institutions of the country, and has already received the support of nearly 200 members of Parliament. The Society as yet has expressed no opinion as to the best form of proportional representation, since this may depend upon the particular circum- stances of each case, nor does it insist that the system should be applied in the first instance to all the constituencies. The main object is to secure that in all constituencies returning more than two members, which after a redistribution of seats are likely to become more numerous, some system of proportional representation shall be retained.

The programme of this Society so forcibly expresses the need of a change in our present system that it is worth quoting at length : "The extension of the Franchise which is proposed in the Bill which Her Majesty's Government have introduced renders the con- sideration of the system under which members of Parliament are elected a matter of urgent importance, it being obvious that the present system of voting will under a uniform franchise tend to diminish that variety in the representation which has hitherto been considered essential to the constitution of the House of Commons.

"This system is also open to grave objections because, while it does not in all cases obtain for majorities their due predominance in the Legislature, it fails to secure for minorities that proportion of representation to which their numbers fairly entitle them. The present system of voting, no matter how the constituencies are arranged, may bring about either, on the one hand, the rule of the minority or, on the other, the political extinction of the minority.

"It renders therefore the result of a general election uncertain and to a large extent a matter of chance ; it leads to violent fluctuations in the balance of political power and consequently in the policy of the country.

"These objections will be greatly aggravated if large constituencies are to return a number of members at all in proportion to their magnitude, unless some plan of proportional representation be adopted. Thus, if Liverpool were to return eight members as an undivided constituency it would be obviously unjust that 31,000 electors belonging to either of the great parties in the State should return eight members while 30,000 belonging to the other should be altogether shut out from representation.

"It would also be most objectionable that it should be in the power of a few voters by changing sides to transfer eight seats from one party to the other, making a difference of sixteen votes on a division.

"Unless some method of proportional representation be adopted, it is probable that Ireland will be greatly misrepresented, and that those who hold moderate and loyal opinions, although numbering more than one-third of the whole electorate, may be every- where out-voted and reduced to silence.

"On the other hand the Irish electors in England have been hitherto almost entirely excluded from direct representation. It would be far better that the Irish electors in our great cities should return members of their own than that their votes should be the subject of more or less secret negotiation with the leaders of the different parties.

"The Proportional Representation Society, in preparing or supporting any measure dealing with the actual details of voting and the machinery of elections, will keep in view the following practical requisites :

(a) That the majority of the representation be secured to the majority of the electors.

(b) That the minority be secured a fair hearing.

(c) That the mode of voting be one easy to be understood and put in practice by the average elector.

(d) That every vote should have its due weight in determining the result of the election.

"Whilst mainly directing its efforts to the improvement of parliamentary representation, the Society will use its best endeavours to maintain the same principles in the election of other representative bodies, such as the municipalities and School Boards of the kingdom, and to support any amendment which may render our representative system still more just and efficient.

"Under any true theory of representation, the elected body should be, as far as is practicable, an accurate reflection of the state of opinion in the country. Without therefore prejudging how far the principle may be subsequently carried out, this Society deems it indispensable, as a first step towards securing the true representation of the electors, that whenever a constituency returns more than two members some form of proportional representation should be adopted.

"The Proportional Representation Society is based upon the acceptance of the foregoing principles, and has been formed for the purpose of promoting, by all means in its power, the adoption by Parliament of such measure of reform in the representation of the people as will secure that, while the majority should govern, every considerable section of the electors should be sure of a hearing in Parliament."

Local associations in connection with the parent Society are already beginning to be formed, and it is hoped before long to organize in this way the friends of proportional representation throughout the country.

In conclusion, it may be well to point out how this system of representation might be introduced into the country without any violent change, and so as to include in itself some of the advantages of equal electoral districts. Let the new Reform Bill provide, in the case of all boroughs returning more than two members, that they be divided into electoral wards equal in number to the members to be elected ; and to such boroughs let the system of alternative voting be applied ; the members, after they have been elected by the voters of the whole borough, choosing for which ward they will sit ; in case of a by-election the voters belonging to the ward of the deceased or retiring member being alone allowed to vote. It would not be necessary that the wards should be the same size, since their only object would be to replace a member who died or retired, and they would have no effect on the answer given by the country to any question submitted at a general election. If this system worked smoothly it might in a few years be extended to all single-member constituencies throughout the country. Lastly, when public opinion had become ripe for it, and the county government system had become firmly established, a Bill might be passed enabling each voter to vote for any candidate standing for any of the seats in the county, whether boroughs or divisions of the county ; the elected members choosing which of the constituencies in the county, if more than one, for which they had been proposed they would represent. In order not to lose the advantages of municipal life, all boroughs large enough to return three or more members should be excluded from the county and made counties of themselves.

To summarize the result at which we have arrived : We have shown that our present system is deficient, since it does not secure either that the majority should govern, or that the minority should be heard, while it prevents a large part of the electors expressing their views on social and other questions which are not matters of party politics, and places the choice of candidates almost entirely in the hands of party organizations. We have pointed out that these difficulties are likely to be increased by the Franchise Bill. We have examined the proposal to form equal electoral districts and have shown that it will not accomplish its objects while it will introduce fresh evils. We have examined the schemes for proportional representation and have shown that they would all secure that the majority would govern on party questions; that all considerable sections of the nation would be heard; and that two of these schemes have been proved by experience to present no practical difficulty in working. We have stated the objections which have been alleged against the third plan—that of alternative or transferable voting—and shown that they can all be avoided, and that this scheme is free from any objection that is found in the present system or in the systems of limited and cumulative voting. We have pointed out the few simple rules which would make its working certain and rapid; and lastly, we have shown that it could be introduced gradually without any sudden changes, and also without the loss of the political life and political history which are to be found in many of our present constituencies.

This is no party question; it is in the truest sense conservative, securing that no one class shall overwhelm the other by its numbers, and preventing any extreme party obtaining from a wave of popular feeling a control over the legislature; but it is equally a Liberal measure, providing for the growth and improvement of our institutions, giving to all parties and classes their share in the government of the country, and enabling the majority of the people always to rule.

Societies for the promotion of these views are now to be found in most of the nations of Europe, and the support they have received seems to point to the near approach of the time when they will be everywhere recognized as necessary to secure a good representative system. England, which has taught the principles of freedom to all other nations, will not, it may be hoped, be the last in recognizing the importance of these improvements in securing that the House of Commons shall be the true exponent of the people.

PARTY STRUGGLES.

From " England and Canada," 1884.

By Sandford Fleming.

The difficulty with our present system lies in the fact that the interests of party must be consulted, whatever the cost, whatever the sacrifice. Party takes precedence of every other consideration. Party seems to cloud the judgments of men who, in many instances, are irreproachable in private life. Public men seem to act on the principle that there is one creed and language for the hustings, the press and parliament, and another for social intercourse.

The Canadian Pacific Railway has been considered a political question during three administrations, and has played an important part in party warfare. Every year, since 1871, motion after motion has been made in Parliament relating to engineering operations and the mode of conducting the work. Seldom have there been such acrimonious discussions. Frequently the whole debate was dictated by the party results supposed to be obtainable. Committee followed Committee, year after year, in the Senate and House of Commons, nominally to investigate matters, in reality to create party capital. Who now can point out the slightest result from all these efforts ? Two Royal Commissions of special enquiry were appointed. The first made no report ; the second prolonged its sittings for two years, at a cost of some $40,000 to the country. What remains of the labours of those Commissions beyond the items of their cost in the public accounts ? The report of the second Commission was contained in two bulky volumes. The record of an attempt for party ends to blast the reputation of men who had given the best years of their lives to the performance of public duty. When this report was considered it was held to be so valueless that it has never been circulated.

In Canada we enjoy a liberal constitution, and it may be affirmed that it is the only principle of authority which, as a people, we would tolerate. It cannot, however, be said that in its present form our system of government is an unmixed blessing.

We may ask if representative government is ever to be inseparable from the defects which form the most striking feature in its application and administration, especially on this continent. Must a country constitutionally governed be inevitably ranged into two hostile camps ? One side denouncing their opponents and defaming the leading public men of the other, not hesitating even to decry and misrepresent the very resources of the community and to throw obstacles in the way of its advancement. Never was partyism more abject or remorseless. Its exigencies are unblushingly proclaimed to admit the most unscrupulous tactics and the most reprehensible proceedings. Is there no escape from influences so degrading to public life and so hurtful to national honor ?

It is evident that the evils which we endure are, day by day, extending a despotism totally at variance with the theory and principles of good government. Possibly Canada may be passing through a phase in the earlier stage of her political freedom. Can we cheer ourselves by the hope that institutions inherently good will clear themselves from the slough into which they unfortunately may be immersed ? May not the evils of partyism at last become so intensified that their climax will produce a remedy ? As by natural laws a liquid in the process of fermentation purifies itself by throwing off the scum and casting the dregs to the bottom, so may we be encouraged to believe that we are approaching the turning period in the political system we have fallen into, and that year by year Parliament will become less and less a convention of contending party men and be elevated to its true position in the machinery of representative government. Public life will then become more ennobling ; it will, indeed, be an object of ambition for men of honour and character to fill places in the Councils of the Nation, when rectitude of purpose and patriotism and truth will be demanded in all and by all who aspire to positions of national trust and dignity.

THE DESPOTISM OF PARTY.

By Herbert Tuttle. From Atlantic Monthly, Vol. LIV., 1884.

The party becomes a species of *imperium in imperio*. Its forms, its agents, its organs are closely patterned after those of the state ; it exercises the great functions of government ; it has its hierarchy of officials, acting within the circumscriptions, and ranging through all the grades which obtain in our political system. These officials feel the responsibility of their positions, which they compare to places of trust in civil administration. The struggles for place within the party are scarcely less keen than the struggles for political life ; the same arts of intrigue and persuasion are used ; the same acquiescence in the result of a contest is always expected, and rarely withheld. Thus the force of imagination alone, excited by the constant spectacle of this vast machine, completely equipped and manned and always in movement, leads people to regard it as a permanent institution, having a corporate existence in the state, and therefore entitled to be treated as an end in itself, and not as a means to the attainment of an end.

It is not, however, by the imagination alone that this illusion is maintained. This of itself would make the error dangerous ; but it has, besides that, led to the announcement of certain audacious propositions, and even to measures of actual legislation, which grossly confuse the distinction between a political party and a political commonwealth, and disclose a fatal tendency toward the very evil against which Mr. Webster so solemnly warned his countrymen. . . . .

Let us inquire for a moment to what, if pushed to its logical consequences, the politicians' view of party would lead. It is known that they abhor independents, and often express the patriotic opinion that every citizen should join a party. The majority in each party should again control its action, and the minority should frankly obey. A careful organization, with executive agents and representative assemblies would furnish the machinery for making the system effective. This seems to be a fair statement of the politicians' ideal. Now what would be the result if this ideal were realized ? The result would be to collect the voters of the country into two or three great parties, held together by inflexible rules of discipline and fealty, and each forbidden in effect to allow desertion or to receive deserters. As no changes of allegiance could take place, the relative strength of parties would be changed from year to year only by the death of existing members, and the enrollment of new ones from young men just reaching their majority, and from newly naturalized immigrants. But even this element of uncertainty can be somewhat reduced. The annual death-rate would probably bear the same ratio to the total membership in all the parties. Again, young men generally follow in the political footsteps of their fathers ; and as the birth-rate in the various parties would be also approximately equal, the balance of power would be little affected from this cause. We are confined, therefore, to the immigrants ; they would hold the key to the situation. If now it be assumed that the Irish would in general go to one party, and the Germans to the other, the issue would really lie between these two classes, which compose the great body of our foreign population. The problem of immigration would assume a new and startling interest. One party would find a potent ally in Irish famines, which encourage emigration from the Emerald Isle. The other would have a keen sympathy with the high taxes and the military system of Germany, which drive so many excellent men from the fatherland. The battles of American politics would be fought out by immigration agents and runners for the rival steamship lines, all liberally supplied with money from the campaign funds of the parties, and perhaps also with platforms, to be posted in the leading seaports and distributed by colporteurs in the interior.

REPRESENTATIVE GOVERNMENT.

By John Stuart Mill, 1884.

Two very different ideas are usually confounded under the name democracy. The pure idea of democracy, according to its definition, is the government of the whole people by the whole people, equally represented. Democracy as commonly conceived and hitherto practised, is the government of the whole people by a mere majority of the people, exclusively represented. The former is synonymous with the equality of all citizens ; the latter, strangely confounded with it, is a government of privilege, in favour of the numerical majority, who alone possess practically any voice in the State. This is the inevitable consequence of the manner in which the votes are now taken, to the complete disfranchisement of minorities.

The confusion of ideas here is great, but it is so easily cleared up, that one would suppose the slightest indication would be sufficient to place the matter in its true light before any mind of average intelligence. It would be so, but for the power of habit ; owing to which the simplest idea, if unfamiliar, has as great difficulty in making its way to the mind as a far more complicated one. That the minority must yield to the majority, the smaller number to the greater, is a familiar idea ; and accordingly men think there is no necessity for using their minds any further, and it does not occur to them that there is any medium between allowing the smaller number to be equally powerful with the greater, and blotting out the smaller number altogether. In a representative body actually deliberating, the minority must of course be overruled ; and in an equal democracy (since the opinions of the constituents, when they insist on them, determine those of the representative body) the majority of the people, through their representatives, will outvote and prevail over the minority and their representatives. But does it follow that the minority should have no representatives at all? Because the majority ought to prevail over the minority, must the majority have all the votes, the minority none? Is it necessary that the minority should not even be heard ? Nothing but habit and old association can reconcile any reasonable being to the needless injustice. In a really equal democracy, every or any section would be represented, not disproportionately, but proportionately. A majority of the electors would always have a majority of the representatives ; but a minority of the electors would always have a minority of the representatives. Man for man, they would be as fully represented as the majority. Unless they are, there is not equal government, but a government of inequality and privilege : one part of the people rule over the rest : there is a part whose fair and equal share of influence in the representation is withheld from them ; contrary to all just government, but above all, contrary to the principle of democracy, which professes equality as its very root and foundation.

The injustice and violation of principle are not less flagrant because those who suffer by them are a minority ; for there is not equal suffrage where every single individual does not count for as much as any other single individual in the community. But it is not only a minority who suffer. Democracy, thus constituted, does not even attain its ostensible object, that of giving the powers of government in all cases to the numerical majority. It does something very different : it gives them to a majority of the majority ; who may be, and often are, but a minority of the whole. All principles are most effectually tested by extreme cases. Suppose then, that, in a country governed by equal and universal suffrage, there is a contested election in every constituency, and every election is carried by a small majority. The Parliament thus brought together represents little more than a bare majority of the people. This Parliament proceeds to legislate, and adopts important measures by a bare majority of itself. What guarantee is there that these measures accord with the wishes of a majority of the people? Nearly half the electors, having been outvoted at the hustings, have had no influence at all in the decision ; and the whole of these may be, a majority of them probably are, hostile to the measures, having voted against those by whom they have been carried. Of the remaining electors, nearly half have chosen representatives who, by supposition, have voted against the measures. It is possible, therefore, and not at all improbable, that the opinion which has prevailed was agreeable only to a minority of the nation, though a majority of that portion of it, whom the institutions of the country have erected into the ruling class. If democracy means the certain ascendancy of the majority, there are no means of insuring that, but by allowing every individual figure to tell equally in the summing up. Any minority left out, either purposely or by the play of the machinery, gives the power not to the majority, but to a minority in some other part of the scale.

. . . . Is it not a great grievance, that in every Parliament a very numerous portion of the electors willing and anxious to be represented, have no member in the House for whom they have voted ? Is it just that every elector of Marylebone is obliged to be represented by two nominees of the vestries, every elector of Finsbury or Lambeth by those (as is generally believed) of the publicans ? The constituencies to which most of the highly educated and public spirited persons in the country belong, those of the large towns, are now, in great part, either unrepresented or misrepresented. The electors who are on a different side in party politics from the local majority, are unrepresented. Of those who are on the same side, a large proportion are misrepresented; having been obliged to accept the man who had the greatest number of supporters in their political party, though his opinions may differ from theirs on every other point. The state of things is, in some respects, even worse than if the minority were not allowed to vote at all ; for then, at least the majority might have a member who would represent their own best mind : while now, the necessity of not dividing the party, for fear of letting in its opponents, induces all to vote either for the first person who presents himself wearing their colours, or for the one brought forward by their local leaders ; and these, if we pay them the compliment, which they very seldom deserve, of supposing their choice to be unbiassed by their personal interests, are compelled, that they may be sure of mustering their whole strength, to bring forward a candidate whom none of the party will strongly object to—that is, a man without any distinctive peculiarity, any known opinions except the shibboleth of the party. This is strikingly exemplified in the United States ; where at the election of President, the strongest party never dares put forward any of its strongest men, because every one of these, from the mere fact that he has been long in the public eye, has made himself objectionable to some portion or other of the party, and is there-fore not so sure a card for rallying all their votes, as a person who has never been heard of by the public at all until he is produced as the candidate. Thus, the man who is chosen, even by the strongest party, represents perhaps the real wishes only of the narrow margin by which that party outnumbers the other. Any section whose support is necessary to success, possesses a veto on the candidate. Any section which holds out more obstinately than the rest, can compel all the others to adopt its nominee ; and this superior pertinacity is un-happily more likely to be found among those who are holding out for their own interest, than for that of the public. The choice of the majority is therefore very likely to be determined by that portion of the body who are the most timid, the most narrow-minded and prejudiced, or who cling most tenaciously to the exclusive class-interest ; in which case the electoral rights of the minority, while useless for the purposes for which votes are given, serve only for compelling the majority to accept the candidate of the weakest or worst portion of themselves.

That while recognising these evils, many should consider them as the necessary price paid for a free government, is in no way surprising : it was the opinion of all the friends of freedom, up to a recent period. But the habit of passing them over as irremediable has become so inveterate, that many persons seem to have lost the capacity of looking at them as things which they would be glad to remedy if they could. From despairing of a cure, there is too often but one step to denying the disease ; and from this follows dislike to having a remedy proposed, as if the proposer was creating a mischief instead of offering relief from one. People are so inured to the evils, that they feel as if it were unreasonable, if not wrong, to complain of them. Yet, avoidable or not, he must be a purblind lover of liberty on whose mind they do not weigh ; who would not rejoice at the discovery that they could be dis-pensed with. Now, nothing is more certain, than that the virtual blotting out of the minority is no necessary or natural consequence of freedom ; that far from having any connexion with democracy, it is diametrically opposed to the first principle of democracy, representation in proportion to numbers. It is an essential part of democracy that minorities should be adequately represented. No real democracy, nothing but a false show of democracy, is possible without it.

Those who have seen and felt, in some degree, the force of these considerations, have proposed various expedients by which the evil may be, in a greater or less degree, mitigated. Lord John Russell, in one of his Reform Bills, introduced a provision, that certain constitu-encies should return three members, and that in these each elector should be allowed to vote only for two ; and Mr. Disraeli, in the recent debates, revived the memory of the fact by reproaching him for it, being of opinion, apparently, that it befits a Conservative statesman to regard only means, and to disown scornfully all fellow-feeling with any one who is betrayed, even once, into thinking ends. Others have proposed that each elector should be allowed to vote only for one. By either of these plans, a minority equalling or exceeding a third of the local constituency, would be able, if it attempted no more, to return one of the three members. The same result might be attained in a still better way, if, as proposed in an able pamphlet by Mr. James Garth Marshall, the elector retained his three votes, but was at liberty to bestow them all upon the same candidate. These schemes, though infinitely better than none at all, are yet but makeshifts, and attain the end in a very imperfect manner ; since all local minorities of less than a third, and all minorities, however numerous, which are made up from several constituencies, would remain unrepresented. It is much to be lamented, however, that none of these plans have been carried into effect, as any of them would have recognized the right principle, and prepared the way for its more complete application. But real equality of representation is not obtained, unless any set of electors amounting to the average number of a constituency, wherever in the country they happen to reside, have the power of combining with one another to return a representative. This degree of perfection in representation appeared impracticable, until a man of great capacity, fitted alike for large general views and for the contrivance of practical details—Mr. Thomas Hare—had proved its possibility by drawing up a scheme for its accomplishment, embodied in a Draft of an Act of Parliament : a scheme which has the almost unparalleled merit, of carrying out a great principle of government in a manner approaching to ideal perfection as regards the special object in view, while it attains incidentally several other ends, of scarcely inferior importance.

According to this plan, the unit of representation, the quota of electors who would be entitled to have a member to themselves, would be ascertained by the ordinary process of taking averages, the number of voters being divided by the number of seats in the House : and every candidate who obtained that quota would be returned, from however great a number of local constituencies it might be gathered. The votes would, as at present, be given locally ; but any elector would be at liberty to vote for any candidate, in whatever part of the country he might offer himself. Those electors, therefore, who did not wish to be represented by any of the local candidates, might aid by their vote in the return of the person they liked best among all those throughout the country, who had expressed a willingness to be chosen. This would, so far, give reality to the electoral rights of the otherwise virtually disfranchised minority. But it is important that not those alone who refuse to vote for any of the local candidates, but those also who vote for one of them and are defeated, should be enabled to find elsewhere the representation which they have not succeeded in obtaining in their own district. It is therefore provided that an elector may deliver a voting paper containing other names in addition to the one which stands foremost in his preference. His vote would only be counted for one candidate ; but if the object of his first choice failed to be returned, from not having obtained the quota, his second perhaps might be more fortunate. He may extend his list to a greater number, in the order of his preference, so that if the names which stand near the top of the list either cannot make up the quota, or are able to make it up without his vote, the vote may still be used for some one whom it may assist in returning. To obtain the full number of members required to complete the House, as well as to prevent very popular candidates from engrossing nearly all the suffrages, it is necessary, however many votes a candidate may obtain, that no more of them than the quota should be counted for his return : the remainder of those who voted for him would have their votes counted for the next person on their respective lists who needed them, and could by their aid complete the quota. To determine which of a candidate's votes should be used for his return, and which set free for others, several methods are proposed, into which we shall not here enter. He would of course retain the votes of all those who would not otherwise be represented ; and for the remainder, drawing lots, in default of better, would be an unobjectionable expedient. The voting papers would be conveyed to a central office, where the votes would be counted, the number of first, second, third, and other votes given for each candidate ascertained, and the quota would be allotted to every one who could make it up, until the number of the House was complete; first votes being preferred to second, second to third, and so forth. The voting papers, and all the elements of the calculation, would be placed in public repositories, accessible to all whom they concerned; and if any one who had obtained the quota was not duly returned, it would be in his power easily to prove it. These are the main provisions of the scheme.

In the first place, it secures a representation, in proportion to numbers, of every division of the electoral body: not two great parties alone, with perhaps a few large sectional minorities in particular places, but every minority in the whole nation, consisting of a sufficiently large number to be, on principles of equal justice, entitled to a representative. Secondly, no elector would, as at present, be nominally represented by some one whom he had not chosen. Every member of the House would be the representative of an unanimous constituency. He would represent a thousand electors, or two thousand, or five thousand, or ten thousand, as the quota might be, every one of whom would have not only voted for him, but selected him from the whole country; not merely from the assortment of two or three perhaps rotten oranges, which may be the only choice offered to him in his local market. Under this relation the tie between the elector and the representative would be of a strength, and a value, of which at present we have no experience. Every one of the electors would be personally identified with his representative, and the representative with his constituents. Every elector who voted for him, would have done so either because, among all the candidates for Parliament who are favourably known to a certain number of electors, he is the one who best expresses the voter's opinions, or because he is one of those whose abilities and character the voter most respects, and whom he most willingly trusts to think for him. The member would represent persons, not the mere bricks and mortar of the town —the voters themselves, not a few vestrymen or parish notabilities merely. All, however, that is worth preserving in the representation of places would be preserved. Though the Parliament of the nation ought to have as little as possible to do with purely local affairs, yet, while it has to do with them, there ought to be members specially commissioned to look after the interests of every important locality: and these there would still be. In every locality which could make up the quota within itself, the majority would generally prefer to be represented by one of themselves; by a person of local knowledge, and residing in the locality, if there is any such person to be found among the candidates, who is otherwise well qualified to be their representative. It would be the minorities chiefly, who being unable to return the local member, would look out elsewhere for a candidate likely to obtain other votes in addition to their own.

Of all modes in which a national representation can possibly be constituted, this one affords the best security for the intellectual qualifications desirable in the representatives. At present, by universal admission, it is becoming more and more difficult for any one, who has only talents and character, to gain admission into the House of Commons. The only persons who can get elected are those who possess local influence, or make their way by lavish expenditure, or who, on the invitation of three or four tradesmen or attorneys, are sent down by one of the two great parties from their London clubs, as men whose votes the party can depend on under all circumstances. On Mr. Hare's system, those who did not like the local candidates, or who could not succeed in carrying the local candidate they preferred, would have the power to fill up their voting papers by a selection from all the persons of national reputation, on the list of candidates, with whose general political principles they were in sympathy. Almost every person, therefore, who had made himself in any way honourably distinguished, though devoid of local influence, and having sworn allegiance to no political party, would have a fair chance of making up the quota; and with this encouragement such persons might be expected to offer themselves, in numbers hitherto undreamt of. Hundreds of able men of independent thought, who would have no chance whatever of being chosen by the majority of any existing constituency, have by their writings, or their exertions in some field of public usefulness, made themselves known and approved by a few persons in almost every district of the kingdom ; and if every vote that would be given for them in every place could be counted for their election, they might be able to complete the number of the quota. In no other way which it seems possible to suggest, would Parliament be so certain of containing the very *élite* of the country.

And it is not solely through the votes of minorities that this system of election would raise the intellectual standard of the House of Commons. Majorities would be compelled to look out for members of a much higher calibre. When the individuals composing the majority would no longer be reduced to Hobson's choice, of either voting for the person brought forward by their local leaders, or not voting at all ; when the nominee of the leaders would have to encounter the competition not solely of the candidate of the minority, but of all the men of established reputation in the country who were willing to serve ; it would be impossible any longer to foist upon the electors the first person who presents himself with the catchwords of the party in his mouth, and three or four thousand pounds in his pocket· The majority would insist on having a candidate worthy of their choice, or they would carry their votes somewhere else, and the minority would prevail. The slavery of the majority to the least estimable portion of their number would be at an end : the very best and most capable of the local notabilities would be put forward by preference ; if possible, such as were known in some advantageous way beyond the locality, that their local strength might have a chance of being fortified by stray votes from elsewhere. Constituencies would become competitors for the best candidates, and would vie with one another in selecting from among the men of local knowledge and connexions those who were most distinguished in every other respect.

The natural tendency of representative government, as of modern civilization, is towards collective mediocrity : and this tendency is increased by all reductions and extensions of the franchise, their effect being to place the principal power in the hands of classes more and more below the highest level of instruction in the community. But though the superior intellects and characters will necessarily be outnumbered, it makes a great difference whether or not they are heard. In the false democracy which, instead of giving representation to all, gives it only to the local majorities, the voice of the instructed minority may have no organs at all in the representative body. It is an admitted fact that in the American democracy, which is constructed on this faulty model, the highly cultivated members of the community, except such of them as are willing to sacrifice their own opinions and modes of judgment, and become the servile mouth-pieces of their inferiors in knowledge, seldom even offer themselves for Congress or the State Legislatures, so little likelihood have they of being returned. Had a plan like Mr. Hare's by good fortune suggested itself to the enlightened and patriotic founders of the American Republic, the Federal and State Assemblies would have contained many of these distinguished men, and democracy would have been spared its greatest reproach and one of its most formidable evils. Against this evil the system of personal representation, proposed by Mr. Hare, is almost a specific. The minority of instructed minds scattered through the local constituencies, would unite to return a number, proportioned to their own numbers, of the very ablest men the country contains. They would be under the strongest inducement to choose such men, since in no other mode could they make their small numerical strength tell for anything considerable. The representatives of the majority, besides that they would themselves be improved in quality by the operation of the system, would no longer have the whole field to themselves. They would indeed outnumber the others, as much as the one class of electors outnumbers the other in the country : they could always outvote them, but they would speak and vote in their presence, and subject to their criticism. When any difference arose, they would have to meet the arguments of the instructed few, by reasons, at least apparently, as cogent ; and since they could not, as those do who are speaking to persons already unanimous, simply assume that they are in the right it would occasionally happen to them to become convinced that they were in the wrong. As they would in general be well-meaning (for thus much may reasonably be expected from a fairly-chosen national representation), their own minds would be insensibly raised by the minds with which they were in contact, or even in conflict. The champions of unpopular doctrines would not put forth their arguments merely in books and periodicals, read only by their own side; the opposing ranks would meet face to face and hand to hand, and there would be a fair comparison of their intellectual strength, in the presence of the country. It would then be found out whether the opinion which prevailed by counting votes, would also prevail if the votes were weighed as well as counted. The multitude have often a true instinct for distinguishing an able man, when he has the means of displaying his ability in a fair field before them. If such a man fails to obtain at least some portion of his just weight, it is through institutions or usages which keep him out of sight. In the old democracies there were no means of keeping out of sight any able man ; the bema was open to him ; he needed nobody's consent to become a public adviser. It is not so in a representative government ; and the best friends of representative democracy can hardly be without misgivings, that the Themistocles or Demosthenes whose counsels would have saved the nation, might be unable during his whole life ever to obtain a seat. But if the presence in the representative assembly can be insured of even a few of the first minds in the country though the remainder consist only of average minds, the influence of these leading spirits is sure to make itself sensibly felt in the general deliberations, even though they be known to be, in many respects, opposed to the tone of popular opinion and feeling. I am unable to conceive any mode by which the presence of such minds can be so positively insured, as by that proposed by Mr. Hare.

PARTY GOVERNMENT.

By Mathew Macfie. From The Contemporary Review, Vol. XLVI., 1884.

If Parties were associated unswervingly with the same set of principles, even though these should sometimes happen to be erroneous, the spectacle of Party greed and reciprocal bitterness would, perhaps, be somewhat more endurable. But both Liberals and Tories have been notoriously fickle and time-serving. Too often have both supported a good cause from a bad motive, ever ready to advocate a new set of principles if by so doing the one party could deal a blow to the other.

We look in vain for principle regulating the conduct of the two great Parties in the State. Truth, honour, and fair dealing, as a rule, are alike surrendered to party convenience. An example of demoralized ethics is thus daily set by our statesmen, which if carried out in the relations of private life would be unsparingly condemned, and the combined religions teaching of the 90,000 preachers of all denominations in the country utterly fails to neutralize the effect of the moral injury thus publicly inflicted.

If Government by Party were identical with Government by the Majority in the Lower House, the faults of the system might perhaps be treated with great leniency. But it has not—although it is fallaciously said to have—even this redeeming feature in its favour. While the Government of the day is chosen from the side showing a majority in Parliament, it is simply a majority of the party which has a majority in the House, and not the majority of the whole House, which governs. Indeed, this majority of a majority, relatively to the totality of members may be, and often is, an actual minority. More than one case could be adduced, since the present Ministry was formed, in which a measure has been introduced, not acceptable to all the members on the Liberal side. Party organization, however, for the most part has triumphed over the dissentients. But it has undoubtedly happened sometimes that the dissentient minority among the Government supporters, secretly opposed to a given measure, when added to the whole force of the Opposition, has represented a distinct majority of the entire House. Clearly, in such a case, therefore, the majority of the majority by whose influence the Bill is carried, would constitute a minority of Parliament. The effect of temporizing Party tactics under such conditions, is that the views of the majority are really misrepresented.

Not the least potent objection to Party Government is that the arrangement is diametrically at variance with the principle of representation. The cardinal idea of the representative system is responsibility to the constituent body only. The basis of Party Government is loyalty to party organization. The Party man merges his representative individuality in the partisan, and votes as an unthinking machine under the direction of his leader. An amusing illustration of this pliant conformity is given in the experience of one of the rank and file who once confessed " that he made it an invariable rule never to be present at a debate or absent on a division, and that he only once, during the course of a long parliamentary life, ventured to vote according to his conscience, and on that occasion he had voted wrong."

PARTY FEELING.

From " Popular Government." By Sir Henry S. Maine, 1884.

The Wire-puller is not intelligible unless we take into account one of the strongest forces acting on human nature—Party feeling. Party feeling is probably far more a survival of the primitive combativeness of mankind than a consequence of conscious intellectual differences between man and man. It is essentially the same sentiment which in certain states of society leads to civil, intertribal, or international war ; and it is as universal as humanity. It is better studied in its more irrational manifestations than in those to which we are accustomed. It is said that Australian savages will travel over half the Australian continent to take in a fight the side of combatants who wear the same Totem as themselves. Two Irish factions who broke one another's heads over the whole island are said to have originated in a quarrel about the colour of a cow. In Southern India, a series of dangerous riots are constantly arising through the rivalry of parties who know no more of one another than that some of them belong to the party of the right hand and others to that of the left hand. Once a year, large numbers of English ladies and gentlemen, who have no serious reason for preferring one university to the other, wear dark or light blue colours to signify good wishes for the success of Oxford or Cambridge in a cricket-match or boat-race. Party differences, properly so-called, are supposed to indicate intellectual, or moral, or historical preference ; but these go a very little way down into the population, and by the bulk of partisans they are hardly understood and soon forgotten. " Guelf " and " Ghibelline " had once a meaning, but men were under perpetual banishment from their native land for belonging to one or the other of these parties long after nobody knew in what the difference consisted. Some men are Tories or Whigs by conviction ; but thousands upon thousands of electors vote simply for yellow, blue, or purple, caught at most by the appeals of some popular orator.

It is through this great natural tendency to take sides that the Wire-puller works. Without it he would be powerless. His business is to fan its flame ; to keep it constantly acting upon the man who has once declared himself a partisan ; to make escape from it difficult and distasteful. His art is that of a Nonconformist preacher, who gave importance to a body of commonplace religionists by persuading them to wear a uniform and take a military title, or of a man who made the success of a Temperance Society by prevailing on its members to wear always and openly a blue ribbon. In the long-run, these contrivances cannot be confined to any one party, and their effects on all parties and their leaders, and on the whole ruling democracy, must be in the highest degree serious and lasting. The first of these effects will be, I think, to make all parties very like one another, and indeed in the end almost indistinguishable, however leaders may quarrel and partisan hate partisans. In the next place, each party will probably become more and more homogeneous; and the opinions it professes, and the policy which is the outcome of these opinions, will less and less reflect the individual mind of any leader, but only the ideas which seem to that mind to be more likely to win favour with the greatest number of supporters.

Historically speaking, Party is probably nothing more than a survival and a consequence of the primitive combativeness of mankind. It is war without the city transmuted into war within the city, but mitigated in the process. The best historical justification which can be offered for it is that it has often enabled portions of the nation, who would otherwise be armed enemies, to be only factions. Party strife, like strife in arms, develops many high but imperfect and one-sided virtues; it is fruitful of self-denial and self-sacrifice. But wherever it prevails, a great part of ordinary morality is unquestionably suspended; a number of maxims are received, which are not those of religion or ethics; and men do acts which, except as between enemies, and except as between political opponents, would be very generally classed as either immoralities or sins.

Party disputes were originally the occupation of aristocracies, which joined in them because they loved the sport for its own sake; and the rest of the community followed one side or the other as its clients. Now-a-days, Party has become a force acting with vast energy on multitudinous democracies, and a number of artificial contrivances have been invented for facilitating and stimulating its action. Yet, in a democracy, the fragment of political power falling to each man's share is so extremely small, that it would be hardly possible, with all the aid of the Caucus, the Stump, and the Campaign newspaper, to rouse the interests of thousands or millions of men, if Party were not coupled with another political force. This, to speak plainly, is Corruption.   *   *

Whether Hamilton looked forward to an era of purity in his own country, cannot be certainly known. He and his coadjutors undoubtedly were unprepared for the rapid development of Party which soon set in; they evidently thought that their country would be poor; and they probably expected to see all evil influences defeated by the elaborate contrivances of the Federal Constitution. But the United States became rapidly wealthy and rapidly populous; and the universal suffrage of all white men, native-born or immigrant, was soon established by the legislation of the most powerful States. With wealth, population, and widely diffused electoral power, corruption sprang into vigorous life. President Andrew Jackson, proclaiming the principle of " to the victors the spoils," which all parties soon adopted, expelled from office all administrative servants of the United States who did not belong to his faction; and the crowd of persons filling these offices, which are necessarily very numerous in so vast a territory, together with the groups of wealthy men interested in public lands and in the countless industries protected by the Customs tariff, formed an extensive body of contributors from whom great amounts of money were levied by a species of taxation, to be presently expended in wholesale bribery.

It is obvious, then, that the simple device of dividing the country into small constituencies, the majority in each of which returns members to Parliament, is at best a clumsy and a haphazard way of approaching the fair representation of the people. In the case of the Metropolis a district more than half Tory threw the balance of its influence in Parliament against the Tory Government, the minority being over-represented and counting as a majority. In the second case the majority had all the members, and the minority was not represented at all. During the last Session, in which the Agricultural Holdings Act was passed through the House, a number of Liberal voters in five agricultural counties, greater than the number of Liberal voters in Birmingham, had actually no voice at all, whilst the party representing the landlord's side of the question was represented by twenty-four votes. Had these five counties been divided into twice as many sections, it is impossible to say whether the result would have been better; it certainly could not have been worse.

These illustrations are enough, I think, to show that the fair representation of the people would not necessarily be secured by the division of the country into equal electoral districts with one or two members to each. I will not here more than simply allude to the still graver, and, as I think, fatal objections which may be urged against the proposal to divide our large constituencies into wards; the utterly artificial character of an arrangement which would break up into fragments a greater political unit like Birmingham, and make Mr. Bright the member for Ward No. 1 or No. 2, and the tendency it would have to provincialize Parliament and to exaggerate petty local interests at the expense of far greater national ones.

If the system cannot be relied on to secure even to the majority its proper weight in Parliament, it is surely self-condemned, apart from the other grave reasons which may be urged against it; and, therefore it is not necessary here to urge them. The nation will hardly be pursuaded to break up its natural political units, and to sacrifice much of its best political life, for an object which cannot after all be attained by the sacrifice.

Are we then to fall back upon large constituencies *without* any direct attempt to secure proportionate voting? Is a bare majority in a large constituency to return all the members of one colour to Parliament?

This brings us back to the point that a system by which the minority in each constituency is eliminated and the majority only is represented in Parliament, cannot be made to secure a fair representation of the people. The objections to it become still more apparent and morally serious when we look at the character of the representation produced by it in each individual constituency, whether small or large—when we consider how easily it may fail in securing a fair representation of the majority itself, and also how often it may give undue representation to elements in the nation which certainly ought not to be over-represented.

It so happens in England, and probably wherever there is government by parties, that in a great number of constituencies the voters are nearly evenly divided between the two parties. In Liverpool and Manchester, for example, two or three thousand voters—a tenth, perhaps of the whole number—swinging over from one side to the other—can convert a minority into a majority, and have done so over and over again. In many boroughs a still smaller fraction holds the key to the result of the election in its own hands; and Professor Fawcett has long ago pointed out with great force and truth that this fraction—this miserably small minority is thus infinitely over-represented, and has artificially placed in its hand a power for good or for evil, altogether disproportioned to its numbers or legitimate influence.

This oscillating class of voters, swinging like a ferry-boat from side to side of the stream, is not composed of the sober-minded men of solid opinion, whether Tory or Liberal. It is too often composed of injured or frightened interests, or of dissatisfied spirits, or of cliques representing special crotchets, and the result of an election at any given time depends far too much upon which way it may cast its votes. It is bad enough that a fickle fraction of the people should have it in their power, by fits and starts, to change the lines of the Government of England, when the bulk of the nation has not changed. But it becomes still worse when a compact and organized clique is tempted to make a test point of its special crotchet or object, however honestly pursued. It is a mockery of representative Government that such a clique should have the power deliberately to force its views upon political parties by putting them in the position of choosing between success and defeat according as they accept or reject its dictates.

This is, in truth, an interference with fair popular representation. It is an act of intimidation analogous to that of the highwayman who demands your purse, pointing a pistol at your breast. It is undue influence of the worst kind, all the more demoralizing in its results, because the stake is so large. And why should we allow so corrupt a practice to continue? The fact is that the power of this fraction of voters, in the absence of proportionate voting, is simply and unnaturally magnified in a large constituency by the unjust and clumsy and artificial arrangement that a bare majority shall shift the whole representation over in a lump from one side to the other, instead of the representation corresponding with the proportionate strength of parties. . . .

I have purposely treated this question from a Liberal point of view. But it is not a party question. When the result of the imperfect system of representing only majorities is considered from a broad point of view, its dangers and its evils are found to be by no means counteracted by the mere subdivision of constituencies, by trusting to the laws of chance, or to the correction which is sometimes obtained in an average result. The last two or three elections have already given proof enough of the reality of the danger of exaggerating the influence of the class of oscillating and dissatisfied voters. For six years the nation was dragged by a majority in the House of Commons, which probably did not represent the majority of voters,[*] into a line of foreign policy which the conscience of a majority of the nation condemned, and from which it is now found possible altogether to retire.

And there is another national danger from which we may be anxious to protect our country—viz., the tendency of minorities remaining long unrepresented hopelessly to retire from political life, leaving the majority without that natural and just and wholesome restraint which the presence of an active minority puts upon their actions. Our faith in the democracy of the future, if it rest upon a rational basis, rests chiefly upon the fair representation of the whole people ; upon the success with which the mass of sound political conviction, which we believe to lie at the bottom of our national life, is secured its due weight by means of fair representation in Parliament ; upon keeping the best minds in the nation interested in politics, and upon the growth in the constituencies of a solid and stable public opinion, which will have its due influence in steering the vessel of the State in a steady course. To attain this object, to save the democracy of the future from the rocks which, in the experience of other nations, have wrecked it in the past, it seems to be essential that true popular representation should be steadily aimed at and as far as possible secured. Nor do I see how to secure that Parliament shall represent the sober sense of the majority of voters in the nation with anything like substantial correctness, without proportionate voting in large constituencies. The question remains how this can best be attained?

. . . A Parliament representing only local majorities, shifted from side to side by the oscillation of the least stable and the least intelligent class of fluctuating voters, is no fair representation of the nation—it may, at certain crises in national history, become government by the mob. A system which robs the sober mass of the nation of its due weight and power in controlling its own destinies, and which puts it in the power of a mere tithe of the nation periodically to drag it against its will into lines of action, which, when the mischief is done, it has at the first opportunity to repudiate, and the evil results of which even a long repentance cannot wipe out, whatever else it is, is hardly in any true sense democratic. And surely the time when the franchise is extended, and a redistribution of seats becomes necessary, is the right time to consider how the sober and solid mass of the nation can best make its voice heard, so that the democracy we are creating may at least be a real one. To refuse to do this because it involves some fresh effort of thought, and some deviation from old-fashioned ways, would be, in my humble opinion, to shrink a responsibility which rightly rests upon the shoulders of this generation of statesmen.

---

[*]There were about 300,000 more Liberal than Tory votes polled in 1874 in the contested constituencies.

REPRESENTATION.

By Sir John Lubbock, Bart, M.P., F.R.S., D.C.L., LL.D.. (1885).

Sir G. C. Lewis, in his work "On the Best Form of Government," tells us that neither his profound study of ancient history, nor his great experience in national affairs, had enabled him to arrive at a decided opinion on this important question.

"The controversy," he says, "is one consisting of a debtor and creditor account; the difficulty lies in striking the balance fairly. The weights in one scale may be less heavy than the weights in the other scale, but they are nevertheless weights. . . The difficulty is to determine which of two sets of valid arguments preponderates."

The remarkable saying of the late Prince Consort that Representative Institutions are on their trial has been so often quoted, that I almost hesitate to do so again.

Yet it might well have seemed that government "of the people, for the people, and by the people," was so obviously wise and just, that it must almost of necessity work well in any intelligent community. This, however, has certainly not been the general experience.

Why, then, has Democracy so often failed in the past? Why have we seen that in State after State power has oscillated from one extreme to the other—from the Tyrant to the Demagogue, and back again from the Demagogue to the Tyrant? The true reason, I believe, is to be found, not in any fault of the principle, but because the principle has not been correctly applied—because, in fact, no country has ever yet adopted a true system of Representation.

This has been well pointed out by a distinguished American statesman, Mr. Calhoun.

"The effect," he says, "of the ordinary systems of representation, is to place the control of the parties in the hands of their respective majorities; and the Government itself, virtually, under the control of the majority of the dominant party, for the time, instead of the majority of the whole community;—where the theory of this form of government vests it. Thus, in the very first stage of the process, the government becomes the government of a minority instead of a majority—a minority, usually, and under the most favourable circumstances, of not much more than one-fourth of the whole community,"

John Stuart Mill has stated the case still more forcibly.

"In a representative body," he says, "actually deliberating, the minority must of course be overruled: and in an equal democracy (since the opinions of the constituents, when they insist on them, determine those of the representative body) the majority of the people, through their representatives, will outvote and prevail over the minority and their representatives.

"But does it follow that the minority should have no representatives at all? Because the majority ought to prevail over the minority, must the majority have all the votes, the minority none? Is it necessary that the minority should not even be heard? Nothing but habit and old association can reconcile any reasonable being to the needless injustice.

"In a really equal democracy every or any section would be represented, not disproportionately, but proportionately. A majority of the electors would always have a majority of the representatives; but a minority of the electors would always have a minority of the representatives. Man for man, they would be as fully represented as the majority. Unless they are, there is not equal government, but a government of inequality and privilege: one part of the people rule over the rest; there is a part whose fair and equal share of influence in the representation is withheld from them contrary to the principle of democracy, which professes equality as its very root and foundation."

And again—

"The majority," he says, "would indeed outnumber the others, as much as the one class of electors outnumbers the other in the country. They would always outvote them, but they would speak and vote in their presence, and subject to their criticism. When any difference arose, they would have to meet the arguments of the instructed few by reasons at least apparently as cogent; and since they could not, as those do who are speaking to persons already unanimous, simply assume that they are in the right, it would occasionally happen to them to become convinced that they were in the wrong.

"Now, nothing is more certain than that the virtual blotting-out of the minority is no necessary or natural consequence of freedom; that, far from having any connection with democracy, it is diametrically opposed to the first principle of democracy—representation in proportion to numbers. It is an essential part of democracy that minorities should be adequately represented. No real democracy, nothing but a false show of democracy, is possible without it."

This evil is remedied by the system of Proportional, or, as it is sometimes called, "Minority" representation. The latter name is, however, misleading.

The supporters of proportional representation have no desire to give the minority a larger share of political power than that to which their numbers justly entitle them. On the contrary, as Lord Sherbrooke said during the debate of 1867 in the House of Commons, he did not "argue for any protection to the minority . . . but that between the members of the constituency there should be absolute equality; the majority should have nothing given to it because it was a majority."

Mr. Fawcett, again, in his last speech to his constituents at Hackney, truly pointed out that

"Far from those who advocate proportional representation wishing to give to the minority the power which properly belongs to the majority, I think I shall have no difficulty in showing that one of the chief dangers which the advocates of proportional representatation desire to guard against, is the minority obtaining a preponderance of representation which ought to belong to the majority."

Nay, so far from this, a true system of proportional representation is—in the words of Mill—"not only the most complete application of the democratic principle that has yet been made, but its greatest safeguard."

In fact, although it may seem a paradox, it is nevertheless true that the system of representation hitherto adopted, not merely through inequalities of area or restrictions on the right of voting, but as a consequence necessarily ensuing from the system of voting hitherto adopted, has had the effect of placing power in the hands, not of the majority, but of a minority.

Lord Spencer also has pointed out in the House of Lords that "in America for many years past great complaints have been made that large numbers of persons, men of influence, of intellect, of wealth and position, refrained from taking any part in political life. Why was that? Because they felt that they were a hopeless minority, whose opinions were crushed by the overwhelming mass of the majority."

It is hardly necessary to point out how the system of single seats limits the freedom of the elector. The Liberal Committee put forward one candidate, the Conservative another, and all the elector can do is to choose between them. Perhaps the elector does not approve of either. This is no doubt one reason why, in large constituencies, we see so many abstentions. But, however little he may be disposed to either candidate, he cannot bring forward a third without dividing his party, and generally ensuring the return of a political opponent.

Professor Ware, of Columbia College, New York, has forcibly pointed out that under this system, though the elector is "nominally free to vote for whom he pleases, the knowledge that his vote is thrown away unless it is given for the regular candidate binds him hand and foot."

Again, this system has a tendency to promote bribery. It often happens that in a constituency the two great parties are evenly balanced, and a few votes suffice to turn the scale. There may be, say, 2,500 Liberals, 2,500 Conservatives, and 250 persons with no political views. In the hands of these last, then, the whole representation rests. If the agent of either party purchases 100, or 50, nay, even 10 of them, the weight of the constituency is thrown into the scale of the party for which he acts.

Those who support the single member system appear to be under the impression that if constituencies were equalized the present mode of voting would—roughly, indeed, but surely —secure that the majority of electors would rule the country. But this is not so. A majority of electors in every constituency is by no means the same thing as a majority of all the electors. Suppose, for instance, a community of 60,000 electors is divided into three divisions, each containing 20,000, and that there are 32,000 Liberals and 28,000 Conservatives, the division might be, and very likely would be, as follows:—

	1st Division.	2nd Division.	3rd Division.
Liberals	15,000	9,000	8,000
Conservatives	5,000	11,000	12,000
	20,000	20,000	20,000

And thus, though in a minority, the Conservatives would actually return two members out of three. This is no hypothetical case.

By the constitution of 1841 Geneva was divided into four colleges. The liberal electors were massed in one ward, which they carried by an immense majority; while the Conservatives, though in a minority, secured the other three ; and the extreme dissatisfaction thus created greatly contributed to the revolution of 1846. In fact, as already stated, a majority of electors in each constituency is by no means the same thing as a majority in all the constituencies.

. . . The recent history of America has peculiar significance. The committee of the United States Senate, to which I have already referred, were of opinion, that if America had adopted proportional representation, instead of single seats, their disastrous civil war might have been prevented.

"The absence of proportional representation," they say, " in the States of the South when rebellion was plotted, and when open steps were taken to break the Union, was unfortunate, for it would have held the Union men of those States together, and would have given them voice in the electoral colleges and in congress. But they were fearfully overborne by the plurality rule of election, and were swept forward by the course of events into impotency or open hostility to our cause. By that rule they were deprived of representation in Congress. By that rule they were shut out of the electoral colleges. Dispersed, unorganized, unrepresented, without due voice and power, they could interpose no effectual resistance to secession and civil war.

"Their leaders were struck down at unjust elections and could not speak for them, or act for them in their own States, or at the capital of the nation. By facts well known to us we are assured that the leaders of revolt, with much difficulty, carried their States with them. Even in Georgia, the empire State of the South, the scale was almost balanced for a time between patriotism and dishonour ; and in most of those States it required all the machinery and influence of a vicious electoral system to organize the war against us and hold those communities compactly as our foes ."

PARTY AND PRINCIPLE.

Quarterly Review, Vol. CLXIII, 1886.

A growing contempt and impatience of the whole machinery of Party; disgust with a method which compels us to accept bad rulers instead of good at the hands of a class, which is as yet incompetent to distinguish good from bad; and shame at the waste of time, the interminable wrangling, and the ignoble ambitions which, in spite of certain splendid exceptions, have marked the course of Party government for some years past, are certainly the most conspicuous phenomena of the present day............

Yet what are we to say? If parties in their old form have died out in the country, it is useless to try to prolong their existence in Parliament by artificial means. If, to repeat what we have already said, the public no longer see sufficient difference between Whig and Tory Conservatives to make them enthusiastic partisans of either, and if parties cannot be redivided into Constitutionalists and Radicals, into those, that is, who wish to preserve, with all necessary improvements, the existing constitution of society, and those who are anxious to subvert it, why go on playing at parties in the House of Commons which correspond to nothing outside of it? This game of ghosts can hardly be expected to satisfy a living people, inspired by a new order of ideas, and anxious for a new kind of political life which shall allow their convictions free play............

In the eyes of ₜthe independent public, we fear the antagonism of parties has latterly seemed little better than a fight for place, to which everything else is sacrificed. What did even Mr. Cowen say on the subject not two months ago? "I am indifferent," he said, "to Party organization: I think the objects which lead men to union very paltry. They bring out the worst features of human nature." We may depend upon it the feeling is spreading very widely. Place! Place! Place! *Si possis recte, si non quocunque modo.* That is the sole meaning which large masses of the nation are beginning to attach to politics..........

The division of the country into Liberals and Conservatives has long been an utterly unmeaning one, a mere form out of which the spirit has departed; and it has been prolonged, as it has been on former occasions, 'by mechanical contrivances to suit the convenience of particular classes and individuals. Artificial differences have been cultivated where no natural ones existed; and, what has been worse, the Whigs, having no differential policy to mark them off from the Tories, have been obliged from time to time to fall in with the designs of the Radicals, in order to impart to their own position some semblance of reality. After the various reforms which have been accomplished, some by one party and some by another, during the last fifty years, there is little left to quarrel over now but the fundamental institutions of the country............

The Party system, then, can no longer be conducted on these terms, terms which compel honourable men to stoop to evasions and subterfuges, which in any other walk of life they would despise; and produce on the public mind the unfortunate conviction, that the game of politics is played only for selfish objects, in which principles have no part.

PARTY AND PATRIOTISM.

By Sydney E. Williams, 1886.

It is the simplest of truths that the aim of politics—like the object of good government and the *raison d'être* of parties—is the welfare of the nation. Yet obvious as it is, the truth fails to exercise anything like its due influence over men's thoughts and actions. Nor is it less true, nor less disregarded, that the good of the nation depends, not upon this or that particular nostrum, nor this or that parochial programme, but upon the development of the national life by means of measures planned not for partial interests but the general benefit, upon the elevation, the unselfishness, the help of all classes and all interests, and upon the greatness and well-being of the empire with which all alike must stand or fall. And this being so it matters little by what party or by what government we are brought nearer the common goal. No government has a monopoly of wise legislation ; nor has any party a monopoly of sound principles. Each has its aspirations and its errors, and each must be judged by its deeds. . . . .

It has been said, with unconscious sarcasm, that our system of government by party does not lay claim to absolute perfection, and that its greatest admirers will bear to be told that it has its drawbacks. But outside the circle of its admirers, which includes few except party politicians, there are many who are beginning to doubt whether its advantages outweigh its disadvantages and whether its use is more conspicuous than its abuse. "Nay, I find England in her own big dumb heart, whenever you come upon her in a silent, meditative hour, begins to have dreadful misgivings about it."

Its chief defect—and a sufficiently grave one in any institution—is that it defeats the very object for which it is intended. Its main object, and the only one that can justify its existence, is to promote the national good. But so little does it attain this end that its chief tendency is to divert the national energy from national objects. It aims at the general welfare by the conflict of opposing parties, each of which claims that it alone is able to promote it, each of which holds out to us the hope of infinite bliss or the dread of infinite woe. We are in short told by the admirers of party government that the only way to attain a common purpose is to wrangle over the means of effecting it. No wonder that the main object is lost sight of. An institution which attracts so much superstitious reverence naturally becomes an end in itself. . . . .

"Party," says Burke in a well-known passage, "is a body of men united for promoting by their joint endeavours the national interest upon some principle in which they are all agreed." And to the institution as thus defined little exception can be taken. But it is manifestly of the essence of the definition as well as of the institution that the object should be to promote the national interests, and to promote them upon some principle in which we are all agreed. How little the institution, as at present seen, answers to this definition we all know. Even Burke, with his exaggerated reverence for the constitution and parliamentary government, might well have had his faith shaken by the present state of affairs. When we see the object of the "joint endeavours" to be the furtherance not of national but of mere party interests, upon principles which are neither sound, stable, or generally believed in, we may well be excused for doubting whether this "excellent mechanism" is "the most satisfactory that the wit of man has yet devised for the management of the affairs of a state."

. . . . Every one is expected nowadays to sacrifice his judgment, and even his conscience, at the shrine of party, even though his party have no policy, and be guided by no intelligent principles. Having once given his adherence he will be expected to support it for all time, however it may change its policy or depart from its principles ; he will be expected to espouse its quarrels, condone its blunders, and credit it with a monopoly of wisdom and right motives. This, it is obvious, is not so much allegiance as mental slavery. Combined action is no doubt necessary in order to carry into effect common opinion. But the necessity for combined action ceases the moment the opinion ceases to be common. Party spirit ought not to be merely *esprit de corps*, but an *entente cordiale*.

The extent to which party dominates politics in the present day is almost unexampled in our history. Party considerations inspire our political programmes, determine the policies of our governments, and decide the result of most divisions. Each party trims its sails to catch the popular breeze, each member gives his vote to keep in office or retain his seat. Hardly a thought is given to the national interest, but rather is it openly avowed that a particular line is taken in the interests of party, and apart from higher considerations.

. . Public spirit is crushed out by party spirit, and with few exceptions our legislators lack the courage to be honest. They seldom, if ever, speak freely the thing they feel, and we wait in vain for a frank expression of personal conviction. When occasions arise which call for plain speaking, our politicians are dumb ; and we can only conclude that they do not know or are too cowardly to say. Nor is this all. What makes matters worse is that there is so little attempt to disguise the fact, and so little general feeling among professional politicians, that the whole thing is unedifying and discreditable. Our High Court of Parliament scarcely affects to be actuated by high motives. Opportunism is the thing thought of, and statesmanship is becoming a byword. What is expedient for the party at the moment, not what is expedient for the country in the long run, is the dominant factor in parliamentary calculations. " Political considerations must prevail," though other and higher objects have to be sacrificed. To get the better of one's opponents is the highest of political ambitions, and to divest oneself of principles likely to jeopardise electoral prospects is the first duty of the modern statesman. . . . .

The chief objection to political organisations is, that though they profess to give expression and effect to public opinion, they in fact do much to control and stifle it. Public opinion is the growing, fluctuating, ever-varying sentiment of society. It is a highly-sensitive and impressionable entity, swayed at times by a breath or moved deeply by a thought, liable both to gradual change and to violent transformation. It it obvious that no permanent organisation with fixed aims can ever hope to represent so intangible a quantity. Nor can any organisation however perfect do otherwise than destroy its mobility, which is really its life and essence. Least of all can any political association with its party name, its party shibboleths, and party prejudice, hope to represent its finer shades, or even, for long, its bolder outlines ; and certainly none such can be trusted to form and mould it.

The natural tendency of all such organisations, whatever their professed object may be, is to manufacture, not represent, public opinion. They can but imperfectly represent it, and must inevitably tend to mar it. They both force and check the common feeling by driving divergent opinions into one rigid mould. They crystallise a sentiment which ought to remain free, and arrest a current which should continue to flow. They encourage mental indolence by supplying electors with a ready-made political creed, and destroy independent thought by asking them to surrender the right to form an opinion.

These are evils almost necessarily inherent in any system of organisation, but they are greatly aggravated in the case of party organisations, by joining which a man undertakes to blindly follow one side and as blindly oppose the other ; to support everything done or proposed to be done by one party, and denounce everything done or proposed to be done by the other. He shuts himself out from taking a true and impartial view of politics by entering an association which encourages political ignorance by looking at questions from only one point of view and by suppressing unpalatable truths. He, in short, relinquishes all claim to that love of fair play which is supposed to be characteristic of Englishmen.

Besides the danger of a mechanical working of the vote in obedience to a small knot of wire-pullers, who are rather partisans than politicians, there is the further danger of a mechanical working of Parliament in obedience to the same high authority ; the practical effect of organisation being to enable a small body of voters to dictate on the one hand to electors for whom they shall vote, and on the other hand to Parliament for what it shall vote. Thus supreme power is vested in an oligarchy who usurp the right of electors on the one hand and the functions of Parliament on the other. . . . .

A member of Parliament is a representative or nothing. He goes to Parliament to represent a constituency, and can never be wholly independent. On the other hand, he is not a mere delegate, the mere mouthpiece of a caucus. If he were wholly independent the country would be unrepresented, and if a mere delegate Parliament would be a mere voting machine. It is impossible for the electorate to determine the details of government and legislation, and any attempt to usurp this function would inevitably tend to lower the character of Parliament. . . . .

Parliament is a deliberative assembly, not a mere voting machine, nor ought its members to be mere lay-figures. They ought, to the best of their ability, to form an honest opinion, upon the arguments placed before them, as to what is best for the whole community. And how can this be possible, as Burke pertinently asks, " when one set of men deliberate and another decide."

A member of Parliament, moreover, ought to be able to see, and does generally see, further and more clearly than his constituents. He should be, and generally is, able to interpret the national will more correctly and more courageously than a caucus. . . . .

It is surely time that the world began to realise how false is the sentiment which would have us believe that to stifle our judgments and our consciences is a high political virtue, and that to possess common courage and honesty is a political stigma. The sentiment is the direct result of party spirit. The party virus has spread over the whole political system till no part of it is free from the taint. And if we do not crush the evil, it will assuredly crush us.

Party spirit, with its evil influence, is more or less inseparable from party government. . . . .

. . . The advantages of party discipline are almost insignificant beside its evils, beside its moral cowardice and insincerity, its want of principle and indifference to the public interest. No one can view without some feeling of disgust the cavilling and bickering, the maligning misrepresentation and calumny, which pass for political criticism, and which are the chief artifices of party warfare. The party system is rotten at the core. Yet this is the system by which we test the purity and usefulness of our institutions and the value of our legislation.

. . . We cannot wonder that high-minded men should shrink from the prospect of becoming mere party hacks and of giving up their self-respect for the sake of being mere puppets on the parliamentary stage. As well might we expect a Salvini to conform to the taste of a transpontine gallery. And it is to the party politician and wirepuller that we owe this deplorable state of things. Between them they are doing their best to make the most independent assembly in the world a mere machine impelled by unworthy motives, and are converting an honourable pursuit into a trade of sharp practice and trickery.

PARTY GOVERNMENT.

From Westminster Review, Vol. LXIX, 1886.

At first sight, a system of government by party seems unfeignedly ridiculous. But the fact that it exists, and that the enthusiasm of most men is attached to the one side or the other, the absurdity of the arrangement must have been painfully evident long ago. That the work of government should be done for a time by one set of men, while another set do nothing but cavil at them, and that when their criticisms have brought about some catastrophe the cavillers should do the work of governing the nation, while those who were lately in power become the critics, does not, at first sight, commend itself to one's mind as at all a rational system. It is difficult to believe that the country has, at any one time at its disposal, two sets of men equally capable of governing ; and even if we were convinced of the fact that it was so fortunate, we should think it a curious waste of the highest moral and intellectual power which the country can produce, that while the one set were doing the work, the other set should be doing their best to make it impossible for the first to discharge their all-important duties. Such a method has never been tried in the transaction of any other business than that of government. Had it had any inherent excellence, surely we should have found it in other departments of affairs. Its continued existence in relation to the art of governing is to be accounted for, as we shall see, not by its efficiency, but by other circumstances which of themselves go far to discredit it, as an institution. But against this view, we have no doubt the startling fact that party government is not a new thing, and that it seems on the whole to have worked fairly well, or at least without positive disaster to the country. We confess our entire allegiance to facts, and are willing to admit, as a rule, that that which works well is a great deal better than that which can be reasoned well about. But the fact that government by party has not been productive of disaster, is only to be accounted for by the circumstance that, whenever an emergency has arisen which would test the efficiency of the system and find it wanting, the common sense of men in and out of office, came to the front, and that which was necessary to be done was done by all concerned without any regard to the system of government by party. Every reader of the daily prints has become familiar with the phrase, "this is not a party question," applied with increasing frequency to matters which would formerly have been regarded, and which in many instances are still regarded, as fair fields for party fights. But that of itself seems to indicate that this system of government is like an unseaworthy ship which may sail well enough on smooth seas, but which will go to pieces under any stress of weather. The wisdom of those on board has been shown in the past by deserting the good ship—Party— whenever the skies threatened............

It is surely too obvious that if party government is the system of ruling, the object of the *ins* will be scarcely so much to govern well as to keep office. The objects of the "outs" will be not to see that the *ins* govern well, but to make it impossible for them to govern at all, and to demonstrate their incapacity to the country, and to secure the power for themselves............

Now the position that the existence of party is essential to healthy parliamentary government does not seem to us to be at all a strong position. And if we can disprove the necessary connection between the existence of popular government and the organization of parties in the State, we shall have disposed of the only reason which seems to be urged for an institution which it is admitted on all hands, has little else to recommend it, and has innumerable features, as these writers have shown, which discredit it.

We have pointed out that at one time, when great dynastic and other questions important to the very life of the nation were in the arena of politics, there was a reason for parties in politics. No doubt civil war can only be carried on by means of parties, but it does not therefore follow that government can only be carried on by a sort of smothered civil war. In our time, were it not that party is a means of raising the temperature of lukewarm enthusiasm—were it not that the war of parties is a foolish survival of primitive savagery which serves the purpose of the few ambitious men who are able to make themselves the leaders of these factions, we are convinced that parties would cease to exist. No doubt when civil war was in question the currents of thought might be well compared to two main streams. They are like rivers which made their own ways through the obstructions of the land. Now, however, party thought is like a watercourse which is made to flow in a certain direction, like a canal, by the artificial banks and locks of party discipline. As it is, as we have tried to show, the interests of the country, the interests of the rank-and-file of politicians, are sacrificed to the ambition of their leaders in much the same way as the common people and the soldiery used to be sacrificed to the pride of kings. It is for this purpose, then, that the irrational distinction between the two parties is maintained. We constantly, in this foolish warfare, hear of tactics, of manœuvres, of party moves, and one leader is proud of the appellation "old parliamentary hand;" and while most of these tricks and tactics are turned against the opposite party, the greatest dupes of all are the parties themselves. The ordinary politician toils years in the vain hope of rising to a position in which he will merit the rewards which it is in the power of party to bestow, and only a few of them ever have the loaves and the fishes which are the end and aim of what by a fine irony is called practical politics. The principle which we have stated as being the ethical foundation of parties—namely, that men may honestly sacrifice minor matters of principle for the sake of party—seems to us to be immoral. We have said that great danger may justify the losing sight of individual opinion. On a battlefield private judgment must be at a minimum. But why in these times we should still keep up this semblance of war in order to make these sacrifices a necessity it is difficult to see. The trick by means of which the juggle of parties is constantly played is that men magnify the points of difference between themselves and their fellows, and shut their eyes to the far more important points of agreement—a process which is dishonest to your antagonist and unfair to yourself. But further, on this matter of sacrificing minor matters of principle at the high behests of party interests, is it not difficult to say where such a process, once inaugurated, is to stop? The advocates of the system say in "small matters," in "minor matters," a man may sacrifice his principles for the sake of the organization. But there is an indefiniteness about this rule which gives spacious latitude to ambitious consciences. It is very dangerous to begin paltering, and when a man has given in the mint and the anise and the cummin for the sake of party, and for the hopes that adhesion to party rear in men's minds, he may easily enough be induced to sacrifice more weighty matters. Where there is room for a conscience in party spirit most candid people have failed to see. But then it is said you cannot work your representative and democratic institutions unless you are willing to put up with these inconveniences. That, as we have seen, is the position which the advocates of party government take up. Well, in the first instance, it is not the highest praise which can be bestowed upon popular government that it can only be worked by means of this immoral and foolish machinery............

Surely the fact that so much in English political life depends upon these party organizations and upon these captains of votes, the wire-pullers, is sufficient of itself to condemn the system and to recommend that which we are here urging as a substitute—the government of the country by the best men, irrespective of party consideration, the permanent tenure of all the great offices during efficiency and good behaviour, and the obedience of the Ministers of the Crown to the expressed wishes of the representatives of the people. Against this system we do not know any reasons of any cogency which can be urged. That there would be less "sound and fury" in politics is one of the recommendations of the system—all the "sound and fury" at present signify nothing; that there would be less enthusiasm brought to bear upon national affairs may be true, but the enthusiasm which arises out of politics in consequence of the war of parties, is like that which is produced on religion by persecution. We may buy our enthusiasm too dear. But to say that there would not remain enough of interest in national affairs to induce the best men to take part in them is, we think, untrue and libellous. While there is great work to be done—and the good government of a country like ours is great work—there will not be wanting the great men to do it. But the party strife, with its chicanery and cunning which form such a large part of party warfare, is a means of keeping some of the best men of the country apart from the work of governing altogether. It is well known that there are many especially able men in America who already keep themselves apart from the din and bustle of politics. The proportion of persons who do not aspire to honour by the road which leads through St. Stephen's is in this country every year becoming greater. That these men would be attracted to the services of the State if they were no longer the reward of party tactics, but were the recognition of special capacity and practical experience, we think none can doubt. Indeed, the objections to the one system are so many, and the objections to the other so few, that it is almost like weakness to argue the matter. It is in deference, not to the reasons which can be urged for government by party that we have said so much, but because we are aware of the long roots which the system has struck into the national life, and of the firm hold it has over the minds of contemporary politicians.

THE DANGER OF PARTY.

By Frederic Harrison. From the Contemporary Review, Vol. XLIX., 1886.

There is urgent need to form a public opinion, independent of Parliament and of all electoral machinery whatever. The fierce rivalry of parties, and the way in which party absorbs all political thought amongst us, is a growing danger. It may be agreed that the healthy organization of party is an essential condition of Parliamentary government. As practised with us, the organization of party tends to crush and stifle the free play of public opinion. Members of Parliament feel it a duty not to embarrass their party leaders by discussing any question which the leaders do not sanction, or by ever criticising anything they do or omit to do. Party men and politicians outside Parliament follow the same cue and encourage the members in silent discipline. The journalists and publicists usually have their party side, and make it a point of honour to stir no awkward topic, but with their whole force to support the party side. Thus, as the whole political energy of our day runs into Parliamentary channels, and is organized with military discipline to secure party victories (and the same thing is even more conspicuous in the United States), the free formation of public opinion is almost as difficult as under the despotism of a Czar or a Napoleon.

In the name of Freedom and Progress let some of us at least keep out of the Parliamentary race-course, out of the party caucus, out of party journalism. Let us in this place attempt to do what we can to organize a real Moral Force. I would claim for Positivists this much : that they are the only organized body of politicians in the kingdom who systematically strive to build up public opinion on other than party lines, with other than Ministerial victories as their aim. Positivism, in its essence, means simply the formation of some moral power as the inspirer of active life, without any coarse stimulus of rivalry or ambition. The Churches busy themselves with theological and celestial questions only. Here is the failure of merely celestial religion. Let us with such help as Conservative, Whig, or Radical will give, try to form high and right canons of public judgment ; let us insist on making the plain moral law dominant in national politics ; let us urge the clear intelligences and the just spirits everywhere to make their voices heard and not slavishly to submit to the loud cries of the many, and the gross verdict of a wooden ballot-box ; let us insist that the first and most crying of public duties is to teach, guide, and lead the people, and as a means to that teaching, to make the people teachable. Let us raise up the spirit of enlightened education in things public and national, strengthening in the people everywhere the idea of being taught and led, convinced and elevated. Politics are not, any more than astronomy or medicine, the province of the mass. They are the province of wise guidance and intelligent co-operation.

PARTY AND PATRIOTISM.

By Alfred Austen. From the National Review, Vol. VII. 1886.

I see symptoms of this demoralization of the public conscience in every direction, and I trace it, for the most part, to the corrupting influence of Party politics, in which unfortunately, the whole community now take part. . . . If one mercilessly thinks it out does it not become painfully apparent, that by the very operation of Party politics, every prominent politician in the House of Commons is being perpetually tempted and tormented by his friends not to be honest, and perpetually assailed and harrassed by his foes in order to be made not to appear honest? Government by Party necessarily entails the continual surrender by a man of his convictions, in order to keep his party together; and if he be in the Cabinet, or in the Ministry, he will be fortunate if he be not called upon at times to defend in debate what he has opposed in council. This is what he has to thank his friends for. As for his foes, they try to trip him up on every possible occasion, to make him look inconsistent, incapable, and generally contemptible. In a word, and to put the operation of Party politics in as succinct a form as possible, each half of the nation is employed, morning, noon, and night, from year's end to year's end, in proving the other half fools and tricksters. For this end, no shaft of ridicule, no craft of speech, no device of invective is spared.

And does anyone suppose that you can demoralize a people politically, and leave them moral and manly in matters into which politics do not or should not enter? . . . Of cleverness in political life, there is an unfailing supply. But one ounce of character is worth a ton of ability, and, unhappily, it is character that is wanting. Conviction, courage, and a tranquil but immovable will, these are the constituents of character. When are we to look for them in public life? . . .

PARTY OR EMPIRE.

From the National Review, August 1886.

The days of Party Government in the old constitutional sense, are numbered. The reign of its decrepitude is to be read alike in the growth and in the collapse of the caucus. . . . We are aware that many will scout the bare idea of such a possibility, and they will point to America as a country in which the Party system has continued to work, though the division of parties has long ceased to carry with it any rational significance. But we deny that any conclusion applicable to England can be drawn from the United States, a nation not weighted with the necessity of a foreign policy, not connected in a common system with a number of independent and alien States, a Government in which the Executive is practically independent of the Legislature and in which the popular House of Representatives plays a comparatively unimportant part. We repeat that in England the days of Party Government are numbered because neither the mechanical ingenuity of the wire-puller, nor the mendacious phrases of the rhetorician can continue to hold together associations of men no longer dependent on principles corresponding with the realities of things. They are numbered because the old causes of division between the two great historical Parties in the state have been removed, and because the Imperial questions that on all sides are pressing for solution are not of a kind that can be thrown with safety into the arena of party strife.

THOUGHTS ABOUT PARTY BY LORD SELBORNE.

Extract from Contemporary Review, Vol. LI., 1887.

" Mr. Justin M'Carthy, in his ' History of the Four Georges,' predicts that ' the principle of Government by party will some time or other come to be put to the challenge in English political life.'

" He refers (I think justly) the origin of the modern form of that system to the days of Pulteney and Walpole. There had been, of course, earlier parties, exercising a powerful influence upon government ; but they had been of a different kind—constitutional, dynastic, or religious.

" ' With Pulteney and his tactics,' says Mr. M'Carthy, ' began the party organization which inside the House of Commons and outside, works unceasingly with tongue and pen, with open antagonism and underhand intrigue, with all the various social as well as political influences—the pamphlet, the Press, the petticoat, even the pulpit—to discredit everything done by the men in office, to turn public opinion against them, and, if possible, to overthrow them. . . . Inside the House he made it his business to form a party which should assail the Ministry on all points, lie in wait to find occasion for attacking it, attack it rightly or wrongly, attack it even at the risk of exposing national weakness or bringing on national danger, keep attacking it always. . . . Pulteney and his companions set themselves to appeal especially to the prejudices, passions, and ignorance of the vulgar herd. They made it their business to create a public opinion of their own. They dealt in the manufacture of public opinion. They set up political shops to retail the article which they had thus manufactured.'

" This Mr. M'Carthy declares to have been ' unquestionably the policy of all our more modern English parties ; ' though he thinks that an English Opposition would be, in our time, more scrupulous than Pulteney and his supporters sometimes were. Some of the outlines and colours of this picture might be taken from life at the present day : the ' social as well as the political influences '—(clubs, ' Primrose Leagues,' whatever may be the name of the imitated article upon the other side)—' the manufacture of public opinion '—and the ' political shops set up to retail the manufactured article.' We have learned better manners (I hope, because we have worthier thoughts of, and more generous feelings towards, the less-instructed multitudes of our countrymen) than to talk of ' the vulgar herd ; '' but appeals from ' classes ' to ' masses ' are still not unknown. The art may have been improved since Pulteney's time ; neither party has a monopoly of it ; nor is it, by any means, confined to the party which may be, for the time being, in opposition. . . . . .

" The Liberal party has also been deemed, by some who have led or who have aspired to lead it, to require a new education, of which the result may perhaps be to accelerate the time foretold by Mr. M'Carthy, when the principle of government by party may be put upon its trial.

" I have alluded in the outset of this paper to what is popularly known as the ' Caucus system,' introduced from abroad into this country, not long since, under high Liberal auspices. It is, I think, an important question whether that system, in any of the forms which it has assumed or may assume, can be permanently reconciled with true Liberality. I cannot myself dissociate political Liberality from Liberty, or Liberty from honest independence of thought and judgment on the part of constituencies, and also of their representatives. It is not, at all events, the *old* Liberal idea, which would remove the centre of gravity of the constitutional system from Parliament to a federation of delegates of political unions ; which would practically limit the choice of Liberal electors, in every constituency, to persons who had first approved themselves to the managers of an inner conclave, holding the local party in leading strings ; which may tend to transform leaders of party and Ministers of State into dictators, by enabling them, through these outside agencies, to ostracise all who, even on subjects vital to the public welfare, have dared in the House of Commons to speak and vote as they think. Formerly, a member who so manifested his independence might have had to justify himself to his constituents, and he generally would have succeeded in doing so if they thought him an honest man, and if he could give good reasons for the course which he had taken. Now, if there were among Liberals no power of patriotism stronger than the bond of party association, he would have to justify himself before some 'council of three hundred,' or two hundred, or whatever else the number may be ; that council itself being under the influence—perhaps in the leading-strings—of a larger 'federation,' of which a very few individuals may be (probably are) the wire-pullers and masters.

" The system of party government will be essentially changed in character, and may soon cease to be tolerable, if it cannot be emancipated from this slavery.   .   .   .

" On all such subjects, the profession of Liberal politics cannot justify a man in making any political leader or wire-puller the keeper of his conscience, or absolve him from the duty and necessity (if he is honest) of making up his mind for himself ; he must act as he thinks, whatever others who pass by the same party name may do. If he approves such measures, he will support them, not because he belongs to a party, but because he thinks them right. If he disapproves, he is under a moral as well as a political obligation to oppose them. That duty is one which no honest man is at liberty to sacrifice to a party name."

A PROBLEM IN POLITICAL SCIENCE.

By Sandford Fleming.   From Trans. Roy. Soc. Canada, Vol. VII., 1889.

I propose to direct attention to a scientific question within the domain of politics or civil government which appears to me to be of great interest. It presents a problem which up to the present time remains unsolved.

The institution of Parliament, as we all know, is of ancient date. In England a general assembly or council of the nation has been held immemorially under various names. Before the Conquest three designations were at various times assigned to it :—

1. Mycel Synoth, or great synod.
2. Mycel Gemot, or great council.
3. Witenagemot, or council of the wise men.

The name of " Parliament " was not given to the National Council in England until after the Conquest, when the French language was exclusively used by the dominant class, and French became the official language of the English nation.

Parliament has greatly changed since its early days. It has grown and developed from century to century, and it may be said to be still in a condition of growth and development.

Whatever may have been the character of the meetings of the wise men before the Conquest, or of the Parliaments which followed, the central idea of Parliament at the present day, is an assembly of individuals representing the whole nation. The functions of Parliament are to act on behalf of the nation as the supreme authority, and representing the nation—it possesses every power and every right and every attribute which the nation possesses. The fundamental idea and guiding principle of Parliament is, that it embraces all the separate parts which compose the realm, that in fact it is the nation in essence.

This is the theoretical and proper idea of Parliament, but it cannot be affirmed that the ideal Parliament has ever yet been realized. Indeed it may be held that the means taken to constitute Parliament cannot, in the nature of things, result in producing a national assembly in which every individual elector may be fairly represented and his voice heard. As a matter of fact, under the existing system, it is not practicable to have in the elective house every part of the nation represented : some parts must necessarily remain unrepresented.

Such being the case, the problem which science may be asked to solve, is simply this : *to devise the means of forming an elective assembly which practically as well as theoretically will be the nation in essence.*

What is commonly known as the "Government" or the "Administration," and how it may be constituted, form no part of the problem, but are separated questions which I do not propose to discuss. I merely submit as a general principle, that the Government may be considered in the light of a committee of Parliament, or executive council to carry into effect the acts and resolutions of Parliament and administer affairs to the approval of Parliament.

Nations differ in their social and political circumstances, but in all free countries, at least, it is generally recognised that the elective assembly is of the first importance. The theory of the elective assembly, is that the whole people or such of the people as are duly qualified to vote shall be equally r epresented. It cannot be said that hitherto this object has been even approximately attained. Its attainment may indeed be impracticable, but the question is of so much importance that it cannot be unworthy of grave consideration. May we not ask if it be possible to devise some means, by which the whole people of the realm may be brought to a central point, to a focus so to speak, in a deliberative assembly or Parliament.

The question of electing representatives to sit in Parliament has received the attention of many political writers and has likewise been investigated at length by many celebrated geometers, who have recorded their dissent from the practices followed. Under the present system, members are elected by a part of the community only, while their election is opposed by another part. It is quite true that the intention is to have the majority of the people represented, but even this is not a necessary result of the existing system ; moreover it does not follow that the majority of members returned will hold the views and opinions of the majority of the people on any subject. It may happen and frequently does happen, as a direct result of the present system, that legislative power is placed, not in the representatives of a majority, but in those who represent a minority. Sir John Lubbock gives an apt illustration of this result. He supposes a country in which there are 1,200,000 electors who vote with party *A*, and 1,000,000 who vote with party *B*. Now if the two parties are evenly distributed over the whole country, it is clear that, under the ordinary system of representation, the weaker party will be utterly swamped. To use a familiar illustration (he remarks) whenever you drop a bucket into the sea, you will bring up salt water. In such a case therefore the 1,000,000 will be practically unrepresented. But we must carry the matter a little further. In the House so elected, let the majority bring forward some bill of an advanced character and carry it by two to one, *i.e.*, by the votes of members representing 800,000 electors and against those representing 400,000 ; in such a case it is clear that the minority in the House would have with them also the 1,000,000 in the country who were left unrepresented ; so that in fact the measure would represent the wishes of only 800,000 electors, and would be opposed by those of 1,400,000. Thus he points out that the result of a system "of Government by majorities, is, on the contrary, to enable a minority of 800,000 to overrule a majority of 1,400,000."

This illustrates only one of the many defects in the present system, but it is quite sufficient to show that the principle of Representative Government, which is inherently good, has not been realised. It is obvious from the very nature of the system practised in electing members, that, every Parliament, not the whole but only a part of the electors are represented, and that the representatives of a minority may frequently over-rule a majority of the people.

Take the present Parliament of our own Dominion, and in doing so we have a case in which all will acknowledge that the Administration at the present moment is supported by a large working majority of members. At the last General Election (Feb. 1887) the total number of voters on the lists in all the constituencies where contests took place was 948,524. Of this number the votes polled for one party were 370,342 and for the other 354,714. That is to say, 39 per cent. of the whole represents one party, and 37 per cent. the other party in Parliament. As the representatives of the 37 per cent. are swamped in Parliament and are in no way recognized in the administration of affairs, it follows that 39 per cent. of the electors through their representatives have complete control, and the remaining 61 per cent. have practically no voice in the government of the country. Moreover, as the election of members representing the 39 per cent. of votes was in every instance opposed by the voters who number 37 per cent. of the whole, it follows that on all questions settled on strict party lines, Parliament speaks and acts in its decisions by the members who represent but two per cent. of the whole body of electors. This is not an accidental but a common and, indeed, a necessary result, of the present system, which must continue so long as we follow the ordinary method of electing members to sit in Parliament.

The question presented is this: Is there any means whatever by which a national assembly can be formed approximating more closely to the ideal Parliament?

Let us begin the inquiry by assuming that the electorate consists of only two electors, that they are equal in all respects, in ability, integrity, in worldly means, in public spirit; that they have each equal claims and equal desires to act as representatives, and each is equally willing to be represented the one by the other.

Under such circumstances what course would be followed by the two to settle the question? Would not the natural method be to cast lots? Assuming that the two electors were left to their own resources, removed from all outside influences, would not this be the only rational means by which they could make a choice?

There are doubtless some minds who would have an innate feeling against resorting to such practice; the casting of lots being more or less associated with dice-playing, lotteries and games of chance, to which objections are taken on good and sufficient grounds; but in the case presented there remains no way of reaching a decision except by lot. What other course could be followed? A contest would not mend matters; a trial of physical strength and endurance would be at once futile and indefensible. If the object be to turn the two into a single representative unit, unanimity is essential, and while agreeing in nothing else they could agree in casting lots. Is the principle of settlement by casting lots in itself objectionable? Was it not considered wise and good in ancient times? And would it not be equally good to-day? It is certainly a time-honored usage for determining difficult questions, and is exemplified in many passages in Holy Scripture; indeed the uniform voice of Scripture goes to show that decisions thus obtained are not only wholly unobjectionable in themselves, but that they were considered to have been overruled and directed by special providential interposition.

I shall cite but one example, the selection of an apostle to take the place of Judas Iscariot. An account of this election by casting lots is given in the "Acts of the Apostles," Chap. I, verses 15-26. It is stated that about a hundred and twenty persons were called upon to select one of their number. They proceeded with deliberate wisdom to follow a usage regarded by them as a means of obtaining the divine mind. They determined by lot who should be the twelfth apostle, and thus they made a selection to which a cheerful acquiescence was unanimously given.

I have assumed a case of two electors, and pointed out the course which might be followed—indeed, the only rational course which could be followed. If the principle laid down be sound, could it not be applied in other cases? Let us assume that the electorate

consists of twenty voters, what could be done in this case? If individual voters in the electorate were equal in all respects, as in the first case referred to, the question would be a very
simple one, as it might be settled by casting lots for one of the twenty equally eligible persons. It may be taken for granted that under the circumstances no one would object to
make the selection in this way, as being the simplest and best mode of making a choice. It
would remove antagonism and promote unanimity ; and, by the very act of casting lots, each
one of the twenty taking part therein would be an assenting party to the choice made. Men
as we ordinarily find them are, however, not alike ; they differ much in their qualifications,
and their opinions are not the same ; we must therefore consider cases in which equal eligi-
bility and uniformity of mind in the whole electorate is not the rule.

First, let us suppose that among the twenty electors, five votes favor the choice of A,
another five B, another C, and the remainder D. We should have A, B, C, D each equally
desired and preferred as the representative of the twenty.

$(A + B + C + D) \div 4$ would therfore be the representative unit of the whole. We cannot,
however, take one quarter of A, B, C, and D, and combine these quarters so as to form one
individual, but we can reduce the four to one by the principle of casting lots. One of the
four can be selected by what may be termed the "Apostolic" method, and the person so
selected would be recognized as chosen by the twenty electors as the common representative
of the whole.

Secondly, let us suppose a case in which there is less diversity of opinion ; two groups of
five electors each favor A, one group of five prefer B, another C. The selected men would
thus stand A, A, B and C, and the representative unit of the whole would be $(2A + B + C) \div 4$.
As in the previous case, this complex would be reducible to a single individual by casting
lots, and it is obvious that the probability of the lots falling upon A would be as two to one.

Third, suppose three groups of five electors desire to be represented by A and one group
by B. In this case we should have $(3A + B) \div 4$, as the representative unit : in selecting one
by lot, there is undoubtedly a possibility of the lot falling upon B, but the probability of
A's being chosen would be three times greater than the probability in B's case. True it may
be said that there should be no possibility of B's being chosen in a constituency where three-
fourths of the electors desire A. We must, however, bear in mind that the object is not so
much to have particular sections of the country, as to have the whole nation, fairly represented in parliament. If we look a little further, if we take four constituencies precisely
similar to the one under consideration, according to the mathematical theory of probabilities,
there would be returned out of the four, three members in sympathy with A and one
member in sympathy with B. Again, if we carry the matter still further if we take into
consideration every one of the constituencies into which for convenience the whole nation
may be divided, it would be found as a general result that the representatives returned to sit
in Parliament would collectively represent the nation and fairly embody the reason contained
in the whole community.

There is one peculiarity of the system suggested which may be noticed ; in every case
the election of a representative would be effected deliberately and without conflict. It
would be accomplished in fact with unanimous assent. Each individual voter would contribute toward a common result—a result which would be reached on principles equally just
and fair to all, and thus command general acquiescence.

These results are attainable only by bringing to bear, on matters of doubt or difficulty,
the principle of settlement adopted by the Apostles. That principle cannot be objected to
on scientific grounds, and those who hold the belief that mundane affairs are over-ruled and
directed, should have no difficulty in accepting it as a means of promoting harmony and
advancing the common good. The belief in a Providence, who takes cognizance of the
affairs of men, is the foundation of all religion ; communities therefore, the social fabric of

which is based on Christianity, should have no hesitation in leaving matters of the highest moment to the arbitrament of an infinitely wise Providence rather than to the settlement of men with all their individual interests and selfish views, all their prejudices, all their passions, and all their errors of judgment.

I have so far, for the purpose of the argument, assumed hypothetical cases; it remains to be considered how the principles laid down may be applied practically. Let us take for example the election of a single representative in a constituency of 2,000 voters. It is desirable in the first place that each voter, or group of voters of one mind, should have perfect freedom of choice in the nomination. Suppose, in order to accommodate every shade of opinion, it be arranged that each hundred voters of one way of thinking name the person whom they would wish to represent them. This would separate the constituency into twenty groups of voters, who would each nominate whomsoever they most favored. It does not necessarily follow that there would be twenty persons nominated in the constituency, as two or more groups might nominate the same person: a circumstance which would increase the probability of his selection exactly in proportion to the number of groups making him their nominee. On the twenty nominations being made, the next step would be for the person nominated to proceed on the principles above set forth, to select one of themselves.

If unable to make an unanimous choice, they might, as in the case of the twenty electors choosing a representative, sort themselves into smaller groups and, by the application of the principles set forth, proceed to reduce the number of voting units, and finally, by the apostolic method, determine the election of one person. The person so chosen would be held to be the common choice of the whole 2,000 to represent the constituency in Parliament.

In the carrying out of such a system, there would be, as in every system, a number of possible contingencies for which provision would have to be made; these I have not deemed it necessary at present to enter into. My object has been briefly to suggest leading principles by which, as it appears to me, the central idea may be realized. If the principles submitted be sound, I venture to think that it is not impracticable to devise proper machinery to elect representatives who, when brought into one deliberate gathering, would, so far as such a thing is possible, be a mathematical concentration of the whole electoral body—would in fact constitute an assembly which would closely approximate to the ideal Parliament.

Referring to the present system an eminent writer asks: "Is government only possible by the conflict of opposing principles?" The familiar expression, "government of the people by the people" cannot be held to mean government of the whole by a part or by the conflict of hostile parts. It must be obvious the united energy and wisdom of a whole nation directed towards one end can only be fully realized, when the supreme power is vested in a Parliament chosen by the whole people, and fairly representing the whole people. This is the great problem for solution and it is manifest that if such a Parliament is ever to be constituted, the people, in choosing members to represent them, must in some way be brought to act not in contestation and conflict, but in concert and in concord.

If it be one of the first of political desiderata to have no large minorities left unrepresented in the national assembly, it appears to me essential to seek for some means of securing the co-operation of the whole body of the electors in the election of members to sit in the High Court of Parliament. To obtain this result it is obviously expedient to adopt a system which necessarily does not develop animosity or provoke hostility; the aim should be to promote friendliness and agreement in a matter which concerns all alike. It cannot be denied that the whole community is concerned in having in Parliament, not men of extreme views, but moderate-minded men of good common sense and good conscience, capable of representing the more enlightened electoral mind. By electing representatives on the principles laid down, these desirable objects would undoubtedly in a large measure be attained; every step would be deliberately taken, free from the excited and heated feelings which so frequently accompany ordinary elections. In every stage of the proceedings there would be a tendency to return only the best men. At the very first step it is obvious that a candidate must be a person respected and supported by a hundred electors. It is presumable that no hundred electors of any class or race or creed would deliberately put forward a base or unworthy or even an inferior individual ; it is not to be supposed that they would choose one of the least intelligent or least honest or least reputable among them as their representative in the candidature. As a rule, electors of one mind would arrange themselves into groups of one hundred, and each group would select some man, who, on his merits as a citizen, would creditably represent them, or who as a statesman would commend himself to their favour. In their turn, those selected by the hundreds would follow the same course, selecting generally the best, the worthiest and wisest men until the final choice was reached and a member selected to represent the constituency in Parliament.

It can scarcely be doubted that if such a system could be put in force, the tendency would be upwards from first to last, and that there would be drawn to the legislature accomplished statesmen, men endowed with wisdom and patriotism, practical knowledge and experience. The inevitable effect would be to allay the spirit of faction and remove political rancour. In a higher degree than under the ordinary method of electing members, the system would attract within the pale of Parliament men in generous sympathy not with a part only, but with the whole people. Thus might be constituted an august body which as closely as possible would be a true mirror of the enlightened mind of the nation to reflect its opinions, its wisdom, and its virtues.

In a Parliament so constituted, perfect unanimity on all questions, perhaps on any question, is not to be looked for, and each separate question would have to be settled, as it arose, by the voice of a majority. Hence it may be said that as every question would in the end have to be determined by a majority, the Parliament as proposed would be no improvement on the present. It will, however, readily be seen that there is a wide difference between a parliament representing the whole people, deciding questions by a majority of its own members, and a Parliament in which a part only of the electors has any voice. The proposed assembly would not consist of men placed in their seats in direct opposition to a large number of the people, but a Parliament formed through the co-operation and assent of the whole body of the electors, to promote their common welfare ; it would approximately be a microcosm, so to speak, of the nation. In and through this Parliament each and every elector would have an equal voice in public affairs.

The proposal is to substitute in our Parliamentary elections the principle of co-operation for the principle of antagonism, and by this means to choose representatives, who when brought together in a deliberative assembly would realize the true idea of Parliament—a " Witenagemot or great council of wise men," representing every part of the realm, and imbued with the spirit of the whole, to act in the name of the whole, and speak the voice of the united nation.

If such a Parliament be an object to be desired ; if it be a fundamental principle that all who bear the taxation should share in the representation ; if it be the sacred right of every elector to have a just and proper representation in Parliament ; then it must be recognized as a paramount duty, and an object worthy of the highest efforts of the progressive statesman, to find some means by which such a legislative body may be realized. A complete solution of the problem may be remote, but as has been stated, Parliament is a growth and development, and in all matters into which the principle of growth enters, the element of time must also enter. The question vitally concerns all free communities, and any change must in the nature of things be preceded by a deliberate and impartial enquiry. I have ventured to submit a scientific solution ; it may not be the best means of attaining the desired end, and I offer it with all diffidence merely as a contribution to the general discussion, in the hope that it may not be wholly barren of utility. I cannot but think that f the strictly scientific habit of mind be brought to bear on the question, some practical method of solving the problem will slowly and surely be evolved. Whatever the solution, I humbly think that it must be based on principles which will not beget the conflicts and contestations which result from political activity under the present system.

It is held by the most eminent political economists that by co-operating two men will do more work and do it better than four men, or four times four men acting in opposition. Is not the rule of universal application? Can there be co-operation without harmony? Can there be antagonism without discord? And are not discord and harmony in the state likened unto disease and health in the human body? This much will be conceded; the chronic feuds between tribes and races which characterized the history of the human family in a less advanced stage of civilization no longer exist. War is manifestly not the normal condition of society in our time. Is it not therefore an anachronism to perpetuate hostility in the internal affairs of a nation? Is it not in the highest interest of the state that each member of the community, in every matter which concerns him as a citizen, should have the fullest opportunity of acting up to the injunction, "Live peaceably with all men?" If the age of belligerency has passed away, is it not eminently fit and proper that we should seek the removal of the last vestiges of a belligerent age which still remain in our political system?

THE DEGRADATION OF OUR POLITICS.

By Dr. F. A. P. Barnard, in " The Forum," Vol. IX. 1890.

Under the early presidents, appointments to office were made in the true spirit of the Constitution. A certain service was to be performed in the interest of the public, and a man possessing the requisite capacity and tried character was looked for to perform it. Appointment as a reward of partisan service, and removal as a punishment for difference of political opinion, were unknown. In the first division of parties, the strength was with the Federalists, and George Washington, their candidate, was elevated to the presidental chair. But George Washington was first of all a patriot, and only in the second place a Federalist; and his earliest executive act was to appoint to the leading place in his cabinet his most conspicuous political opponent, since known as the father of American Democracy, Thomas Jefferson; while Alexander Hamilton, the champion of the party which had just triumphed in his own election, was assigned to a lower seat at the same council board. And in this large and liberal and magnanimous spirit were made all the appointments to office during the administration of that great man. If under his earlier successors the same noble magnanimity was not the invariable rule, there was at least no large departure from it for more than thirty years. There came a time at length, however, when the chair of state was filled by a man who chose to make himself the chief of a party and not of the country, or, rather, in whose view no country existed except the party supporting him. Under the iron rule inaugurated by this energetic chief, every incumbent of a federal office, no matter how insignificant, who was presumed not to have been favorable to the revolution which brought the new dynasty into power, was unceremoniously ejected from the public service; and in filling the multitude of places thus vacated, the qualifications demanded were no longer honesty, competency, and fidelity to the Constitution, but, instead of these, activity and zeal in the service of the party and devotion to the party chief.

From that time to the present, the character of the civil service of the country has been steadily falling lower and lower. Among the servants of the public, the public interest is the last thing thought of. Rather, on the other hand, the public treasure is regarded by those into whose hands it has fallen not otherwise than as the merchandise of a rich caravan is regarded by the Bedouins of the desert—a legitimate booty, to be seized with favoring opportunity and divided among the members of the successful band. Not even in the beginning was any attempt made to conceal the mercenary character of the new system. It was even defended as a just system in the highest legislative council of the nation, by a very prominent leader of the party which first profited by it, whose pithy enunciation of its fundamental principle will never pass from the memory of man—"To the victors belong the spoils." But it is no longer the system of a particular party. It has become the recognized system of all parties, until the continually-recurring political struggles by which the country is agitated have ceased to be contests over great questions of constitutional law or governmental policy, but have degenerated into discreditable squabbles to determine which of two bodies of political cormorants, both equally unworthy, shall be permitted to prey upon the public. Under its operation the very character of our government has been changed.

This violation of the spirit of the Constitution in prostituting the power of appointment to be an instrument of reward and punishment, originated as we have seen, in the will of a single man, strong enough in an abnormal popularity to force his own measures upon the country in spite of a hostile legislature, and to convert the government for a time into a practical despotism. He was accustomed indeed to speak of the government as "my government," and of himself as one " born to command"; and had he been asked to define the state, would, probably, like Louis XIV., have answered, L'état c'est moi. But his imperial mantle fell upon a successor fashioned in a far inferior mould and infinitely less daring in temper, who, though not suited to the bold role of avowed dictator, was possessed of an astuteness which amply compensated for this defect. It was his boast to tread in the footsteps of his illustrious predecessor, and in some respects he certainly improved upon the example his predecessor had set him. To him is believed to have been due an important discovery, if not in the science of political economy, at least in the economy of scientific politics—that the power of governmental patronage may be indefinitely increased by the ingenious expedient of employing middle men in its dispensation. The middle man, who must be a man worth buying, is bought by the privilege of bestowing the benefaction; the final recipient is bought by the benefaction itself. The men most worth buying by this participation in the power of appointment are naturally to be found, and they were found, among the members of the legislative body; and by firmly attaching a sufficient number of these, in interest as well as in sympathy, to the recognized head of the party in power, there was secured to the executive the incalculable advantage of a never-failing and indiscriminate support, in that body, of all his measures. The system thus introduced speedily and effectually took root, and has since become the established system of American politics. No matter what party is in power, it is always practiced. But it has wrought, in the experience of years, a consequence which the inventor certainly never anticipated; for the privilege which the middle men at first received with thankfulness, they now, in virtue of a long-undisturbed possession, boldly demand as a right. The spoils of victory are claimed as the common property of the victorious band; the right of the chief to control its distribution is set at defiance; and thus the executive, with which the system originated, has been shorn by it of the power to name its own subordinates, and the government of the Constitution has practically ceased to exist.

In its place has grown up something which admits of no classification among systems of government ancient or modern. Republican in form, as nominally representative, it is yet not a republic; for its representatives, though chosen by the people, are not the people's choice. Democratic in methods, as seemingly resting on universal suffrage, it is yet not a democracy; for the periodical appeal to the popular voice is a ceremony as empty and unreal as a plébiscite under the Second Empire. Though the government of a class, it is not an aristocracy; for it is largely composed of elements least of all deserving of respect. And though the government of a few, it is not an oligarchy de jure, though it is such de facto : for it exists by no recognized right, and its existence is not even confessed. The imperfection of language has necessitated the invention of a new form of words to describe it; and this has been supplied, by those most familiar with its workings, in the felicitous expression, "machine government." No phrase could have been better chosen. A machine is a contrivance in which numerous separate elements are combined for the effective application of force to a determinate object. Such is the political machine. It is composed of a class of men who make politics a profession, and whose ruling aim in life is to make their profession profitable. In order to do this, it is necessary to secure the possession of all places of trust and emolument under the government to men of their own class. And in order to do this again, it is further necessary that the people shall be deprived of the option to choose other men. The effectiveness of the machine is most strikingly illustrated in the thoroughness with which this object is accomplished. So long as forms of popular election are maintained, party divisions among the people are, of course, inevitable. And it is as true of parties as of armies, that without organization, unity of purpose, and concert of action, there can be no success. To control the party organization is therefore the aim of the professed politician, and experience has shown that this is comparatively easy. The process is a curious combination of fraud and farce.

The first step in it, is what is known as "engineering the primaries." The primaries are in theory assemblies of the sovereign people. Their province is to select delegates to a representative convention, having for its function to set forth publicly the principles for which the party ostensibly contends and to name its standard-bearers. The primaries are easily engineered. Their business is carefully prepared for them in advance, even to the designation of their own officers. At the appointed hour, the captains of tens and the captains of fifties are prompt in attendance; a machine politician is called to the chair by a vote without a count; a machine politician proposes the nominees; the nominations are declared to be adopted; and the engineering of the primary is complete. The management of the convention is almost equally simple. Being made up of machine politicians, it knows very well what it has to do, and it does it. The really important part of its work has been prepared for it in anticipation of its meeting by a process conducted in secret, known among machine politicians as "making up a slate." In general, the slate, after the observance of certain decorous formalities, is duly ratified; but occasionally, as there will now and then be factions within factions, the slate may be broken, and a new one produced—a result, however, of no importance to the country, since it is perfectly understood that the winning party in any case shall have the use of the machine. The portion of the work of the convention which is designed for popular effect, is the declaration of principles, technically called a "platform." This is a beautiful piece of composition, glowing in every line with patriotic and virtuous sentiment, setting forth with earnest emphasis a variety of indisputable propositions, and embellished with a choice selection of those glittering generalities which sound so well and, when we think of it, seem to mean so little. These may be varied from time to time according to circumstances; but there are one or two specifications which, as being always in place and particularly well-sounding, are quite indispensable to any properly-constructed platform. These are, first, a peremptory demand for the retrenchment of the public expenditure; and, secondly, a proper denunciation of the ungrateful miscreants who would rob our brave soldiers and sailors of their well-merited pensions. The platform being duly promulgated, the work of the convention is done.

In the meantime, the opposing party has been going through with a performance entirely similar; and the result is that the simple citizen, or the "man outside of politics," has no alternative but to stay outside altogether, or to choose the machine with which he will run. There remains, of course, the expedient of independent action; but such action is only labor wasted, unless it be so wisely concerted, so thoroughly organized, and so energetically prosecuted as to become powerful enough to break both machines. It must be attempted, if at all, under enormous disadvantages. The advantage of experience is against it; it must oppose raw volunteers to disciplined and veteran troops. The advantage of position is against it; one of the parties is already in possession of the government. The advantage of instrumentalities is against it ; the custom house, the post office, the internal-revenue bureau, the land office, and all the other ramifications of the civil service, are so many engines in the hands of the enemy. And, finally, the advantage of access to the public ear is against it ; for the periodical press is largely either subsidized by existing parties or in sympathy with them. . . . . .

It would be an office wholly ungracious thus to set forth the evidences of our moral and political decadence, were there not a hope behind, that, out of the unpleasing exhibit, there might grow some suggestion of good. It is only by portraying the evil in its fullest magnitude that we can be thoroughly impressed with the lesson of its accompanying danger. For there is before us a danger greater and graver than any we have yet encountered. Hitherto the forms of our Constitution have been respected, though the spirit has been perverted. Hitherto our personal rights have been secure, though our political franchises have been practically lost. We need but travel a little further on the downward road, and even those relics of our liberties will be swept away. In the grand corruption which made for a time the commercial metropolis of our country an illustration of the ills the people suffer when the wicked bear rule, we had almost reached the point at which law itself ceases to have efficacy, and the most sacred rights of person and property become the sport of the caprice of any adventurer bold enough and bad enough and strong enough to throttle justice in her own temples. The example of that tyranny was typical of the system which rules the country. It was only a little in advance of the general progress. But nothing is more surely written in the book of destiny than that, unless effectual remedies be speedily devised to arrest this downward tendency, what was true of New York in 1870 will, long before the close of another century, be true universally ; and more than that, the career of defiant corruption will culminate inevitably in the downfall of all law, and a sea of anarchy and a social chaos will engulf all rights of the citizen, personal or political.

Are there, then, remedies for these evils ? Undoubtedly there are, but they are remedies which, if applied at all, must be applied by the people themselves, and which can only, or will only, be applied by a people thoroughly aroused to their danger and their duty.

The wide departure from the principles of the Constitution which is the source of all our woes, has been owing to the abuse of power in the hands of the men who hold it. We need, therefore, no change in the Constitution, but a return to the Constitution ; no change in the laws, but a great change in methods of administration ; and to this end we must have men in power not wedded by habit to existing abuses, or bound to them by interest. How shall this object be secured ? . . . . .

We should teach our youth, therefore, that the first duty of every good citizen is at present to use his most energetic efforts for the breaking up of machine government ; for it is through the political machine that the people have been practically divested of their rights, and subjected to the rule of a usurping and unscrupulous oligarchy.

In order to this, effort must begin at the bottom. If the system of what is called regular nominations is to be continued, the nominations must be honest nominations of honest men. The primary meetings in which they originate must be really meetings of the honest voters, must be organized and controlled by the honest voters, and must express the will of the honest voters ; instead of being what they have so long been heretofore, close caucuses of petty pot-house politicians, employed to give the outward forms of regularity to corrupt arrangements already perfected in secret. And this they will be, as soon as honest voters do their duty, by direct and personal participation in the selection of the men who are in turn to name their rulers.

Our young men should also be instructed as to the nature and use of parties in political affairs, and taught to distinguish the limitations within which the action of such is healthful, and beyond which it may be destructive of the ends of good government. Upon every great measure of public policy, and upon every great question of constitutional interpretation, opinions will necessarily be divided ; and on these divisions will inevitably arise opposing parties, which, in spite of their differences, may be equally honest and equally patriotic. But it is in the nature of things human that these points of difference cannot be eternal. Questions of public policy cease with the occasion out of which they grew. Questions of constitutional law must in some form or other be at length adjudicated. But though with the disappearance of the original cause of difference the reason of their being is itself removed, it is rarely the case that parties recognize the fact that their usefulness has ceased, and voluntarily dissolve themselves. For while the questions dividing them were living questions, it was unavoidable that the struggle over these should take the practical form of a struggle for the possession of the government, and these being lost, the possession of the government becomes itself the object of contention, the greed of gain becomes the bond of union, and selfishness takes the place of patriotism as the ruling motive.

PARLIAMENTARY *VS.* PARTY GOVERNMENT.

Address at Queen's University, by Chancellor Fleming, 1891.

The matter which I take upon myself to bring to your notice involves the consideration of an evil to which it is impossible to shut our eyes, and in the removal of which every honest minded person is directly interested ; and this fact will I am sure be accepted as my reason for dealing with it specifically. Wherever there is a public evil, there is a public wrong to be righted ; and it becomes a duty, which we owe to the community, to apply our utmost intelligence to discover the proper remedy, and act with energy in its application. The theme of my address is *Party Government* versus *Parliamentary Government*.

At the recent prolonged meeting of parliament at Ottawa, there was brought to light a series of transactions, which have given a shock to the moral sense of many of our people. These revelations will little surprise those who are familiar with public affairs in the United States.

I believe I am correct in saying, that in Canada we have not reached the length which our neighbours have attained in what passes by the name of "politics." Methods and practices have, however, been introduced into our public life, in some respects the same as theirs, and if our system has not yet reached the same development we may reasonably expect that if we continue on the path which they have followed and which we have entered upon, we shall in course of no long time arrive at the same goal.

In a work recently issued from the press, "Bryce's American Commonwealth," there are twenty-three chapters devoted exclusively to the subject of government by party, and many of the other chapters have a bearing on the same matter. Within the pages of this valuable and instructive work we find a full and detailed account of the party system which prevails among our neighbours. The author describes at length the business of the politician, the machinery of parties, how it works and what it effects. He reveals the fact that the machinery has many and costly ramifications, and that a great deal of money is required to keep it in motion. Where the money comes from is another question. He points out that "the politicians themselves belong to, or emerge from a needy class" and the funds generally must come from other sources than the pockets of the men most actively engaged, but from whatever source money may in the first place be obtained, the startling conclusion is irresistibly reached that "the whole cost in the long run is thrown on the public."

At the first glance it is not easy to see that this conclusion can apply to the party out of power and in no position to help themselves. The author, however, explains that its members live on hope ; they hope that they will eventually succeed in overthrowing their opponents and are buoyed up with the belief that the minority of to-day will be the majority of to-morrow. He points out that as a fund must be raised meanwhile to carry on the struggle, the vassals of the party are assessed and subscriptions levied on manufacturers, contractors, office seekers and expectants generally. Thus, claims are established on the spoils which sooner or later will come under the control of the party. When the victorious day arrives, the expectants do not as a rule allow their claims to be forgotten.

One thing clearly brought out by the author is that enormous sums are expended by each party contending for the mastery. Those, engaged in the conflict, maintain journals, employ writers, speakers, canvassers and agitators ; in fact an army of professional politicians finds employment in this kind of warfare. The necessity of a party fund is apparent. If money is the root of all evil, it is likewise the main-spring of party activity ; the greater the activity, the larger the demand on the purses of those who have something to give, or something to expect.

Party organizations on both sides are on an elaborate scale, and nothing is left undone by each contestant to advance party interest. It is civil war on a gigantic scale. There are hostile camps everywhere. The nation is formed into two divisions, each division contending and struggling for the supremacy. The rank and file are drilled by the professional politicians, who manage the nominations, dictate who are to be the candidates, and generally direct the contest so as to carry the elections. The party managers are, for the most part, men who make politics the sole, or chief business of their lives, and who live and flourish by the occupation. The list, not seldom, includes ministers of state, or those who expect to be ministers, members of congress, or those who expect to be members ; it also comprises those, who make the party to which they are attached a stepping stone to power and place ; and who if they do not at once attain their ends, are rewarded meanwhile if in no other way by the excitement which is stimulated by contest.

The fullest and most painstaking enquiry into the whole system leads the author to describe the general result in the following words : " The tremendous power of party organization has been described. It enslaves local officials, it increases the tendency to regard members of congress as mere delegates, it keeps men of independent character out of local and national politics, it puts bad men into place, it perverts the wishes of the people, it has in some places set up a tyranny under the form of democracy."

This conclusion arrived at by the latest independent authority is not disputed in any quarter. It is supported by every writer of any note. Albert Stickney in " Democratic Government," 1885, says : " The practical result of the present political system in the United States, which at first sight seems in form so thoroughly democratic, has been to develop the most ingenious and remarkable tyranny known in all political history. . . . The political life of the nation is a never-ending struggle for political power between rival factions—all of them brought into existence by the same cause, obeying the same laws, using the same methods, compelled, whether they wish to or not, to prostitute the power of public office to personal ends. The result is a new kind of tyranny—the tyranny of the election machine. Under this system political freedom for the citizen cannot exist."

Henry George in " Social Problems,' 1890, writes : " Speaking generally of the whole country from the Atlantic to the Pacific and from the lakes to the gulf, our government by the people has in large degree become, is in larger degree becoming, government by the strong and unscrupulous. . . . Money and organization tell more and more in elections. In some sections bribery has become chronic, and numbers of voters expect regularly to sell their votes. In some sections large employers regularly bulldoze their hands into voting as *they* like. In Municipal, State and Federal politics the power of the ' machine ' is increasing. In many places it has become so strong that the ordinary citizen has no more influence on the government under which he lives than he would have in China. He is, in reality, not one of the governing classes but one of the governed. . . . And he is beginning to accept the situation and leave politics to politicians, as something with which an honest, self-respecting man cannot afford to meddle. . . The type of the rising party leader.

is not the orator or statesman of an earlier day, but the shrewd manager who knows how to handle the 'workers,' how to combine pecuniary interests, how to obtain money and how to spend it." The same writer in another place referring to the party organization, says : " Its members carry wards in their pockets, make up the slates for nominating conventions, distribute offices as they bargain together, and—though they toil not neither do they spin—wear the best of raiment and spend money lavishly. And who are these men ? The wise, the good, the learned ; men who have earned the confidence of their fellow-citizens by the purity of their lives, the splendour of their talents, their probity of public trust, their deep study of the problems of government ? No ; they are gamblers, saloon keepers, pugilists, or'worse, who have made a trade of controlling votes and of buying and selling offices."

An equally well-known writer, Dr. Goldwin Smith, remarks : "A national conflict every four years for the Presidency, and the enormous patronage that is now annexed to it, must bring everything that is bad to the top, and will end in the domination of scoundrels. The moral atmosphere is darkened with calumny, bribery and corruption and all their fatal effects upon national character. How can the political character of any nation withstand forever the virus of evil passion and corruption which these vast faction fights infuse ?"

We have thus described to us the character of the machinery which controls political affairs in the republic. Writers generally affirm that public life has become so foul that the best men and the finest intellects take no part in the business of the nation ; that these have been driven off the field and politics have now to a large extent become a prey to unprincipled plunderers.

It is well to know something about the road we are travelling, and I read these extracts so that we may understand whither we are going, and what is before us if we continue as we have commenced. So long as we travel smoothly and pleasantly we do not think of making enquiries concerning the way. But when we come to "bad spots," then we ask the next traveller we meet the condition of the road before us. This is exactly our case in political affairs. We have stumbled on a stretch of rough ground ; we enquire the character of the way we have to pass over, and those familiar with it tell us, that it becomes worse and worse, terminating in a quagmire. With this information, unless we are fatuously blind and criminally indifferent to our fate, we call a halt and consider as to the attempt we should make to find a better route.

The political path followed in the United States is "partyism," and we plainly see where it has landed our neighbours. In Canada we have not yet travelled so far, but if anything be wanting to show that we are hurrying on in the same direction, let me read a few sentences from a good authority, the Halifax *Herald*, the chief organ of one of the parties in Nova Scotia. Within the last few days (Oct. 12), that newspaper, in a leading article, expressed these opinions : "Those who are acquainted with the political methods of either party might, we presume, furnish the public with an interesting experience of the use and abuse of campaign funds. . . Party government is an institution in itself, recognized under the political constitution of the country. The organization of a party, its maintenance, and successful working all necessitate large financial outlay. . . The money must be raised, and those who refuse to contribute their fair share, only increase the temptation ever present to the party workers to obtain funds from those who have a financial interest in the success of one party or the other. It is useless to ignore existing conditions. The struggle between rival parties will continue. Funds for political purposes must be raised. It is, therefore, the duty of all good citizens to contribute according to their means ; and if they fail to do so, the political organizations of rival parties must be thrown more and more into the hands of those who contribute to their support from corrupt or selfish motives."

I believe I am warranted in saying that in Canada partyism is not yet developed to the extent described in the United States, but recent disclosures show the tendency in public life, and it is perfectly clear that if we act on similar principles and follow the same headlong course, we cannot fail to reap the same or similar evil consequences.

We know that there are good men on both sides of politics. It is not the want of men, patriotic, public-spirited and able, that we have to deplore, it is the malign influences of the

system by which they are enslaved. The best men are dragged downwards by the party mael-
strom, and once within its vortex they become powerless to escape from its baleful embrace.

The low tone of public life which we Canadians have already reached, is evidenced by the
fact, that no ordinary man in his private dealings, would do that which by a singular obliquity
of moral sense is considered unobjectionable in party ethics. It seems to be well understood on
both sides, that dishonesty in almost any form only becomes an offence when detection follows ;
and if we judge our politicians as described by themselves or by the partisan press, there are few
indeed of whose public or private character it is possible to form an exalted opinion.

It is not necessary to go far a field for evidence of the demoralizing tendency of the
political system practised in our own land. The proceedings of the last few months clearly
indicate that we have already made a most disquieting progress in our downward course. Can
nothing be done to turn it in a right direction? The universal law is that there must be progress.
Nothing remains stationary. If we permit the system to remain as it is, the progress will continue downwards ; and the experience of our neighbors teaches us that as time rolls on we will
make the descent at a greatly accelerated speed.

We may one and all ask the question what in this emergency are we to do? We do not
want retrogression or degradation. We do not desire to go from bad to worse. Our object
should be improvement and advancement.

If this be our aspiration there are certain things which we must not do. We must not fold
our hands in despair and leave politics and political affairs wholly to the politicians. We must
not close our eyes to the misdeeds which have been brought to light in our own land, or to the
experience derived from the United States. The past history of politics in both countries will be
of benefit to us if we only determine to profit by it. We must not listen to that school of politicians, who tell us that government by party is the only means of carrying on free institutions ;
that it is impossible to attain to good government without opposing parties. We must be prepared to dismiss from our minds the dogma that partyism is a necessity, however ably or by whatever number the assertion be made.

Government by party has been practised in the United States for a hundred years ; in
England for two centuries ; in Canada it may be traced from the first year of her legislative
existence. In all three countries it has been tried and found wanting. I think I cannot be
wrong in laying down the axiom, that no system, however deeply rooted by long usage, however
strengthened by prejudice, if founded on evil or productive of evil, can be considered a finality.

The party system divides a nation into two halves ; in itself an evil. It is based on principles which nurture some of the worst passions of our nature. It is productive, as everyone must
admit, of intolerable evils ; and on every ground we are warranted in the conclusion, that this
system should not be held as sacred, or unassailable and unalterable.

If that much be conceded to us, we may venture a step further and consider if it be at all
possible to make a change for the better, a wise and beneficial change. It must be clear to
everyone that we cannot continue in the old way, shutting our eyes to what is going on around
us. Do not all the facts, all the testimony from every quarter, establish that the old way leads
downwards to a lower and lower plane of political demoralization ?

It is historically true, that the spirit and force of party organizations have, in past generations, been an essential, possibly in some cases, the chief factor in Government. At this day,
the system is upheld by men of eminence whose opinions deserve to carry weight. There is
indeed a traditional idea of wide prevalence, that the party system alone will suit a free people ;
and that the principles upon which it is based are essential to purity of government. Do the
facts, may we ask, establish that the party system has resulted at any period of our history in
purity of public life, or has it effected the opposite result ? Has it been proven, that the contentions and discords and conflicts of partyism are in any way conducive to our national well-
being? Is it the case that subjection to traditional party spirit is indispensable to our freedom?

Let every thoughtful man, whatever his predilections, consider these questions carefully and dispassionately, and it will become more and more clear to him, that the party

system of government, which we have inherited as the accompaniment of representative institutions, is no longer a necessity ; that its usefulness has come to an end, that it has in its latest development grown to be a positive evil ; and that it should now be replaced by another system better adapted to the improved intelligence and altered circumstances of the age.

Within the present century, scientific methods have made conquests over traditional methods in nearly every sphere of life.   In agriculture, in commerce and in mechanical art the traditional spirit has disappeared, and given place to the scientific spirit.   We find that in spinning, weaving, printing, lighting, heating, telegraphing, travelling by land and sea, and in nearly every human engagement we can name, the scientific method has irrevocably superseded traditional methods.   Is the great question we are now discussing to prove an exception ?   Is the art of government to remain outside the pale of progress ?   Surely parliamentary development has not reached its ultimate stage, and public affairs for ever must be administered according to the principles of the prize ring.   Heaven forbid !   Can we not discern some little glimmerings of light, following perhaps the deepest darkness preceding the dawn ?   Is it not the case that in modern times the power of tradition has been weakened and that its authority is steadily declining ?   May we not, therefore, cherish the hope that it may be dethroned in political life ; that we shall not always remain victims of a superstitious belief in the system of government by party ; and that this fair land shall not forever be the battlefield of gregarious politicians?   What this young nation wants is not endless political conflict with all its accompanying evils, but settled rest and peace.

Our people essentially democratic, and attached to representative institutions, will bear in mind that parliamentary government and party government are not identical, indeed, that they are totally distinct.   True they have been so long associated that they have come to be considered inseparable, but reflection will make it clear to us that the connection, even if it be historical, is accidental, and that it is an erroneous popular notion, that a connection between them is a necessary consequence.

The tendency of events suggests that important changes must eventually be made in the structure of parliament itself.   Such changes are needed in the direction of unity, simplicity and strength.   Our parliament is supposed to represent the nation ; but as at present constituted it practically comprises but the representatives of two parties.   The theory of parliament is an assembly of persons chosen by the whole body of electors with supreme authority to speak and act for the nation.   The ideal parliament is the nation in essence, but the system followed in the election of members utterly fails to attain this desired end.   Under the party system it is absolutely impracticable to attain even an approximation to the ideal parliament.   It is true that parliament, formed by means of the existing system, assumes the functions of a perfectly constituted national assembly ; but its members represent only a part of the nation, and those who support the administration of the day, and keep it in power, form a still smaller representative part.   Take for example the parliament formed after the general election of 1887.   The government had on this occasion the largest support given to any administration since Canada became a Dominion ; and yet, including every vote polled for government candidates who were defeated at the elections, the supporters of the administration represented only 39 per cent. of the whole body of electors.   The opposition members represented 37 per cent. of the whole, counting also the votes polled for the defeated candidates on their side.   Thus it becomes perfectly obvious, that a large majority of the people, whatever party may rule, has no part whatever through representatives, in the administration of public affairs.   In the case referred to 61 per cent. of the whole body of electors had no share in the government of the country.   The administration was supported by the representatives of 39 per cent. and it was opposed by those of 37 per cent. in every measure carried in the house by a party vote ; leaving as a net balance the representatives of only two per cent. of the electors to determine legislation, to settle the policy of the government, and to speak and act for the nation with the whole weight and supreme authority of parliament. I have presented no extreme case.   If we take the results of the recent general elections (1891), it will be found that the number of votes cast for government candidates was only 33 per cent. of the electors, and the government net majority in the house represents but one-and-a-half per cent. of the total number of voters on the list. As a matter of fact, the system of government by party enables a minority, frequently a small minority, to seize and hold control of the affairs of state, and award to its friends office, power and patronage with every one of the prizes of party victory. All outside the lines of the successful party are systematically ignored. Do not the facts prove that party government is opposed to the true theory of parliamentary government ? Is it surprising that in working out the party system the struggle becomes so fierce, and that ways and means are resorted to which shock the sensibility of even party men when they come to be exposed to the light of day ?

What is the remedy for the state of things which now prevails ? It is not far to seek, and it involves no great constitutional change. We have simply to obey the law of perpetual evolution so that our parliament may become freer and better than it ever has been. We have only to free it from the trammels of party and obtain an assembly which will represent the people in fact as well as in name. Hitherto we have had the shadow, now let us have the substance. In all previous parliaments a part only of the electors, and not necessarily the best part, has been represented. Why should any portion be excluded ? Should not the supreme national assembly command the confidence and reverence of the whole people? To obtain their confidence and reverence it is obvious that our parliament should represent the whole, and consist as far as possible of the wisest and best men the entire nation has to offer.

This is the true conception of a parliament for a democratic people such as we are, and we must seek to obtain such a parliament if we wish to escape from the evils which at present beset us. Denouncing the politicians for the inevitable consequences of a bad system, as some of our people do, is an easy matter ; but it is folly to suppose that this alone will bring any permanent remedy. Politicians are human as we are, and they become precisely what the people make them, or allow them to make themselves. If the people so will, and take the proper course to effect their purpose, the school of politicians which flourishes to-day will disappear.

Having the clearest evidence that we have never had and never can have a perfectly constituted parliament under existing political usages ; having the best grounds for the belief that the system which prevails is hastening us to a condition of political subjection, to an oligarchy of the worst kind, such as we find in the United States ; being satisfied on these points, every good citizen must feel the responsibility resting upon him that he should do his utmost to avert such a national calamity.

The first important step is to take means to have a perfectly constituted parliament. In Canada we have accepted the great fundamental principle that "the people is the source of all law and all power," we must therefore strive to constitute our parliament so that it will represent not a part, as now, but the whole nation. This step cannot be taken without effecting other changes which would tend to the common welfare ; the chief of which would be that a new complexion would be given to the government. We would no longer have a party government ; the executive would proceed from the national assembly and thus would be the veritable focal point of the whole nation. The best and wisest members returned by the people could be chosen by parliament from its own members to sit at the same council board to guard public interests, administer the laws, and speak and act for the nation.

In a paper published in Volume VII. of the Royal Society proceedings under the heading "A problem in political science," I have endeavored to show that by the scientific adjustment of votes and the application of sound principles, the true parliament could be constituted.* I can-

---

* The object of my paper "A problem in Political Science," was simply to demonstrate that Parliament could be formed so as to represent truly the whole nation.

I do not wish it to be thought that I have given the only solution to the problem. I merely wish it to be understood, that having established the possibility of constituting the national assembly with scientific accuracy, I felt warranted in urging that an effort should be made to abolish government by party and substitute government by the whole people.

I do not doubt that features open to objection in the solution presented in my Royal Society paper can be eliminated or that better means may be devised, of attaining the desired object. If a "will" become apparent in the public mind, a "way" will not be wanting.   S. F.

not here enter into any extended explanation of the proposition. I must content myself with the statement, that in my judgment it is perfectly practicable by the proposed plan, even if no better can be devised, to extend to every elector full and equal representation, thus removing the anomalies I have pointed out.

The details of the machinery cannot here be discussed. Indeed, it would be premature to deal with details in advance of principles; but the machinery may be of the simplest character, and being entirely national the cost would be made a direct charge on the state, as the cost of taking the census or of any other public service is borne by the public exchequer. The practical working of the system would be conducted by public officials, specially appointed and held responsible for the proper performance of their duties in the manner of other public officials. The cost of the proposed system of choosing representatives might be considerable: but it would fall far short of the cost of the present system, when the expenditure under two party organizations and every accessory charge are taken into account. Moreover, the whole would be open and above suspicion, and there would be no room for improper practices. Whatever the cost, it would render party organization nugatory, and the gain to the public would be incalculable. Legislation would certainly be greatly simplified. The sessions of parliament would no longer be prolonged through the interminable and profitless discussions which proceed from party strife. There would be great economy of time and money; but however great this economy, it would be of small moment compared with the more important benefits which would result generally from the overthrow of a pernicious system, entirely out of joint with the march of events.

Partyism has an historical origin. It was born in troublesome times, when the spirit of antagonism between the classes was general, and when the masses of people were in a ruder condition than they now are. As the ages succeed each other, the spirit of humanity changes with the advance of civilization. We have long passed out of the age of fierce and cruel persecutions. We have left behind us the spirit of conflict and destruction, and have entered the marvellous period of construction and production. Our lives are now more happily passed in the peaceful era of human justice and human reason. If we have left behind the belligerent ages, would it be in advance of our time to abandon political methods in civil life, which keep alive the spirit of conflict and maintain usages which are opposed to true progress? In intelligent communities at the present day partyism can be viewed only as an anachronism.

Consider for a moment the consequence if partyism were introduced into modern commercial life. Take a bank, an insurance company or any large business concern. Introduce the principle of partyism into the management, what would follow? We should in each case have a house divided against itself, and how long would it stand?

Suppose the directors of a railway company were divided, as parties are ranged in parliament. The persistent endeavour of one portion of the board would be directed to keeping the trains in motion; while the other portion as persistently would do their utmost to throw obstacles in the way. Would the public reap any advantage from the antagonism? Would the shareholders receive dividends?

Take this university. How long would it prosper, how long would it maintain its ground and be useful to the community, if partyism gained a footing so as to cause continual contentions and strife among the trustees, or the senate, or the council?

Consider the consequences if partyism were allowed to enter into the proceedings of the great annual assemblies of the several religious denominations. Would it be justifiable on any ground? Would any one of these important bodies perform its functions so speedily and so well? Each one of these great gatherings partakes of the character of parliament, and might with advantage in some respects be imitated. An enormous amount of business is brought before them, and ordinarily they do more in one week than they could in ten weeks if party tactics, such as are displayed at Ottawa, prevailed.

Take a much humbler well-known illustration. Take an ordinary row boat, allow the crew to fight among themselves, or suppose the rowers determine to pull in opposite directions. It is needless to say there would be much agitation of the water, but little or no satisfactory progress.

These several illustrations will bring out the well established fact, that to the extent that conflict is provoked, satisfactory results are lessened ; and that under all ordinary circumstances, conflict is a wasteful expenditure of force. This rule must apply to political and national affairs as to everything else ; and viewing the question before us from all points, we are led to the conclusion that there is no logical justification for partyism in this age. In order to supersede partyism, it is not at all necessary to broach any new doctrine, revolutionary in its character. In reality the opposite is the case. The desire is to maintain the institution of parliament and make it more efficient, more perfect and more stable. The design is to realize the ideal national assembly in which every elector may have an equal voice. The aim is to maintain all that is good in the parliamentary system of government, and take away all that is defective and bad ; to remove the worn out vestures of the past which are ill adapted to the growth of the nineteenth century. The great primary object is to establish unity and promote amity, and thus remove far from us the desolation which proceeds from, a "kingdom divided against itself."

In my humble judgment the question of parliamentary representation is capable of scientific treatment, and it is safe to say that if so treated, partyism, as it now exists, with its baneful[1] influences and demoralizing effects, would irrevocably be swept away. There are few questions which more deeply affect society and civilization. In the heat of party warfare it cannot be discussed fruitfully, and it is only in the intervals between conflicts, or under conditions removed from the struggle that calm reflection will avail. This question is the great problem of to-day ; it has the strongest possible claim on the attention of every well-wisher of his country who has the qualifications to consider it carefully and dispassionately. I fear it has small chance of being so considered by those who place party triumph higher than country, or who regard fealty to party more binding than the laws of the decalogue. Such men are wanting in intellectual freedom to approach this subject appreciatively. Even those whose relations with political organizations are not close, so far as they are partisans are they wanting in the qualifications necessary to take a disinterested view of it ? There are many men with whom party advancement and success have been the ruling motives; such men will naturally have a settled unwillingness to part company with old associations, and the party spirit inherent to them. They will cling with tenacity to their deeply rooted habit of thought. They will extol the advantages of party government. They will reiterate that government by party is the only possible means of carrying on representative institutions. They will declare that the abolition of party would mean an end of all order and progress, and would prove the beginning of general desolation. Certain it is that government by party will never be reformed from within, and we may be well assured that every honest attempt to effect a change will be ridiculed as utopian or branded as a mischievous innovation. True partisans are not the men to yield without a struggle. They will never pull down their own ramparts and surrender their own citadel. The stronghold of partyism can only be sapped and mined by the slow process of public education, and eventually demolished through the common sense of the nation.

Whatever the present political condition, we may rest satisfied that the great heart of Canada is sound. We may depend upon it that so soon as the nation comes to understand the true nature of the malady, and that a remedy is possible and applicable, from that moment party government will be doomed.

There is but one cure for the disease under which we suffer. Laws may be passed to prevent scandals begotten of party exigencies ; but ways will be found to elude them, let them be ever so stringent, so long as partyism exists. There is a rankling sore in the body politic. We may heal an ulcer on the surface, but the ulcer is but one of the symptoms, and so long as the deep-seated disease remains it will again break out in another spot or appear in another form. The true physician directs his attention to the source of the ailment, and by proper treatment removes the first cause of the evil and thus purifies the whole system. In this national matter in order to succeed, the same course must be followed ; and whenever the mind of the nation becomes satisfied that it is the only effective means of getting rid of our political evils, then, and not till then, will partyism be dethroned.

How is the mind of the nation to be reached on this cardinal problem ? The national mind is made up of many individual minds, each one of which is a minute fraction of the whole. These fractional parts must in the first place be moulded and instructed by men of rectitude, whose powers have been matured by study and observation, men who are watchful of the highest interests of the people. What class better qualified by the nature of their calling for this noble and patriotic duty, than teachers, both lay and clerical, throughout the land ? Obviously we must look mainly to the school, the college and the pulpit for the agencies to enlighten and elevate the individual mind, and, through the individual, the collective mind of the nation. We must first form private opinion, from which public opinion will slowly and surely form itself.

It may be objected that ministers of the gospel should not meddle with politics. If politics, degenerating into partyism, have become vicious and impure, so much the more is it the imperative duty of clergymen to employ every proper means to promote a sound and healthy moral tone for the benefit of the community. Is not Canada a Christian land ? Does not the census inform us that, with the exception of a few tribes of Pagan Indians and a few hundred Jews, we are from sea to sea all Christians ? On what ground then should a Christian teacher be debarred from assuming all the duties of his office ? Can he indeed throw off the grave responsibility which rests upon him ? Can he neglect the high duty of using every opportunity to restore public life to a healthy and more upright character ? Merely party issues in which no moral element is involved should be absolutely excluded from every pulpit discourse ; but a great question, such as this, in which the public morality, the purity, the honour and the lasting welfare of the whole nation is involved, should be fearlessly dealt with by every clergyman in the land. The influence of the pulpit has been and always will be great, and no better or more effective means can be found of enlightening the masses and elevating public opinion to a higher level. It was written a century ago : " the true cure for darkness is the introduction of light." Who better able to introduce light than those who have obtained its possession—the wise and the learned ? Who more fitted to purge politics of its evils than those whose lives have been dedicated to morality and uprightness ?

In this young country it is only in harmony with nature that everything should be in a condition of healthy growth. I know of no reason why our parliamentary system should not partake of the general improvement and advancement. At Ottawa a corner of the curtain has been raised sufficiently high to admit of our seeing evidences of fundamental defects in governmental methods, and traces of grave obstacles to our progressive well being. I ask should it not be the earnest aim of every Canadian with the true patriotic spirit to seek to eradicate these defects and remove every obstacle which retards our growth and elevation as a people.

If this be a Christian country surely the entire moral code of Christianity should be binding on all, and on none more than our law-makers. It is of unspeakable importance that we should find effective means to purify the fountain of legislation. It is a matter of public economy, public morality and public honour, and our hopes must rest on the three great educational factors which I have named In this question, is involved the first and last needs of the Dominion, and we must appeal to our best teachers of all creeds and in all places to set about the task of lifting politics out of partyism into a loftier and healthier atmosphere. True, there are enormous difficulties to be overcome, but the task is as noble as it is necessary and it is rendered nobler even if more difficult by the fact that we shall look in vain for a precedent, no other nation having led the way in any successful attempt to bring parliament up to its true ideal condition. The scientific movement of the nineteenth century has accomplished marvellous success, it has been crowned with peaceful victories far more wonderful and far more glorious than military conquests. If, in the new field, the calm voices of science and of reason can be heard through the din of party strife, it may be that Canada will do something to accomplish her destiny, by establishing a precedent which all nations possessing free institutions may follow.

We remember the familiar phrase " Canada first." These two short words have a strong sterling ring about them. Let Canada be the first in a movement towards a rectification of the national administration, and a recognition of happier political methods. Let the sons of Canada determine to be first in all that is good, to be in the front rank of the great family of British nations. What loftier ambition can we have than to elevate our country, and present Canada before all the nations of the earth, a bright example of vigorous, upright youth, in every respect worthy of the historic races from which we spring ?

PLAN FOR MINORITY REPRESENTATION.

By Prof. J. R. Commons in " Review of Reviews," Vol. IV., 1891.

One of the features of the Australian ballot reform is the provision whereby parties or groups of men, whose numbers give them little political significance, can yet secure representation upon the common public ballots. This provision, however, is incidental to the character of the Australian ballot, and was not the main argument for the striking popular approval of that measure. It was the promise of freedom from bribery and corruption that led to this approval. The American people are not yet sufficiently alive to the rights of minorities to make thoughtful efforts to bring about minority or proportional representation for its own sake. Yet if some plan at once simple and efficient were devised, it is probable that the advantages of such representation would be clearly brought to view. If you can show *how* to do a good thing, it doesn't take long for the people to see *why* it should be done. The difficulty with all projects of minority representation has been their awkwardness. It requires a professor of mathematics to apply them. They are not suited to the rough needs of our democratic mass-meetings. This is true of the Hare system, the only one that has received anything like wide attention. This system is now employed in the election of alumni trustees for Amherst and Harvard Colleges, where its unwieldiness is not apparent, since these elections are conducted by correspondence. What is wanted is a plan that can be used not only in elections for college trustees, but in turbulent political meetings, in all kinds of conventions, societies, and corporations, so that the plan can become a part of the popular habit, just as the motion for the previous question or the distinction between the executive, legislative, and judicial branches of government is a part of popular habit or way of thinking. In this way such a plan could gradually grow into favor and finally win its way into the highest political organizations, such as Congress and the legislatures.

Among the multitude of new things proposed or adopted at the recent state convention of the People's party of Ohio was a plan for minority representation which seems to meet these requirements. This plan was devised by Dr. L. Tuckerman, an alumnus of Amherst College, and a prominent Nationalist and labor reformer of Cleveland, Ohio. Dr. Tuckerman has been experimenting upon this plan and perfecting it for several years. He had a definite project before him ; how to harmonize and unite the different incongruous labor elements of the city of Cleveland, such as Nationalists, Socialists, Knights of Labor, Trades Unionists, etc. Under the current plan of elections, the result of attempts to unite such elements resulted in something as follows : Suppose that at a union meeting of these organizations it was voted to elect a committee of five to draft a series of resolutions. Each clique would put forward its own ticket. But only one ticket could be elected. This might include representatives of the two strongest elements, but those which were in the minority would be left out. Consequently a bolt and hopeless antagonisms would be the result. This evil of unrestricted majority-rule is apparent especially in political conventions. Suppose we have a convention of one hundred delegates, divided into two factions. It is proposed to elect a committee of five for some purpose. If one faction numbers fifty-five delegates and the other forty-five, the first faction will elect the entire committee and the faction numbering almost half, will have no voice in moulding or tempering the action of the convention. Their only recourse is to bolt, and thus risk the defeat of their party altogether. The evil is recognized by our political conventions, and recourse is taken to the Czar-like policy of putting the nominations of committees in the hands of the chairman. As a result the minority gets representation, but it is in the person of some insignificant figure, who is wholly ignored by the strong characters of the majority. The committees of the American House of Representatives offer an exhibition of this fact.

The Tuckerman plan provides for *weighing the choices* of each elector. If there are five offices to be filled the elector writes on his ballot the names of five candidates in the order of his preference. Then the tellers, in counting the ballots, allot to each name on the ballot a weight of choice corresponding to the position held by that name on the ballot. Thus if the candidates A, B, C, D, E, are written on a single ballot in the order given, candidate A will have five units credited to him, candidate B will have four units, C three units, D two units, and E one unit. After all the ballots are counted the units opposite the names of the candidates are added up, and the five having the highest number of units are declared elected. Thus only one ballot is required to elect five officers. Continuing the example given, suppose the candidates A, B, C, D, E are voted for in the order named by each of the fifty-five delegates. The weight of choice would be as follows :—

Choice.	Units.		Electors.	Total Units.
A.	5	×	55	275
B.	4	×	55	220
C.	3	×	55	165
D.	2	×	55	110
E.	1	×	55	55

But candidates F, G, H, I, K receive the support of the minority of forty-five electors. The proponderance of choice will run :—

Candidates.	Units.		Electors.	Total Units.
F.	5	×	45	225
G.	4	×	45	180
H.	3	×	45	135
I.	2	×	45	90
K.	1	×	45	45

Consequently the successful candidates are A, B, C, F, and G. The majority faction has three representatives, and the minority has two—their first and second choice. According to the current method they would have been unrepresented : but with this plan they can in no possible way be excluded so long as they number one-fifth of the total electors. In such case their first choice would receive one hundred units, bringing him in ahead of the fifth choice of the majority.

In the manifold applications of the plan there would be variations from the examples given, but the principle is eminently simple. Its results are about the same as those of the Hare system, so far as the representation of the minority is concerned—in fact the plan is merely a simplification of that method. It differs from the Hare plan in the device of employing the units to compare the weight of choice, and thereby does away with recounting the ballots and dropping the names of the lower candidates on the scale. Its best results are found in the election of boards and committees consisting of more than one member. But where only one officer is to be chosen, as president or chairman, the gain comes in the prevention of a deadlock, and this is no small gain, because, as every one knows, it is in the attempt to break a deadlock that our legislatures in electing senators have been the scenes of bargaining and bribery.

In municipal, state or national elections for representative assemblies, the operation of the plan would be the same, and can be illustrated by taking the typical example of a state house of representatives. Let the State for the purpose of electing members of the lower house be divided into districts of such a number that each district would elect five representatives, this being the most convenient number. Then each elector would vote for five representatives in the order of his choice, with the result above shown in the election of committees. If there were three parties in the field, it is probable that the third party would elect members from different districts, by means of this cumulative voting, and the state legislature would be in fact an exact mirror of public opinion.

Among the other advantages of the general adoption of this plan might be mentioned the following : —

It would prevent one-man rule such as that exercised by the Speaker of the House of Representatives. Committees could be elected on a general ticket at a single balloting. Minorities would have no excuse for bolting conventions, since they would have their ablest men on the committees. Committees would be truly representative. This would also prevent many of the opportunities for ring rule in politics.

Electors of a minority or third party, besides securing their own first choice, could throw some weight in the scale between the candidates of the other parties.

In the case of private corporations this plan would seem to offer the means of avoiding some of the most flagrant abuses. It furnishes a very simple device for cumulative voting for directors and officers.

Finally, the freedom from machine rule, and the possibility of selecting the ablest men of the community without recourse to bargains, is one of the first necessities for the reform of our politics. Cumulative voting and minority representatives would bring this about. If this kind of voting can be simplified, as it has been done by Dr. Tuckerman, there seem to be conclusive reasons for adopting it. Perhaps in the election of city councils and boards of aldermen is the place to begin.

PARTY SPIRIT AND ITS VICES.

By E. de Laveleye, from " Democratic Government," 1891.

THE SPIRIT OF PARTY AND ITS DEFECTS.

The spirit of party is the necessary motive power of the representative system, and is at the same time its scourge, when institutions in place of combating its excesses aid in its development by the offer of encouragement and reward.

The spirit of party resembles the spirit of sect ; it calls into being a special conscience which believes everything permissible for the good cause. The faults of friends are never avowed ; they are never even perceived. The good faith of its adversaries can never be admitted. On their side are only seen fraud, falsehood, injustice, perfidious plots. The desire is to repress them, or without pity to strike them down ; because while they were leading to the abyss of ruin, on the other side the true interests of the country were being defended. With the republican every monarchist is an obscurantist, an abettor of despotism, one full of ambition greedy for favour, an ignoble soul aspiring for servitude. For the monarchist every republican is an apostle of disorder, a disciple of guillotine—the grandson of Marat. Parties engaged in this contest, under the form adapted to the political manners of our days, are nothing else than those hordes of antiquity who in the heart of the forest disputed for their prey, or the factions which fought with arms in their hands in the Italian republics of the middle age.

The spirit of party is so intolerant, and the *credo* so rigid, that whoever fails to defend it as a whole is a traitor. All independence of thought disappears ; every one becomes the slave of the official programme. The statesman with originality of mind becomes a peril ; he is "a horse which kicks out in the ranks"—he must be reduced to the yoke or expelled.

The government of party appoints to the vacant offices its partizans only, without regard to merit or the claim to consideration. On their side those thus appointed to office only act to increase the influence of their friends and to maintain them in power without thought of the general good.

To win numbers with a democracy, what is needed is a simple and striking watch-word, a general idea, which resumes and makes manifest the whole facts by their most salient side. Those who place themselves without scruple and without reserve in obedience to this watch-word and who know skillfully in the matter to appeal to the passions and prejudices of the crowd, are the destined ringleaders of parties.

Those eminent minds which consider affairs under all their phases, which desire that circumstances should be considered, which, knowing the past foresee the future, are held in distrust.

Parties in the struggle must organise themselves, as hostile armies. Their partizans are brigaded into the association ; committees which direct the campaign are placed at their head ; blind obedience must be given to these chiefs ; the strictest discipline is imposed under penalty of ruin. Two or three large masses advance to the vote in serried columns under the same flag. The most numerous carry the day, and govern in the name of national sovereignty

The sovereign then is not reason, but number.

As the representative system is the condition of a free government, and party spirit is the indispensable motive power, there can be no question as to its suppression ; but it is essential that the attempt should be made to prevent its attendant abuses. Experience indicates the means of attaining this result. They are the following : Representation of minorities ; system of voting by which the secret of the vote and its sincerity is assured ; to take from the government in the most effective manner the disposal of offices to bestow on its political friends.

UNJUST INFLUENCES IN ELECTIONS.

When the interference of government is present by threats or promises, it lowers or corrupts the national character. In England in the eighteenth century, the votes of deputies were purchased by favours, or by even ready money. To-day the proceeding is different ; it is the body of electors which is purchased, by the promise of public works, a post, a wharf, a road, a railway, subsidies for the corporations.

Every candidate for parliament promises that government will dispense millions for their district. When the budget for the public works is presented it is an interminable narrative of such requirements.

The minister replies to all, concedes all or part, promises what is desired, in order to obtain the votes of members and, above all, that of the electors. Everyone desires to dip into the public chest, as if it were replenished by its own force. It is not understood that each province pays its part in the local outlay. The State gives. But who pays ? Always the taxpayers. There is an illusion that it is a gratuitous gift as it comes from the public chest. Often to accord to each province an equal part of the cake, works entirely useless are voted and hastily determined.

THE POLITICIANS OF TO-DAY.

From " The American Commonwealth," by James Bryce, 1891.

The greatest parties are the Republicans and the Democrats. What are their principles, their distinctive tenets, their tendencies ? Which of them is for free trade, for civil service reform, for a spirited foreign policy, for the regulation of telegraphs by legislation, for a national bankrupt law, for changes in the currency, for any other of the twenty issues which one hears discussed in the country as seriously involving its welfare ?

This is what a European is always asking of intelligent Republicans and intelligent Democrats. He is always asking because he never gets an answer. The replies leave him in deeper perplexity. After some months the truth begins to dawn upon him. Neither party has anything definite to say on these issues ; neither party has any principles, any distinctive tenets. Both have traditions. Both claim to have tendencies. Both have certainly war cries, organizations, interests enlisted in their support. But those interests are in the main the interests of getting or keeping the patronage of the government. Tenets and politics, points of political doctrine and points of political practice, have all but vanished. They have not been thrown away but have been stripped away by Time and the progress of events, fulfilling some policies, blotting out others. All has been lost, except office or the hope of it. . . . .

The chief practical issues which once divided them have been settled. Some others have not been settled, but as regards these, one or other party has so departed from its former attitude that we cannot now speak of any conflict of principles.

When life leaves an organic body it becomes useless, fetid, pestiferous : it is fit to be cast out or buried from sight. What life is to an organism, principles are to a party. When they which are its soul have vanished, its body ought to dissolve, and the elements that formed it be regrouped in some new organism :

> " The times have been
> That when the brains were out the man would die."

But a party does not always thus die. It may hold together long after its moral life is extinct. Guelfs and Ghibelines warred in Italy for nearly two centuries after the Emperor had ceased to threaten the Pope, or the Pope to befriend the cities of Lombardy. Parties go on contending because their members have formed habits of joint action, and have contracted hatreds and prejudices, and also because the leaders find their advantage in using these habits and playing on these prejudices. The American parties now continue to exist, because they have existed. The mill has been constructed, and its machinery goes on turning, even when there is no grist to grind. . . . .

In America we discover a palpable inducement to undertake the dull and tiresome work of election politics. It is the inducement of places in the public service. To make them attractive they must be paid. They are paid, nearly all of them, memberships of Congress and other Federal places, State places (including memberships of State legislatures), city and county places. Here then is the inducement, the remuneration for political work performed in the way of organizing and electioneering. Now add that besides the paid administrative and legislative places which a democracy bestows by election, judicial places are also in most of the States elective, and held for terms of years only ; and add further, that the holders of nearly all those administrative places, Federal, State, and municipal, which are not held for a fixed term, are liable to be dismissed, and have been hitherto in practice dismissed, whenever power changes from one party to another, so that those who belong to the party out of office have a direct chance of office when their party comes in. The inducement to undertake political work we have been searching for is at once seen to be adequate, and only too adequate. The men for the work are certain to appear because remuneration is provided. Politics has now become a gainful profession, like advocacy, stockholding, the dry goods trade, or the getting up of companies.

People go into it to live by it, primarily for the sake of the salaries attached to the places they count on getting, secondarily in view of the opportunities it affords of making incidental and sometimes illegitimate gains. Every person in a high administrative post, whether Federal, State, or municipal, and, above all, every member of Congress has opportunities of rendering services to wealthy individuals and companies for which they are willing to pay secretly in money or in money's worth. The better officials and legislators—they are the great majority, except in large cities—resist the temptation. The worst succumb to it, and the prospect of these illicit profits renders a political career distinctly more attractive to an unscrupulous man.

We find therefore that in America all the conditions exist for producing a class of men specially devoted to political work and making a livelihood by it. It is work much of which cannot be done in combination with any other kind of regular work, whether professional or commercial. Even if the man who unites wealth and leisure to high intellectual attainments were a frequent figure in America, he would not take to this work ; he would rather be a philanthropist or cultivate arts and letters. It is work which, steadily pursued by an active man, offers an income. Hence a large number of persons are drawn into it, and make it the business of their life ; and the fact that they are there as professionals has tended to keep amateurs out of it. . . . .

Having thus seen what are the causes which produce professional politicians, we may return to inquire how large this class is, compared with the corresponding class in the free countries of Europe, whom we have called the Inner Circle.

In America the Inner Circle, that is to say, the persons who make political work the chief business of their lives, includes :—

Firstly. All members of both Houses of Congress.

Secondly. All Federal office-holders except the judges, who are irremovable, and who have sometimes taken no prominent part in politics.

Thirdly. A large part of the members of State legislatures. . . . .

Fourthly. Nearly all State office-holders, excluding all judges in a few States, and many of the judges in the rest.

Fifthly. Nearly all holders of paid offices in the greater and in many of the smaller cities, and many holders of paid offices in the counties. . . . .

Sixthly. A large number of people who hold no office but want to get one. This category includes, of course, many of the "workers" of the party which does not command the majority for the time being, in State and municipal affairs, and which has not, through the President, the patronage of Federal posts. It also includes many expectants belonging to the party for the time being dominant, who are earning their future places by serving the party in the meantime.

All the above may fairly be called professional or Inner Circle politicians, but of their number I can form no estimate, save that it must be counted by hundreds of thousands, inasmuch as it practically includes nearly all office-holders and most expectants of public office.

It must be remembered that the "work" of politics means in America the business of winning elections, and that this work is incomparably heavier and more complex than in England, because :—

(1) The voters are a larger proportion of the population ; (2) The government is more complex (Federal, State, and local) and the places filled by election are therefore far more numerous ; (3) Elections come at shorter intervals ; (4) The machinery of nominating candidates is far more complete and intricate ; (5) The methods of fighting elections are far more highly developed, *i.e.*, they are matters requiring more technical knowledge and skill ; (6) Ordinary private citizens do less election work, because they are busier than in England, and the professionals exist to do it for them.

I have observed that there are also plenty of men engaged in some trade or profession who interest themselves in politics and work for their party without any definite hope of office or other pecuniary aim. They correspond to what we have called the Outer Circle politicians of Europe. It is hard to draw a line between the two classes, because they shade off into one another, there being many farmers or lawyers or saloon-keepers, for instance, who, while pursuing their regular calling, bear a hand in politics, and look to be some time or other rewarded for doing so. When this expectation becomes a considerable part of the motive for exertion, such an one may fairly be called a professional, at least for the time being, for although he has other means of livelihood, he is apt to be impregnated with the habits and sentiments of the professional class. . . . .

I shall presently return to the Outer Circle men. Meantime let us examine the professionals somewhat more closely ; and begin with those of the humbler type, whose eye is fixed on a municipal or other local office, and seldom ranges so high as a seat in Congress.

This species, like the weeds which follow human dwellings, thrives best in cities, and even in the most crowded parts of cities. It is known to the Americans as the "ward politician," because the city ward is the chief sphere of its activity, and the ward meeting the first scene of its triumphs. A statesman of this type usually begins as a saloon or bar-keeper, an occupation which enables him to form a large circle of acquaintances, especially among the "loafer" class who have votes but no reason for using them one way more than another, and whose interest in political issues is therefore as limited as their stock of political knowledge. But he may have started as a lawyer of the lowest kind, or lodging-house keeper, or have taken to politics after failure in storekeeping. The education of this class is only that of the elementary schools : if they have come after boyhood from Europe, it is not even that. They have of course no comprehension of political questions or zeal for political principles ; politics mean to them merely a scramble for places. They are usually vulgar, sometimes brutal, more rarely criminal, or at least the associates of criminals. They it is who move about the populous quarters of the great cities, form groups through whom they can reach and control the ignorant voter, pack meetings with their creatures. . . . .

These two classes do the local work and dirty work of politics. They are the rank and file. Above them stand the officers in the political army, the party managers, including the members of Congress and chief men in the State legislatures, and the editors of influential newspapers. Some of them have pushed their way up from the humbler ranks. Others are men of superior ability and education, often college graduates, lawyers who have had practice, less frequently merchants or manufacturers who have slipped into politics from business. There are all sorts among them, creatures clean and unclean, as in the sheet of St. Peter's vision, but that one may say of politicians in all countries. What characterizes them as compared with the corresponding class in Europe is that their whole time is more frequently given to political work, that most of them draw an income from politics and the rest hope to do so, that they come more largely from the poorer and less cultivated than from the higher ranks of society, and that they include but few men who have pursued any of those economical, social, or constitutional studies which form the basis of politics and legislation, although many are proficients in the arts of popular oratory, of electioneering, and of party management. . . . .

In this general description I am simply repeating what non-political Americans themselves say. It is possible that with their half-humorous tendency to exaggerate they dwell too much on the darker side of their public life. My own belief is that things are healthier than the newspapers and common talk lead a traveller to believe, and that the blackness of the worst men in the large cities has been allowed to darken the whole class of politicians as the smoke from a few factories will darken the sky over a whole town. However, the sentiment I have described is no doubt the general sentiment. "Politician" is a term of reproach, not merely among the "superfine philosophers" of New England colleges, but among the better sort of citizens over the whole Union. "How did such a job come to be perpetrated ?" I remember once asking a casual acquaintance who had been pointing out some scandalous waste of public money. "Why, what can you expect from the politicians ?" was the surprised answer.

PROPORTIONAL REPRESENTATION—THE GOVE SYSTEM.

Extracts from Notes on Electing Representatives by John M. Berry, Worcester, Mass., 1892.

. . . In the general chorus of national pride, is there not a constant undertone of dissatisfaction bewailing political decadence ?   Is it not evident to all that we are too much exposed to mercenary influences ? . . . .

It may almost be said that political corruption is getting to be deemed the rule rather than the exception ; we expect even more than we lament it.   The affairs of state are prostituted to serve the ends of those in power.   Office is not the free gift and choice of an intelligent constituency.   It is secured by barter between those who would profit by it.   Candidates climb to leadership by the promise of spoils.   Bribery has become so common in legislative bodies that it no longer surprises any one.   Political rings and lobbyists direct and control the legislature for personal gain and aggrandizement.   Scarcely a matter that comes up is fairly and honestly considered upon its merits without prejudice or influence.   High minded and honorable men in the legislature find themselves sadly at variance with their surroundings, and sometimes feel that the censure of the legislative body is no disgrace, but that its fellowship and good will may be.   But yesterday, as it were, we saw a member of the legislature of one of our oldest and proudest states, a state second to none for legislative virtue and honor, resign his seat, disgusted at the unworthy and trifling manner in which his associates were accustomed to deal with important public matters.   If the ordinary construction of language can be applied to the reported utterances of Senator Ingalls, in a recent speech*, he boldly avows that politics is a battle in which any means are justified which enable the party using them to win.   When such an open confession is made to the world by the president *pro tempore* of the senate without protest from his fellow members of congress, it is unnecessary to seek further for proof of political degeneracy and the need of radical reform.

The place where this reform is most needed is in our system of representation, condemned by such vile products.   Had we sunk so low as a people as we must if the legislative bodies just spoken of fairly represented us, sad, indeed, would be our condition, and hard the task to discover a remedy.   But it is not so.   Our legislators are the real choice of but a few. The fault is in our defective system of election.   It is an essential feature of our government that it professes to be representative.   In that essential point it has failed, and reform is bitterly needed.   The right to vote, indeed, is carefully guarded by the constitution.   But voting does not necessarily secure representation.   It should do so ; that is its proper object ; but the means are so poorly adapted to the end that it almost completely fails.   Of what avail is the dropping of a ballot if it does not count to elect a representative ?

At the last general election (1888) over five million citizens voted for representatives in congress, yet failed to secure representation ; and in some states these formed a majority of those who voted.   In round numbers eleven million votes were cast for representatives in congress in all the states ; three million of these elected the Republican majority and therefore control legislation, while more than five million who voted did not elect a representative.   It is estimated that five million more of voting age and sex omitted to vote at all, largely influenced we may fairly infer by the feeling, warranted by the above facts, that such action would be futile, a result sure to occur if they belonged to a hopeless

* "The purification of politics is an iridescent dream.   Government is force.   Politics is a battle for supremacy.   Parties are the armies.   The decalogue and the golden rule have no place in a political campaign. The object is success.   To defeat the antagonist and expel the party in power is the purpose.   In war it is lawful to deceive the adversary, to hire Hessians, to purchase mercenaries, to mutilate, to kill, to destroy.   The commander who lost a battle through the activity of his moral nature would be the derision and jest of history. This modern cant about the corruption of politics is fatiguing in the extreme.   It proceeds from the tea-custard and syllabub dilettanteism, the frivolous and desultory sentimentalism of epicenes.'

minority in their respective districts.   Over one-seventh of the Northern representatives were elected by an actual minority (although a comparatively large one) of voters in their districts.

Political parties are so equally divided that the sum of the voters on the losing side in the various districts comprises nearly one-half of those who vote, and none of these have a representative, or rather they are misrepresented by one whose views are opposed to theirs. In reply to this consideration it is mistakenly urged, by some who do not justly appreciate true representation, that the defeat of a given party in one district is balanced and compensated by its success in another, so that the parties are fairly represented after all.   Were this so, the individual voter still loses his right to a voice in the selection. . . . .

To the unrepresented members of the defeated one of the two great parties in each district are to be added the members of still smaller parties.   If these vote, they do it with almost the certainty of failing to secure representation, and in the present congress none of these minor parties has even a single representative.   Taking both of these elements together the wholly unrepresented often form a majority of all who vote at any election.   Yet these unrepresented citizens contribute their share toward the expenses of government.   Thus we have taxation without representation, the very thing which was thought by our forefathers just cause for war.   If under a king this was just cause for a bloody revolution, it is not a greater wrong under a free representative government where the people are supposed to be guaranteed equal rights, and is it not time to seek if possible, means for a peaceful revolution in this respect?   The whole population of the colonies was less than two million, yet here at the present time are over five million of unrepresented tax payers who voted, and if we add to their number those who did not vote, it swells our unrepresented population to nearly two-thirds of the inhabitants having the right of suffrage.

It may be said that it is the privilege of the citizen to vote only and that many must necessarily be outvoted, yet that they have no ground for complaint, as the majority must rule.   This is no answer to the complaint of loss of votes cast for a representative.   If the votes were directly upon a proposed law or measure, as in voting upon a proposed amendment to a state constitution, the principle would be as stated ; but in voting for representatives, the people are not voting directly, but are choosing delegates to vote for them upon measures. Consequently if one's vote does not count to elect a representative, he is not merely outvoted ; he loses his vote altogether upon the questions brought before the legislature ; he has no voice directly or indirectly in the making of the laws.   Our legislative system is not a government by majority.   It is government of a majority of pluralities in separate districts.   Consequently we have actually minority rule.   It is customary to call the plans proposed for remedying the evil, plans to secure minority representation.   The term is a misleading one.   The plans do aim to give a voice to those now left in the minority in the various districts, but the final result aimed at is the rule of the majority through the equal representation of all.

. . . It is usual to attribute such results to gerrymandering.   That the evil is occasionally aggravated by this cause is unfortunately true, but the main reason for it lies far deeper.   Let districts be arranged as justly as possible, a minority usually large in each, must necessarily be defeated and left without representation, the sum of these minorities being usually sufficient to elect several representatives.   Moreover, the party in the minority in the state will usually obtain much less than its fair proportion of representatives, while it is always possible that it may obtain far more than the fair proportion.   The evil is inherent in the system itself, which is radically defective.

The result of the last election shows the district system to be unjust and delusive. Unjust, because less than half who voted at the North, secured 202 of the 211 representatives from that portion of the country.*

---

* The Southern States are purposely omitted to avoid any complication on account of the alleged suppression of the negro vote.   If the whole country were included the showing would undoubtedly be far worse.

Delusive, because the popular belief is that a majority of those who vote control through the representatives they elect.

Yet in the election of the present congress in the Northern states, new states included,—

3,172,999 citizens elected 167 representatives, a majority of the 332 in congress from all the states both North and South, while—

3,304,692 who voted in 167 Northern districts, failed to elect any. . . .

One half the Northern Representatives were elected by less than a quarter of the Northern voters, and more than twice as many who voted in the same states did not elect even one.   To secure anything like justice or equality the result should be far different. One quarter of the voters should elect one quarter of the representatives, and twice as many voters should elect twice as many representatives.

It may be that men like Senator Ingalls, disregarding all broad considerations of justice and public welfare, may see in these figures only a satisfactory partisan advantage.   But the majority party itself can by no means afford to look with equanimity upon this unjust method, although for the moment gaining an unfair advantage from it.   Its position is too precarious.   No very great change of vote, whether from change of opinion or from corruption of voters, instead of making a proportionate change in the representation, might completely reverse the relative position of the parties.   Less than three per cent. of the Northern vote could have been so changed as to tip the scale and give an entirely different majority in congress for all the states.   The power of so few voters to change entirely the complexion of congress is too strong a temptation to be left open to unscrupulous politicians, and hangs a Damocles sword over the head of the winner. . . . .

Some object to the representation of all, on the ground that the ignorant so far out-number the wise that they would rule, but this objection cannot be sustained.   The ignorant are found in all parties, and so far from making common cause against the educated, would almost without exception vote for the ablest man of their own party if they knew who he was.   But even if the objection was well founded, the remedy would be an educational qualification, or some change in the law instead of devices to cheat a voter by giving him the appearance of political power without the reality.   In any case intelligence will rule. At present we are ruled by intelligent demagogues, and if the same amount of brain power now applied to personal and party ends was applied to lofty unselfish statesmanship we should be ruled by intelligent patriots.

Aristotle argued that the wisdom of the whole people included and exceeded the wisdom of the few who were wise.   Therefore let us utilize the wisdom of the mass by granting to all their right of representation.   All the great beneficial movements among mankind have been the work of determined minorities.   Therefore let the wiser minority also be represented.

Various attempts have been made to secure a more just system of representation and much thought has been expended upon it.   It is only necessary for us to become once thoroughly alive to its importance and a way can readily be devised to apply an effective remedy.   We have seen how the present system fails.   Let us in conclusion take a glance at some of the propositions made to introduce a better one.

In 1869 the United States Senate appointed a committee on representative reform.

. . . The committee were of opinion that had there been equal representation, our disastrous civil war might have been prevented. . . . .

In 1870 Mr. Marshall proposed a measure to give equal representation and was supported by Mr. S. S. Cox, Mr. Garfield and others, and almost carried the House with him. . . .

There has been in Denmark for thirty-five years representation by the single transferable vote.   An estimate is made of the number required to elect, by dividing the votes cast, by

10

the number of representatives. Any candidate receiving this number is declared elected, and any surplus or ineffective votes are transferred to assist in electing others of the same principles. This system, (Mr. Andræ's, best known as Mr. Hare's) is endorsed by Mr. John Stuart Mill, Sir John Lubbock and others, and seems the most just of any yet put to practical test. Harvard College and some other institutions and corporations have elected officers by this method. By this plan there is the least possible loss and waste of votes, and the greatest possible number of individual voters represented.

Retaining all these excellencies and including some new and desirable features, is a system offered and recommended to the Massachusetts Legislature in 1888.

The New York Evening Post in commenting on it, says :

" It presents a scheme which seems to us the most complete and practical that we have seen. It is worked out in detail with great care and elaboration so as, we should think, to leave no loophole for blunder or fraud. The fundamental principle is that of Mr. Hare's plan, the transference of surplus votes to other candidates, by which every representative has an equal constituency, and every voter has a representative for whom he voted. But while Mr. Hare distributes the surplus votes by a complicated and perplexing method, the plan before us requires each candidate *before the election* to say to whom his unnecessary votes shall be transferred. Each voter, therefore votes for a single name, but with the knowledge that his vote for A, may count for B, C or D, and the transference of the surplus votes is made by a simple rapid process, always to a candidate or candidates in general agreement with the one voted for."

So general is the conviction among the best thinkers that some reform in representation is demanded, that the time is not far distant when it must come. Remedies have been sought in other countries as well as our own, a system of voting by which no votes shall be lost, or at least no considerable number, and every vote shall count for the election of a person who is the choice of the voter.

Appeal has been made to congress, but a system that elects legislators, too often blinds them to its injustice. Only the opposition of men conscious of their unfitness for the places they occupy, and conscious that in a fair and just representation of all voters other and better men would supersede them, has so long delayed reform. When that comes, and every citizen exerts an influence, true statesmen will hold the suffrage of the people and legislation will be for their benefit and the best good of the country, and not to conciliate parties or sections with a view to re-election. Then the purest and best men will stand at the helm, their aspirations satisfied in a true statesmanship, free from debasing intrigues which now excludes many of them from all participation in matters of government. . . .

A majority of representatives in the present congress (52nd 1892) were elected by less than 21 per cent. of the votes, while over twice as many cast at the same election did not elect any.

In the Northern States at that election, using round numbers, 33 hundred thousand Democratic votes elected 121 representatives, while 34 hundred thousand Republican votes cast in the North elected only 83 representatives.

In the Northern states—
2,703,976 votes elected 167 representatives a majority of congress from both North and South, while
3,420,246 in the North voting at the same time could not elect even one.
Other countries suffer from the same evil. In Great Britain there are—
6,067,133 registered voters.
The House of Commons has 670 members. In the present House 449 seats were contested, 221 were uncontested.
3,160,755 votes were cast for the 449 contested seats.

1,302,081 votes are represented, having elected 355 members (19 more than a majority of the whole House) while a larger number—

1,303,812 votes cast at the same elections are unrepresented being wasted on defeated candidates. . . . .

THE GOVE BILL.—LEGISLATIVE REPRESENTATION.

COMMONWEALTH OF MASSACHUSETTS, ⎫
In the Year One Thousand Eight Hundred ⎬
and Ninety-one. ⎭

RESOLVE.

To amend the Constitution relative to the Election of Senators and Representatives.

Resolved, By both houses, that it is expedient to alter the constitution of this Commonwealth by the adoption of the subjoined article of amendment ; and that the said article, being agreed to by a majority of the senators and two-thirds of the members of the house of representatives present and voting thereon, be entered on the journals of both houses, with the yeas and nays taken thereon, and referred to the general court next to be chosen ; and that the said article be published, to the end that if agreed to in the manner provided by the constitution by the general court next to be chosen, it may be submitted to the people for their approval and ratification, in order that it may become a part of the constitution of the Commonwealth.

ARTICLE OF AMENDMENT.

Section 1. In order to provide for a representation of the citizens of this Commonwealth, founded upon the principle of equality ; any resident of this Commonwealth, eligible under the constitution to the office of senator, may be nominated as a candidate for said office by any person.

No such nomination shall be valid unless the following conditions are complied with :—

(1.) The nomination shall be in writing, signed by the person making it, and shall contain the name and place of residence of the candidate.

(2.) An acceptance of the nomination signed by the candidate shall be endorsed thereon.

(3.) It shall be deposited in the office of the secretary of the Commonwealth not more than three months nor less than five weeks before the day of election.

(4.) There shall be deposited with the nomination the sum of fifty dollars, or such other sum not exceeding one hundred dollars, as the legislature may hereafter by law direct.

Sec. 2. Not less than four weeks before the day of election, the secretary of the Commonwealth shall furnish to each candidate and to every voter who shall request it, a printed list containing the names of all the candidates in alphabetical order with the place of residence of each, and the name of the person by whom each was nominated.

Sect. 3. At any time after his nomination and not less than three weeks before the day of election, any of said candidates may furnish to the secretary of the Commonwealth a statement in writing, signed by himself and acknowledged before any magistrate authorized to take acknowledgment of deeds, which statement shall contain the names of one or more others of said candidates with whom he believes himself to be in accord upon the most important public questions, and to one or more of whom he wishes to transfer any ineffective votes cast for himself.

Sect. 4. The secretary shall prepare a new list of candidates similar to that named in section two of this article, but containing also against the name of each candidate the names in alphabetical order of all candidates named in the list, if any, furnished by that candidate, as provided in section three ; and he shall, not less than two weeks before the day of election, furnish to the clerk of every city or town a sufficient number of copies of said new list. Every such clerk shall, immediately upon the receipt thereof, post conspicuously, and open to the inspection of the public, one copy of said list at each and every place in his city or town where votes are to be received at said election, and shall also immediately furnish one copy to every legal voter resident in said city or town who shall demand the same.

Sect. 5. Every legal voter wherever resident, shall be entitled to cast his vote for senator in favour of any person whose name appears in the aforesaid list of candidates ; but no person shall vote for more than one candidate, nor for any person whose name does not appear upon the aforesaid list of candidates.

But whenever a candidate duly nominated [is omitted from the list published by the secretary of the Commonwealth, votes may be cast for him with the same effect as if his name appeared on said list.

If the secretary shall make such omission intentionally or through wilful neglect of duty, he shall, upon conviction thereof, be ever after incapable of holding any office of trust or profit under the Commonwealth.

Sect. 6. The returns of votes having been transmitted to the secretary of the Commonwealth as provided by the constitution, the secretary shall make a list of all candidates voted for, with the vote received by each candidate in each precinct or voting place, and his total vote, and said list shall be transmitted, published and distributed in the same manner provided in section four, concerning the list therein named ; and after the secretary shall have ascertained who are the persons who appear to be elected, he shall make a list of the successful candidates with the computation by which their election has been ascertained, and shall forthwith furnish a copy of the same to each candidate and also to every voter who shall request it.

Sect. 7. Ineffective votes shall be transferred according to the request of the candidate for whom they were originally cast, to a person named in the list furnished by said candidate as provided by section three.

The forty candidates then having the highest number of votes shall be declared elected and the secretary shall issue certificates of election to them.

In case two or more candidates have the same number of votes, the candidates residing at the greatest distance from the state house shall be deemed, for the purpose of election, to have the highest number.

Sect. 8. The following shall be deemed ineffective votes, and shall be transferred in the order named :—

(1.) Any votes cast for a candidate in excess of one-fortieth of the entire vote cast, beginning with the candidate receiving the largest vote, and proceeding to the one next highest and so on.

In the case of two or more receiving the same vote, the transfer shall be from each alternately, in alphabetical order.

(2.) Votes cast by candidates who have since their nomination died or become ineligible in the same order.

(3.) Original votes cast for candidates who fail of election, beginning with the candidate receiving the smallest total vote, and proceeding to the next lowest, and so on ; in case of two or more receiving the same vote the transfer to be made from each alternately in alphabetical order.

No votes shall be transferred from any candidate who has not furnished the statement named in section three.

Sect. 9. Every ineffective vote of a candidate shall be transferred to the candidate named in his said list, living and eligible at the time of counting the vote, for whom the largest number of votes were originally cast and whose vote by transfer or otherwise does not equal one-fortieth of the whole vote cast, until all are transferred as far as possible.

If the same number of votes were originally cast for two or more candidates named in said list, the candidate residing nearest the one from whom the votes are to be transferred shall be preferred.

Sect. 10. The secretary shall at once transmit to the treasurer and receiver-general all sums of money received as provided in section one.

Immediately after declaring the names of the persons elected senators, he shall draw on the treasurer and receiver-general a warrant for the payment of the sum received with one nomination, and issue the same to the person nominating each candidate who shall appear by the returns to have received one thousand or more original votes, and all such warrants shall be paid by the treasurer and receiver-general on presentation. The remainder of the sums paid under section one shall be and remain the property of the Commonwealth.

Sect. 11. In case a vacancy shall occur in the senate after the declaration of election provided in section seven, the votes cast for the member whose seat shall have become vacant together with any ineffective votes assigned to him, shall be re-distributed in the same manner as if he had died or become ineligible before the canvassing of the votes, and the candidate not before elected, who, after returning to him any votes originally cast for him, shall then appear to have largest number of votes shall be declared elected.

Sect. 12. The supreme judicial court, upon the petition of twenty-five legal voters, shall have jurisdiction to enforce by mandamus the correction of any erroneous or improper issue of such certificate of election, when such error can be made to appear from the face of the returns issued by the secretary as provided in section six, upon canvasing said returns in the manner provided in section seven, eight and nine.

But the senate shall continue to be the final judge of the election of its members.

Sect. 13. The legislature may at any time provide by law that representatives be elected in substantially the same manner as is herein provided for senators, and by such law may, if it so decides, divide the Commonwealth into not exceeding six electoral districts, from each of which the candidates voted for in that district must be taken, and by voters within which such candidates must be nominated. The number of voters in each of these districts to be as nearly equal as possible.

PARTIES AND PARTY GOVERNMENT.

By Henry Sidgwick. From " The Elements of Politics," 1891.

The dual system seems to have a dangerous tendency to degrade the profession of politics: partly from the inevitable insincerity of the relation of a party leader to the members of his own party, partly from the insincerity of his relation to the party opposed to him. To keep up the vigour and zeal of his own side, he has to maintain the fiction that under the heterogeneous medley of opinions and sectional interests represented by the "ins" or the "outs" at any particular time there is a fundamental underlying agreement in sound political principles; and he has to attribute to the other side a similar agreement in unsound doctrines. Thus the best political talent and energy of the country acquires a fatal bias in the direction of insincere advocacy; indeed the old objection against forensic advocacy as a means of obtaining right judicial conclusions—that one section of the experts employed are professionally required to make the worse seem the better reason—applies with much more real force here than in the case of the law-courts. For in the case of the forensic advocate this attitude is frankly avowed and recognized by all concerned : every plain man knows that a lawyer in court is exempt from the ordinary rule that binds an honest man only to use arguments which he believes to be sound ; and that it is the duty of every member of a jury to consider only the value of an advocate's arguments, and disregard, as far as possible, the air of conviction with which they are uttered. The political advocate or party leader tends to acquire a similar professional habit of using bad arguments with an air of conviction where he cannot get good ones, or when bad ones are more likely to be popularly effective ; but, unlike the forensic advocate, he is understood, in so doing, to imply his personal belief in the validity of his arguments and the truth of the conclusions to which he desires to lead up. And the case is made worse by the fact that political advocacy is not controlled by expert and responsible judges, whose business it is to sift out and scatter to the winds whatever chaff the pleader may mingle with such grains of sound argument as his brief affords ; the position of the political advocate is like what that of a forensic advocate would be, if it was his business to address a jury not presided over by a judge, and largely composed of persons who only heard the pleadings on the other side in an imperfect and partial way.

What has just been said applies primarily to the leading members of a party who undertake the task of advocacy. But the artificiality of combination which the dual system involves has to some extent a demoralising effect on other members of the legislature ; they acquire a habit either of voting frankly without conviction at the summons of the "whip," or of feigning convictions which they do not really hold in order to justify their votes.

And the same cause impairs the security for good legislation, apparently furnished by the fact that a measure can only be passed if it has the approval of a majority of the legislators ; since it increases the danger that measures may be passed which are only desired and really approved by a minority—it may even be a small minority if sufficiently fanatical or selfish;—such measures being acquiesced in by the rest, under the guidance of their leaders, in order to maintain the party majority.

Of the gravity of these disadvantages it is difficult to form a general estimate, as it depends largely on the condition of political morality, which is influenced by many causes more or less independent of the form of government : but we may reasonably regard the disadvantages as sufficiently grave to justify a serious consideration of the means of removing or mitigating them. The available remedies are partly political, partly moral : the former will naturally vary much according to the precise form of government adopted. If the Supreme Executive is practically dismissible at any time by a Parliamentary majority—even with the possibility of appealing to the country—the danger of transient and shifting Parliamentary majorities is so great and obvious, that a nation in which the two-party system is firmly established is hardly likely to abandon it. But the case is different with other forms of Representative Government. For instance, where there is a supreme executive appointed for a fixed period, without the power of dissolving Parliament, there is less manifest need of this system than where the executive holds office on the English tenure, and less tendency, *ceteris paribus*, to promote its development : since, in the former case, the party struggle in parliament is not kept always active—as it is in the latter case—by the consciousness that the Cabinet or the Parliament may come to an end at any moment. It is true that the example of the United States might be quoted on the other side, since there the fixed tenure of the Presidency has not interfered with the fullest development of dual party government that the modern world has seen. Here, however, I conceive that the election of the President by the people at large, and the "spoils" system, have operated powerfully to foster this development : if there were a Supreme Executive elected by the legislature, with subordinate officials holding office independently of party ties, I think it probable that the tendency to a dual division of parties—and generally the influence of party on government—would be materially reduced.

Assuming that a Parliamentary Executive is retained, the bad effects of two-party government might still be mitigated in various ways. Substantial portions of legislative and administrative work might be withdrawn from the control of the party system, under the influence of public opinion, aided by minor changes in parliamentary rules and in the customary tenure of executive offices. ·Firstly, as I have before suggested, on certain important questions, not closely connected with the business of the executive departments, the preparation of legislation might be entrusted to parliamentary committees other than the executive cabinet : and the natural tendency to different lines of divisions on different subjects might thus be allowed fair play.

Secondly, certain headships of departments, in which a peculiar need of knowledge, trained skill, and special experience was generally recognized, might be filled by persons not expected normally to retire with their colleagues, when the parliamentary majority supporting the government of which they were members was turned into a minority ; but only expected to retire when the questions on which issue was joined between the parties related to the administration of their special departments.

Again, it would seem possible, by certain changes in the customary relation between the Cabinet and Parliament, to reduce the danger of excessive instability of government consequent on allowing free play to the natural tendency to a multiplicity of parties. Thus, it might be the established custom for ministers not to resign office because the legislative measures proposed by them were defeated,—unless the need of these measures was regarded by them as so urgent that they could not conscientiously carry on the administration of public affairs without them—but only to resign when a formal vote of want of confidence was carried against them in the House of Representatives. This change would at once promote, and be facilitated by, an increased separation of the work of legislation from that of administration.

Again, the introduction of the "Referendum"—even to the limited extent suggested in chapter xxvii.—would at any rate reduce the danger that a minority, concentrating its energies on narrow political aims, may force through legislation not really approved by a majority of the assembly that adopts it.

Finally, the operation of the party-system might be checked and controlled—more effectually than it now is in England and the United States by a change in current morality, which does not seem to be beyond the limits of possibility. It might be regarded as the duty of educated persons generally to aim at a judicial frame of mind on questions of current politics, whether they are inside parties or outside. If it is the business of the professional politician to prove his own side always in the right, it should be the point of honour of the "arm-chair" politician, if he belongs to a party, to make plain when and why he thinks his party in the wrong. And probably the country would gain from an increase in the number of persons taking a serious interest in politics who keep out of party ties altogether.

BURKE'S DEFENCE OF PARTY.

By Dr. Goldwin Smith. From "The North American Review," Vol. CLIV., 1892.

The great sponsor for the morality and the necessity of party is Burke, whose words in "Thoughts on the Present Discontents" have been cited a thousand times. Burke is a magnificent writer, but unless read with reference to time and circumstance he is very apt to mislead. He is the Prince of Pamphleteers, but he is a pamphleteer, and, like all pamphleteers, to some extent makes his philosophy for the occasion. "Thoughts on the Present Discontents" is the manifesto of the Rockingham connection of Whigs against the cabal of "King's Friends," who were striving to put an end to constitutional government, and instal the personal government of George III. in its place by backstairs intrigue, jobbery and corruption. To vindicate any connection of constitutional statesmen against backstairs intrigue, jobbery, corruption, and the personal government of George III. was not difficult. But as a general vindication of the party system, if it was so intended, this renowned passage will not bear examination. "Party," says Burke, "is a body of men united for promoting by their joint endeavors the national interest upon some particular principle in which they are all agreed." The particular principle apparently can be nothing but their joint opinion on the great question or questions of the day. But the great question or questions of the day will in time be settled. When they shall have been settled, what will there be to render the bond of party moral or rational ; what will there be left to hold the connection together but the common desire of political power and pelf? The party will then become a machine, and its cohesion will be maintained either by mere personal association or by motives and influences more or less corrupt. By the philosophy which is always forthcoming in defence of existing arrangements, particularly those arrangements in which many persons have an active interest, it has been alleged that men are naturally and almost providentially divided from their birth into conservatives and liberals. But this bi-section of humanity is a politician's dream. Temperaments vary through an infinite series of gradations, and the same man is conservative on one subject and liberal on another. Youth as a rule, perhaps, is prone to innovation, while age is reactionary. Yet nobody is so violently reactionary as a young aristocrat. Is the community then to be artificially divided into two sections, at perpetual war with each other, for the purpose of carrying on the system? How is the apportionment to be made, and why, if the existence of the two parties is necessary, should each of them be always traducing and striving to annihilate the other? Burke's glowing language about a generous contention for power on manly and honorable maxims, and without proscription of opponents, sounds like a satire on party politics as they are. The reality is that which he would exclude by contrast,— "delusion of the ignorant by professions incompatible with human practice and followed by practices below the level of vulgar rectitude." If he could only have seen the machine and the bosses ! If he could only have looked into the office of Mr. Schnadhorst ! If he could only have been present at a nominating convention for the Presidency or witnessed a general election in the England of these days ! A convention of Whig magnates gathered round the dinner table of the Marquis of Rockingham to settle the policy of the connection, and distribute the pocket-boroughs at its command, was the only sort of convention that he had ever seen. Party, unless there is some great question, such as parliamentary reform or slavery, to justify its existence, can be nothing but a fine name for faction, of which the ties are passion and corruption, and which always must be in the end, as it always has been, the ruin of the commonwealth.

Yet how under the representative and elective system are we to dispense with the party machine? There is the problem. How are the individual votes to be combined and directed so as to elect the representatives and form the basis for the government?

PARTY GOVERNMENT.

By Charles Richardson. From Annals of the American Academy of Political and Social Science, January, 1892.

Among the most important functions of these organizations are the selection of candidates and the adoption of a platform or declaration of principles. These responsible duties are intrusted to conventions, composed of delegates chosen for the purpose at the party elections, known as the primaries.

Those who have so far conformed to the rules of a party as to be entitled to vote at its primaries may be divided into two classes, as follows : 1. Citizens who have no special advantages to gain, and whose only motive for participation is their desire for good government.

2. Those who are actuated by personal ambition or hopes of securing office, contracts or pecuniary benefits.

In order to carry the primaries a considerable amount of time and labor must necessarily be expended. The voters must communicate with each other : views must be compared and harmonized ; candidates suggested, interviewed and agreed upon ; tickets prepared and supplied, and concert of action secured.

This labor is undertaken with eagerness and enthusiasm by the men who are working for the offices or other personal benefits, and are actuated by purely selfish motives. But the majority of citizens, engrossed as they are with private business and family cares, have neither time nor inclination for such tasks. And when their reluctance is overcome, as it occasionally is by their sense of public duty, they are likely to find that their opponents have no hesitation in resorting to misrepresentation, trickery or fraud, in order to control the result. Under these circumstances a small, but well-disciplined, energetic and unscrupulous minority can generally defeat the honorable and patriotic majority. It is therefore not surprising that honest and industrious citizens are apt to conclude that it is useless for them to take part in such contests.

The growth of this feeling is particularly noticeable in our large cities. Efforts to arrest it are only successful in rare instances, and it seems inevitable that the primaries must continue to be gradually abandoned more and more to the control of the class generally designated as politicians.

These gentlemen may have great abilities and many good qualities, but for the reasons just stated, their positions cannot, except in rare cases, be either won or retained unless their dominant motives are personal and partisan advantage ; moral principles and the interests of the public being secondary considerations. Public offices, contracts and patronage are what they work for and what they must have, by fair means if possible, but if not, then by whatever means may be necessary. For this purpose they are obliged to combine among themselves and submit to such leaders as may seem best able to direct their efforts, and to secure and apportion among them the prizes they covet. Having once acquired complete control of a nominating convention, their natural desire, is of course, to nominate such candidates as will best serve their own personal interests, and in the absence of factional fights among themselves, the only real check upon this desire is their fear of losing enough of the more independent voters to turn the scale in the general elections.

This conflict between what they would like to do and what they dare to do, usually results in their nominating such men as have no more honesty and independence than may seem to be absolutely necessary for ultimate success. And if they can secure candidates who are generally believed to be able and honorable, but who will really obey and assist the spoilsmen, the temptation to nominate them, and thus deceive and outwit the people, can hardly be resisted.

In the construction of a party platform the leaders are naturally governed by similar motives, and, instead of publishing a frank statement of their real objects and intentions, they are disposed to adopt whatever may seem most likely to attract the voters. In their effort to do this they seek to treat almost every subject of public interest, but there are necessarily some points in regard to which even the members of their own party are divided, and it is one of the defects of party government that while many voters find sentiments which they disapprove in each platform, they can see no alternative but to cast their ballots for one or the other, and thus seem to endorse and support ideas to which they are really opposed.

It would appear, therefore, that our system of political parties must necessarily tend to place the selection of our candidates and the declaration of our principles in the hands of a small minority of able but comparatively selfish and unscrupulous men. If this tendency was confined to either party, it might be possible to hold it in check by voting for the nominees of the other; but the present system practically confines the choice of the people to the candidates of the two principal parties, all of them having been selected and nominated by similar methods, and therefore characterized by a similar lack of unselfish patriotism and moral principle. However dissatisfied the voters may be with the candidates of their own party, they are naturally disposed to believe that the candidates of the other party, having been chosen in the same way, are at least as bad. They have therefore no means of expressing their preference for better men, and their votes must be determined by the attractions of a more or less 'unsatisfactory and untrustworthy political platform, rather than by any considerations of personal honor or fitness.

Under such a system, if a candidate belongs to a party which happens to be on the most popular side of some leading question, like the tariff or silver coinage, his lack of integrity or personal ability must be very glaring to prevent his election. And when he takes his seat in a legislative body, and it becomes his duty to make a careful study of some important question, to sift the evidence and reach a wise and just conclusion, he, who should be like an impartial judge or an unprejudiced juryman, may find that he is only the bond servant of the leaders of his party, a mere automaton for the registering of their decrees. It is in this way that our legislative assemblies are slowly losing their character as deliberative bodies, and yielding more and more to the dictation of irresponsible partisan chiefs, or the decrees of a secret caucus.

While it is true that there are many 'exceptional instances, and occasional popular uprisings, it is difficult to avoid the conclusion that our general submission to the rule of political parties tends to lower our moral standards, corrupt our people, and subject our National, State, and Municipal governments to a class of men who care far more for personal and partisan success than for either the honor or material interests of those they profess to serve.

PROPORTIONAL REPRESENTATION.

By Professor J. R. Commons. From Annals of the American Academy of Political and Social Science, March 1892.

An earnest effort to abolish the "gerrymander" will probably lead to the conclusion that the district system must be abandoned. To do this in Congressional elections, it will not be necessary to return to the system of a general state ticket elected by the majority party of each state, which was the custom in the first quarter of the century, and which is still employed in the case of the presidential electors. A modification of that discarded system could be adopted by introducing some simple device of proportional representation.

Proportional representation is not a new thing in politics, although it has heretofore received but limited application. Twenty years ago there was abundant discussion of plans for minority and proportional representation, and out of the discussion in our own country a crude plan of cumulative voting was adopted by some of the municipalities of Pennsylvania, and for the election of members of the lower house of the Illinois legislature. This plan is still in force. It has been recently applied to all private corporations by the new constitutions of Kentucky, North and South Dakota and Montana. The Illinois system for the election of state representatives was submitted to the people by the Constitutional Convention of South Dakota, but was defeated at the polls. In Denmark, another plan of minority representation has been in force since 1856. But the most important application of proportional representation has been made by the Canton of Neuchatel, in Switzerland, and more recently by the Canton of Ticino. Something like the Swiss plan could be profitably adopted in the election of all our representative assemblies and boards.

For Congressional elections, let each state elect its entire quota of representatives on a general ticket. Let each party in the state convention nominate the entire list, or as many candidates as it could probably elect, adding a few names for favorable contingencies. Then, in canvassing the returns, let the representatives be assigned to each party in proportion to the popular vote of the party, giving preference to the candidates according to their standing on the vote.

For example, Ohio, in the elections of 1890, cast 713,152 votes for Congressmen. The number of Congressmen to be elected was twenty-one. This gives a quota of 33,959 votes to each Congressman. The Republicans cast 362,624 votes, which gives them ten representatives and a remainder of 23,034 votes. The Democrats cast 350,528 votes, giving them ten representatives and a remainder of 10,928 votes. The Prohibition vote was 21,891, and the Union Labor vote 3,223. There being twenty-one representatives to elect, and the Republicans having a remainder above their ten quotas larger than the Democratic remainder, and larger than the total Prohibition or Union Labor vote, they get the additional representative. Thus, the Ohio delegation would stand eleven Republicans and ten Democrats. At present, under the gerrymander of 1890, it is seven Republicans and fourteen Democrats.

In the election of state legislatures, the state could be divided into districts, each electing five, seven, or some odd number of representatives, and the electors of each district would vote for the entire list of names on their party ticket, the quotas and proportions being obtained as above. For example, the county of Cuyahoga (including the city of Cleveland) sends repeatedly a solid delegation of six Republicans to the Ohio State Legislature, elected on a general county ticket, and not one Democrat. By the proportional system, there would be three Democrats and three Republicans. The county of Hamilton (including the city of Cincinnati) sends to the Sixty-ninth General Assembly a solid delegation of nine Democrats. The Republicans of that county are unrepresented. With proportional voting, the delegation would stand five Democrats, four Republicans. Other counties in the state send one representative each. They could be grouped into districts of five, and could then vote on the proportional plan.

In cities, election districts for councils and boards of aldermen could be constructed on a similar basis. Where there are two branches of the city legislature, the smaller branch could be chosen on a general ticket for the city at large by the proportional system, and the more numerous branch by districts of five.

In all elections upon this plan, the different party tickets could be printed on a single ballot, according to the form of the Australian ballot. The order of names on each ticket would be determined by the state convention of each party, and this would indicate the order of preference of the party. Voters would not vote for individuals, but for the ticket. If individual voters took the liberty of changing the order of names, they would lose their vote altogether. This provision is necessary in order to simplify the counting of the ballots. But "bolters" could nominate a new ticket, and at the same time assist in electing the party ticket, simply by placing their first choice at the head of their ticket and following it by names taken from the regular ticket. If they were sufficiently numerous to comply with the law, the privilege could be obtained of having this new ticket printed separately on the Australian ballot. If, now, the voters of this ticket could command a quota of the entire vote, they would elect their first choice, and any remainder above the quota would go to the next name, thus helping to elect one of the regular party nominees. The new system would thus involve no waste of votes.

The plan here outlined is a modification of one devised by Dr. L. B. Tuckerman, of Cleveland, Ohio, who has developed it with special reference to the election of committees by conventions or mass-meetings. In such assemblies the one-man power of the chairman is done away with, and each party can be fairly represented on committees by its own first choice.

To set forth all the advantages of proportional representation would require an extended study of politics and parties, and a careful weighing of remote causes. For the present, it is possible to point out only a few of the patent benefits it would confer. In the first place, the gerrymander would be absolutely abolished. No other feasible plan can be thought of that will do this. The gerrymander inheres in the district system. So long as it is possible to redistrict a state, it is hopeless to expect that a party in power will refrain from doing so to its own advantage. The changes in population necessitate redistricting at least once in ten years. If legislatures be prohibited from passing such an act within a period less than ten years, the party which happens to be in control of the legislature at the legal time will fasten its own gerrymander on the people for a decade, with no possible chance for redress. It is better to let the two parties play against each other.

Public opinion cannot stop the gerrymander, because public opinion rejoices in this kind of tit-for-tat. The fact that one party has infamously cut up the state is good reason for the other party to retrieve itself when it gets the power. If Congress should take the matter out of the hands of the State Legislature, it would be simply to do its own gerrymandering, while state and municipal gerrymandering would still go on as before. Constitutional restrictions, requiring equal population and contiguous territory, are easily evaded. Notwithstanding such restrictions, the populations of Congressional districts in New York vary from 107,844 to 312,404. In no state is the Constitution on this point observed. And as for contiguity, a glance at the diagram of the English district of North Carolina or the First and Third districts of South Carolina will show on what a slender thread this fiction may be made to hang.

It seems plain that with proportional representation abler men would be attracted into legislative careers. The area of choice would be enlarged, and the leaders of a party could not be driven from legislative halls where their ability is needed, as was done at the last Congressional election. The feeling of responsibility to the whole people would be increased in the leaders of parties, because they could stand on their record before the state at large, and not be compelled to dicker with petty local magnates. A man is at present elected to Congress, not on account of public service, but according to his ability in turning spoils and appropriations into his district. He does not represent before the country any great policy on which to stand or fall. He must depend on local wire-pulling and the exchange of favors. If he has done some distinguished service for his party, or has reached eminence in politics, the whole strength of the National party of the opposition is thrown into his district, and if possible, he is gerrymandered out of office.

Right here, however, will arise the principal popular objection to this plan, namely, that districts would not be represented. But a slight thought will show that this objection has no force. The gerrymander has taken nearly all the virtue out of a district that it may ever have possessed. There are few Congressional districts that have a unity of any kind, either economical, political, topographical, geographical or historical. The county of Huron, in Ohio, has been in five different combinations during the past twelve years, and now it is in the western part of a district one hundred and twenty miles long and twenty wide ; its Congressional representative lives sixty miles away, and had, previous to the last gerrymander, very little knowledge of or interest in the county. In this, and hundreds of other cases, the candidates in some districts at the other end of the state are better known to the voters of the district than are the candidates in their own district. On the other hand, the state is a historical and political unit. Its great men belong to no one district. At present only two of them can go to the United States Senate, and others are shelved as governors, or are compelled to seek some Presidential appointment. Under proportional representation those who are unavailable for Senators would lead their party delegations in the House.

Arguments for proportional representation have usually been advanced in behalf of minorities. But they are equally valid as a defence of the majority. Under the system of districts and primaries less than ten per cent. of the voters of a party often dictate the policy of the party. Machines and ward bosses are the party rulers, and the majority does not dare to "bolt" at the polls, because the opposite party would then come into power. Proportional representation would permit independent movements within the party without risking the defeat of the entire ticket, simply by allowing the nomination of a new ticket composed partly of independents and partly of the regular ticket. If the independent candidates are elected and there is a surplus of voters above the quota, the surplus goes to the regular ticket. The majority of the party would be benefited as often as the minority. The present system on the face of it means the rule of the minority. The gerrymander overthrows majority rule.

The fact that voters could not vote for individuals, but must cast their ballots for the straight ticket, may seem at first sight a serious objection. But the objection is not valid as against the present system, because even now the voter has no choice except between party tickets, while under the proposed plan independent movements are made possible without risking the complete defeat of the party.

Other objections might be noted. A small third party would be likely often to hold the balance of power. The probability is, however, that there would be no occasion for third parties, because reforms inside the old parties would promptly gain a hearing, and compromises would head off radical "bolts."

The strongest objections are those which come from inertia and the dread of change. Constitutional amendments will be necessary in some cases, though Congress has complete power in the matter of National representatives. Nevertheless, representative government is not something absolute and fixed in the nature of things. It is the result of circumstances and experiments without any great amount of political analysis or design. It grew out of the primitive mass-meeting, or folk-moot, simply because distant electors could not conveniently come up to the annual meetings. In the folk-moot the minority was, of course, fully represented. How they should be represented in the delegate assembly was at first a problem, but its solution was abandoned. The history of Colonel Maryland shows, in an interesting way, how this came about. The original deliberative and legislative body was a primary assembly, where any freeman might speak and vote. In the second assembly—1638 —voting by proxy was allowed to those freemen who could not be present in person. Abuses of this device led to the issuing of writs to the local divisions, instructing them to return representatives. But realizing that those who did not vote for the successful candidates would be unrepresented, individuals who were in the minority were allowed to appear in their own right. The third assembly was therefore an anomalous body, comprising the governor and his nominees, the duly elected representatives of localities, those individuals who had not consented to the election of representatives, and the proxies of other unrepresented individuals. Such a heterogenous mass was neither representative nor primary, and was so threatening to the representative element that the hope of minority representation was given up in despair and the assembly defined its own constitution by limiting popular representation to the elected deputies, and ruling out proxies. Doubtless other colonies went through similar experiences.

The system finally adopted is rigid in the extreme. It has endured because there has been no special strain. But the growing intensity of class divisions and the immensity of the interests involved call for a more elastic system. Proportional representation seems to meet this requirement in every essential particular.

THE CONSTITUTION AND ELECTORAL LAW OF THE KINGDOM OF DENMARK.

Abstract and Analysis made and translated by R. J. Wicksteed, LL.D., B.C.L., &c. Barrister.

THE CONSTITUTION.

(Adopted 1849, revised and promulgated 28th July, 1866.)

Section 1. The form of government is a limited monarchy.

2. The legislative power is exercised concurrently by the King and the Rigsdag. The executive power belongs to the King. Judicial power is exercised by the tribunals.

13. The King appoints and dismisses his ministers.

15. The Assembly of the ministers forms the Council of State. The King presides.

19. The King each year convokes the Rigsdag, for its ordinary session.

20. He may summon the Rigsdag for an extraordinary session.

22. The King may dissolve one or both of the chambers of the Rigsdag.

24. The consent of the King is necessary to give the force of law to a resolution of the Rigsdag. The King orders its promulgation, and superintends its execution.

29. The Rigsdag is composed of two Chambers, the Folkething and the Landsthing.

30. Every person is an elector to the Folkething who possesses an unblemished reputation, who is a citizen, and of the full age of 30 years, provided always he is not in the service of a private person and has no household of his own ; that he has not received or is not in receipt of public assistance, which he has not been forgiven or which he has not paid back ; that he can dispose of his own property ; that he has had a domicile for one year previous to the election, in the electoral district or town wherein he resides.

31. Any person is eligible to be returned as a member of the Folkething, with the exceptions one, two and three mentioned in the last preceding section, who possesses a blameless character, is a citizen, and is of the full age of 25 years.

32. The number of the members of the Folkething bears the proportion to that of the inhabitants of 1 to 16000. The elections are carried out in electoral districts. Each district elects a representative.

33. The members of the Folkething are elected for 3 years. They receive a daily indemnity.

34. The number of the members of the Landsthing is 66,—of whom 12 are appointed by the King,—7 by Copenhagen,—and 45 by the electoral districts, 1 by Bornholm and 1 by Faroe.

35. No person can take part directly or indirectly in the elections of the Landsthing, unless he has fulfilled the conditions required of the electors of the Folkething.

36. In Copenhagen the united electors appoint electors of the second degree, in the proportion of 1 to 120. An equal number of electors of the second degree are appointed by the electors who the preceding year were in receipt of a taxable income of, at least, 2000 rixdollars. These two classes of electors of the second degree proceed together with the election of the Landsthing for Copenhagen.

37. In the country parts the united electors appoint one elector of the second degree in each rural commune.

Provisions as to certain towns.

38. All are eligible for election to the Landsthing who are eligible to the Folkething.

39. The royal members are appointed for life; but must be chosen from among those who have been or who are elected members of the representative Chambers of the Kingdom. The other members of the Landsthing are elected for 8 years,—the moiety of the members is renewed every four years. The members of the Landsthing receive the same indemnity as those of the Folkething.

40. The elections for the Landsthing are conducted according to the proportional system. The electoral law fixes the other provisions respecting the elections.

THE ELECTORAL LAW.

The law of elections put in force on July 12th, 1867, in the reign of Christian the Ninth, at Copenhagen.

1. FOLKETHING.

ELECTORAL RIGHTS AND PRIVILEGES.

Section 1. All persons of unblemished reputation, possessing the right of citizenship, and of the full age of 30 years, are electors to the Folkething.

2. No one is considered as enjoying a spotless reputation who has been found guilty, by a court, of an act dishonorable to the man, in the eyes of the public.

3. No one in the service of a private person can enjoy electoral rights, unless he has a household of his own.

4. No one who has received assistance from the Government, which has not been repaid or forgiven, can exercise electoral rights.

5. No person in pupillage or bankruptcy can be an elector.

6. One year's domicile within the city or electoral circle where he resides at the time of the election, is required. Those who are domiciled in various places may themselves elect the place where they will vote.

7. Every person is eligible for election to the Folkething who enjoys an unblemished reputation, has the right of citizenship and is of the full age of 25 years, —unless he comes within the provisions of sections 3, 4, and 5.

Electoral Lists.

Section 8. The governing bodies in the Communes are obliged to prepare the lists of the electors domiciled within each commune.

9. The names of the electors are in alphabetical order on the electoral lists; which ought also to include their name, age, business and domicile.

10. The electoral lists are prepared every year. A special list is prepared of those who have not fully accomplished the required conditions.

11. The electoral lists must be completed within the last fortnight of February. Doubtful points are decided by the communal government.

12. From the 1st to the 8th of March, inclusive, the electoral lists are exposed in a convenient place to the public view.

13. Complaints respecting errors are made, within three days of the exposure of the lists, to the communal authorities.

14. The claims and protests are examined by the communal authorities at a session within the following fortnight ; to which are summoned the complainants and the parties complained of.

15. The president of the commune which does not contain the place for holding the election, sends certified copies of his election lists to the president of the commune where the election is held.

16. The president of the commune where the election is held is bound, within the three days following the 1st of April, to inform a qualified bailiff what lists are wanting.

17. The bailiff, by imposing suitable penalties, procures the missing lists.

18. If the lists are not revised in the manner authorised by law, a bailiff compels the communal authority, by means of a penalty, to conform to the provisions of the law, the legal delays being shortened.

19. Examinations of protests in Copenhagen.

20. If the communal authority refuses the right of voting to any person, the latter may appeal to the courts.

21. The electoral lists are available for elections from the 1st of April to the 31st of March in the following year.

Electoral Circles and Committees.

22. Each electoral circle returns a member to the Folkething.

23. In each circle is formed an electoral committee, composed of delegates from all the communes belonging to the circle. Each commune elects one member of the committee whatever its population. The communes of 3,000 souls appoint two, and one more for each 1,500 of population. The members of the committees are elected by the communal authorities, so soon as the circle is called together for an election.

24. The member or members of the committee elected by the commune where the election is to take place make all the preparations, receive the notifications of the candidates, &c.

25. The original electoral lists are brought by the members of each commune representing it, to the electoral committee.

26. If the original list is wanting recourse is had to a true copy.

27. The electoral commit ee in each of the electoral circles of Copenhagen.

28. The electoral committee where the election is had, keeps a minute book of proceedings, correspondence, &c. This is kept by the communal authorities where the election takes place. Eight days after an election, the president of the electoral committee forwards to the proper minister a certified copy of these minutes, who in turn presents this copy to the Folkething.

Electoral Candidates.

29. No person can be elected to the Folkething unless presenting himself as a candidate ; He must also be recommended by one of the electors of the circle, who is not a member of the electoral committee.

30. The candidate must present a written notification of his intention to be a candidate. He must also present himself, on the pain of nullification, on the day of the election.

31. The candidate need not justify before the electoral committee.

32. No person can offer himself as candidate in more than one electoral circle.

Election Meetings.

33. Elections for the Folkething are made for each circle in electoral meetings which are open to the public.

34. The day, hour, and place of meetings are announced, 8 days in advance, in the official Journal of the locality, or, in rural communes, in the churches, for two Sundays preceding the election.

35. At the meetings, the president presents the candidates and their sureties to the meeting. The candidates and their sureties address the meeting in alphabetical order. They also answer questions. No member of the committee is allowed to speak.

Voting by Uplifted Hands.

36. Voting for the candidates then takes place. The electors voting in alphabetical order. The one obtaining the majority of votes is elected member of the circle for the Folkething.

37. If there is only one candidate he must obtain more than one-half the votes in order to be elected.

Voting by Names.

38. A defeated candidate, or his sureties, may demand a vote by names. When only one candidate, fifty electors present may demand a vote by names. This demand must be made within one quarter of an hour after the proclamation of the result.

39. In voting by names the electors decide between the candidate elected by the show of hands and the opposing candidates.

40. The various electoral lists are distributed among the members of the committee, who collect the votes.

41. The electors give verbally their votes in the order in which they come forward. The member of the committee in charge of the list inscribes on it opposite the name of the elector, the name of the candidate for whom he votes. Before the elector retires the name of the candidate for whom he has voted is read over to him.

42. When all present have voted, the chairman declares the election closed. The members of the committee sign the lists and give them to the chairman.

43. The committee, when met, again proceed to examine the lists and add them up. The result of the vote is recorded in the electoral register and announced to the meeting. The electoral lists and the lists of votes are returned to the respective communes,—signed by the members of the committee.

45. Elections in the Bailiwick of Holback.

46. Elections in the Faroe Islands.

2. LANDSTHING.

ELECTORAL RIGHTS AND QUALIFICATIONS.

47. Electors to have the same qualifications as those to the Folkething.

48. Members of the Landsthing to possess the same qualifications as those of the Folkething.

Circles of the Landsthing.

49. Besides the 12 members appointed by the King, the Landsthing is made up of 54 members elected by circles.

11

50. The elected members of the Landsthing are elected for 8 years,—one half being renewed every four years.

Election Committees.

51. The Landsthing elections are directed by special committees for each circle.

52. The committees are composed of a chairman, appointed by the King, and of two members for each of the bailiwick councils comprised within the electoral circle, and of one member of the communal authority of the largest town of each of the bailiwicks of the circle. Special provisions as to Copenhagen and divided Bailiwicks.

Electoral Lists.

53. As the basis of the electoral lists, the proper minister publishes yearly, before the 15th January, the number of rural communes throughout the country, and within each circle of the Landsthing.

54. In the elections of electors of the second degree, the electoral lists in use for the Folkething are employed, with supplementary ones respecting the electors of the first degree.

55. These supplementary lists are prepared in the same manner as those of the Folkething.

56. Preparation of the lists of the electors of the first degree in Copenhagen. Exposure, protests, &c., same as in the case of lists for the Folkething.

57. Lists of electors of the second degree prepared in other towns, by the communal authority. Exposures, claims, and protests as in Folkething.

58. Any person whom the electoral committee refuses to put on the lists mentioned in sections 56 and 57, may appeal to the courts as in section 20.

59. The lists of those electors in the country parts who are most highly taxed and who take part directly in the Landsthing elections are prepared by the committees of their respective circles (see sections 51 and 52).

60. In the preparation of these lists the revenue officers must, before the 15th January in each year, forward to the electoral committees a statement of the rate-payers who have paid to the state and to the commune of the bailiwick the highest taxes,—giving three times the number of such ratepayers as there are rural communes in the district served by the inland revenue office. This statement contains the amount of the taxes paid, and the rural commune where the ratepayer has his domicile.

61. The electoral committees have, before the 1st February, with the assistance of the statements before mentioned, to prepare a list of the ratepayers, who, in the proportion of two for each of the rural communes in the corresponding circle of the Landsthing, are allowed to take part directly in the elections of the Landsthing, ranking them according to the value of their taxes. Printed copies of this list are sent to each communal council of the circle as soon as possible to be exposed for the same time and at the same place as are those for the Folkething. Protests are invited to be fyled within 3 days following the conclusion of the exposure. The committee pronounces upon the protests at a meeting in the end of March; summoning the interested parties to it, three days in advance.

62. Any person who is refused enrolment on the list may appeal to the courts.

63. Immediately after the sitting mentioned in section 61 at least before the end of March, the committee prepares the final list of electors who pay the highest taxes, which contains a number equal to that of the rural communes of the circle. To provide for vacancies, a supplementary list is prepared, on which are placed the names equal to half the number of the rural communes of the circle, of those next in order of highest taxation.

64. Notice is given to the direct electors of their being such, and of the time and place of election. The list of the direct electors must be prepared at least 8 days before the election of the electors of the second degree. The electors are bound to present themselves on pain of penalty.

65. The calculation of taxes. All the taxes that a person pays to the state, no matter where the properties are situate, are reputed as being paid in the locality in which he is entered as an elector to the Folkething.

Election of Electors of the Second Degree.

66. These elections, in Copenhagen, are carried out as in the elections to the Folkething. Outside they are carried out by each commune separately, under the direction of their respective communal authorities. The same lists are used as in the Folkething elections. The domiciled electors in the commune or the circles can alone be electors of the second degree. The electors of the second degree may be chosen by the highest ratepayers from out of the general body of the electors.

67. The elections of the electors of the second degree are fixed by the electoral colleges at Copenhagen, and by the highest ratepayers in the other towns. The day and place are announced as in section 34.

68. At Copenhagen all the electors on the Folkething lists appoint the electors of the second degree in the proportion of one to 120. An equal number of electors of the second degree are appointed by the ratepayers who had, the previous year, a taxable revenue of at least 2000 Rixdollars,—they are divided among the different circles of the Folkething, as much as possible proportionately to the number of the highest ratepayers in each circle. A list of those elected in the first manner is sent to the circles to prevent dual elections.

69. In the country places all the electors appoint one elector of the second degree in each rural commune. The committee of each circle sends to all the communal authorities within the circle a list of all the highest ratepayers who take a direct part in the Landsthing elections, and who therefore cannot be elected as electors in the second degree.

70. Elections in towns.

71. The voting takes place openly in a convenient place. The circles may be divided into several voting divisions. The electors each vote for as many electors of the second degree as have to be elected within the circle.

72. Three hours after the opening, if no one offers to vote, the election is declared closed. The majority decides. In case of a tie the decision is by lot.

73. The names of those elected are inscribed on a register authorised by the communal authority.

74. Every person appointed an elector of the second degree is bound to accept the trust unless he can plead a legal objection.

75. Every elector of the second degree who makes default or abstains from voting is subject to a penalty of 20 rixdollars, which penalty is absorbed by the poor box of the commune; or the municipal treasury.

76. The duties of the electors of the second degree terminate with elections of the Landsthing—unless a re-election is ordered.

77. The electors of the second degree are not bound by the instructions of their constituents nor by any engagements they may have made with them respecting the elections.

78. The electors of the second degree receive an indemnity of 18 skillings per mile, from their domicile to the place of voting for the Landsthing.

Elections of the Members of the Landsthing.

79. The place of election of certain circles is fixed by the King. The day, hour, and place is announced by the electoral committee, as in section 34.

80. The electors of the second degree and the direct electors must be present at the place, and hour of election.

81. The election meeting is public. All the electors are present, and, after identification, receive a ballot paper containing as many divisions as there are members to elect.

82. The elections for the Landsthing are conducted according to, what is known as, the proportional system.   The electors proceed to vote by filling up their ballots.   The number of ballot papers handed in to the chairman divided by the number of members of the Landsthing to be elected, forms a quotient which is taken as the basis of election.   After the ballots have been lodged and cast into an urn, the chairman draws them out one by one and reads out in a loud voice the name which stands at the head of each ballot.   So soon as a name obtains the number of votes equal to the quotient above mentioned the reading is stopped, the ballots verified, and the candidate proclaimed elected. The reading of the remaining ballots is continued, taking care to consider the name of the candidate already elected, and which may be found at the head of the list, as effaced, and to consider the next name at the head of the list.   A second candidate is obtained, as before, when his name reaches the quotient;—and so on until the ballots are all drawn out.

83. If there still remain members to be elected, the names of those who have obtained the greatest number of ballots are selected to fill the remaining places, provided always that the person to be elected must obtain at least one-half of the quotient in the number of votes cast for him.   In case of ties the lot must decide.

84. If there still remain elections to be completed, the ballots are read over again, and out of the candidates placed at the head of the ballots, who have not already been elected, a sufficient number is taken to fill the number of members required.

85. Special provisions as to Bornholm and Faroe.

86. The committee cannot reject votes because they have been given to men whose qualifications are doubted.   The Landsthing determines questions of this kind, when they present themselves before it.

87. All that passes at the election meeting is entered in the Register, and examined by the chairman.   This Register must contain exact and particular information,—the number of ballots cast, the number of those who were elected, and the number of votes given to each, the ballots rejected and the reasons therefor.   The ballots are then sealed up and preserved. The chairman then notifies the elected members of their election.   If they do not refuse to act within 8 days they are taken to consent.

Eight days, thereafter, the Chairman sends a copy of the Register to the Minister in charge.   He, in turn, lays it before the Landsthing when they meet.

General Provisions.

88. General elections, every three years for the Folkething, and every four years for the moiety of elective members of the Landsthing.

89. A member of the Rigsdag elected to replace another serves for the time that the member whom he replaces would have served.

90. The king fixes the day of the general elections.   The elections for the Folkething coming first.   For bye-elections the date is fixed by the proper minister.

91. Every person elected to the Rigsdag receives a letter, signed by the electoral committee to that effect.

92. Any person, neglecting the duties imposed by the present law, is subject to a fine of from 10 to 200 rixdollars ; unless a severer penalty has been imposed.

93. The costs of the elections to the Folkething are, broadly speaking, paid by the treasurer of the commune.

94. Travelling allowances of 48 skillings per mile are allowed to the members of the electoral committees for verifying lists, &c. The electors voting directly are not allowed any kind of indemnity. This refers to the Landsthing.

95. All the costs of the Landsthing elections are paid by the chairman of the electoral committee. He prepares a statement which is verified by the council of the Bailiwick, where the election occurs.

96. After this statement is verified, the chairman divides the costs of the election among the communes of the circle, according to the number of electors of the second degree each commune has to appoint. One month after the receipt of notice the communal authorities are obliged to reimburse the chairman the proportion to be paid by them, under a penalty.

97. The chairman of the committee of each of the Landsthing circles (except Copenhagen and Faroe) is authorised to secure an advance from the treasury of the Bailiwick where the election occurs of the necessary sum, on condition of repayment within 3 months following the election.

98. Costs of elections how paid in Copenhagen and Faroe.

99. Every member of the Rigsdag receives an indemnity of three rixdollars per diem while the session lasts. Travelling expenses are also allowed.

100. Repeal of laws.

VOTING BY COMMAND.

By Dr. Wicksteed. From " The Week" May 13th, 1892.

In order that the Canadians may fully appreciate the importance of the question of compulsory voting, I desire to place before them the following statements submitted to the members of the Select Committee of the House of Commons of Canada, to whose consideration has been referred the Bill of the present session entitled, " An act to make voting compulsory ":—

Relying upon the desire which actuates the members of this committee, the desire to calmly and thoroughly investigate and pass upon the principles involved in the Bill before them, I venture to put forward, in writing, a few extracts from the works of others, bearing upon the subject of compulsory voting in elections for the House of Commons.

The question whether an elector in Canada should be compelled to vote may be discussed from four standpoints, viz. : the moral, the ethical-political, the ideal-political and the practical-political.

Extract "A," in the appendix hereto, from the pen of Dr. R. W. Dale, a Congregational minister of Birmingham, England, is a good example of the argument on religious grounds.

In extract "B," we have the views of the late Dr. Francis Lieber, as expressed in his " Manual of Political Ethics." The " Encyclopædia Britannica" includes this work when stating : "The political writings of Francis Lieber are held in great estimation by all publicists."

Nearly one-third of the electors of Canada refrained from voting in the elections of 1891, as is shown in quotation "C."

All scriptures, both sacred and the honest profane, are written for our learning; and he is a foolish statesman who acts without informing himself beforehand, from the history of nations and the writings of their best men, what had been advocated under similar circumstances by rulers and philosophers, and how their teachings were borne out and resulted when put to actual test.

Extract "D," taken from that dialogue of Plato called "Laws" is given as showing the compulsory manner of voting enjoined by this philosopher in his ideal commonwealth for the Athenians, written about 350 years before Christ. This is the philosopher of whom it has been said that "he has anticipated nearly all the questions that have swelled into importance in the meta-physical and ethical speculations of these later ages ."

The only modern instance, we can discover, of the compulsory voting being made use of in state elections is that of the kingdom of Denmark. In 1866, a new electoral law was passed, in which the principles of compulsory voting and proportional representation were embodied. According to the Danish ambassador at Washington, this law has worked well; and according to the "Encyclopædia Britannica" "notwithstanding her dismember-ment (in 1864) Denmark has prospered to an astonishing degree, and her material fortunes have been constantly in the ascendant."

Let us return to Canada. Under the Dominion Elections Act it is provided that all persons possessing certain qualifications "on the day of the polling at any election for any electoral district, shall be entitled to vote at any such election for such electoral district, and no other persons shall be entitled to vote thereat." How does this Act work in practice? In 1891, as shown by appendix "C," out of 1,132,201 electors on the lists, only 730,457 voted. This fact might not be so much deplored but for the prophecy of the wise Lieber: "they whose voting is the least desirable are the surest to be at the poll." In Canada the surest to be at the poll are the venal, the bribed, the boodler, the place-hunter, the weak, the worthless, while the brains, the sinew, the substance of the State keep away from the poll. The latter do not answer to the question, What are the duties of your station? as does the elector in Bolingbroke's political catechism: "to endeavour, so far as I am able, to preserve the public tranquility, and, as I am an elector, to give my vote to the candidate whom I judge most worthy to serve his country."

The law of the land governs all: it declares that (for good reasons) certain persons (the majority) shall not vote; and declares that certain others—the privileged, the representative minority, the trustees of the Dominion people at large—are entitled to vote. What we want from the Bill is to substitute the words "must vote" for the words "shall be entitled to vote." The reason why they were not substituted at first was the argument that, although all electors could vote, yet some of them abstained; still the machinery of the law would not be affected, inasmuch as sufficient votes would be cast to carry out the intentions and the provisions of the Act. The bare provisions, as expressed in words, perhaps, but surely not the intentions of our law-makers. But we find that the machinery, for want of or from improper feeding, although it works, turns out bad work or inferior work. The work turned out by the electoral machine is not representative of the truest and best manhood of Canada—which it would be in time if the one-third laggards were whipped to the polling booth, and some of the now voters were whipped at it. If the army machine of England were not fed with sufficient recruits of good quality—what would happen? why, at once, a compulsory recruiting or conscription Act would be passed.

We have seen that on religious, moral, ethical, political, historical and practical grounds all electors should vote or be punished. We therefore call upon the members of the House of Commons to pass the Bill making voting compulsory. We ask those members who are ready to punish one of their number, who, having heard the question in the House, declines to vote; we ask them to punish electors in their electoral districts, who, having heard the pronouncements and appeals of the various candidates, decline to vote. In what do these two bodies differ?—they are both representatives, they are both trustees—the electors of the nation, the Commoners of the electors.

APPENDIX.

Authorities, Citations, Opinions and Extracts in favour of.

A.—"The great outlines of national legislation and policy are laid down, not in Parliament, not in the Cabinet, but at the polling booths. It is the electors who make war or maintain peace, who repeal old laws and pass new ones, who interfere, justly or unjustly, between landlords and tenants, masters and servants, parents and children. Those who abstain from voting, determine the national policy as truly as those who vote. The responsibility of the Parliamentary franchise cannot be evaded. . . . . . According to the Divine order civil authority is necessary to the existence of civil society. Civil rulers are 'ministers of God.' But they are not designated to their office by a voice from heaven. In this country the sovereign and the peers inherit their position by birth; the rest have to be selected, directly or indirectly, by those who possess the franchise. It is surely a part of God's service to determine who shall be 'God's ministers,' and for the manner in which we discharge this service we are responsible to God. Not to vote is to act the part of the unfaithful servant who hid his talent in the earth and made no use of it. To vote corruptly is felony; it is to appropriate to our own purposes what we have received as trustees for the town or the nation."—From the Laws of Christ for Common life, by Dr. R. W. Dale.

B.—"The question has been made, whether a citizen, possessing the right to vote, ought not to be legally bound to vote for general elections, as the citizen is obliged to serve on juries Why, it is asked, should those for instance, who possess most property and receive the full benefit of the law, from indolence, superciliousness or cowardice be allowed to refuse to join in that manner of expressing public opinion or of appointing law-makers which the law of the land establishes? It cannot be denied that affixing a penalty for unexcused omission of voting would have this advantage at least, that the public opinion respecting the obligation of every citizen lawfully to aid in the politics of his country, and the discountenance given to politicial indifferentism, would be fixedly pronounced by law. . . . . . We have treated already of the bad motives and mischievous tendency of political apathy or superciliousness. A man who from indolence or blamable disdain does not go to the ballot-box knows little of the importance of the whole institution of the State, or must be animated by very little public spirit; or he deserves the mantle of lead which Dante apportions to cowards in the lower regions. There seem to me to be two rules of perfect soundness and elementary importance in politics:—

1. There is no safer means of preventing factious movements of any kind, and the State from falling a gradual prey to calamitous disorders, wherever the franchise is enjoyed on an extensive scale, than the habitual steady voting of all who have the votive right at all primary elections.

2. The moral obligation of depositing without fail one's vote increases in the same ratio as the right of suffrage extends, which right will necessarily more and more extend with modern civilization, so that with increasing civilization this obligation of voting increases.

. There is no great principle which has ever actuated mankind that has not had likewise its inconvenience for the individual ; so has the main moving principle of our times ; but we are not on that account absolved from conscientiously acting upon it and acting it out.   Therefore, if we have a mind honestly to join in the great duties of our period, we must act as conscientious citizens, and, if we mean to do this, we must go to the poll.   It is, I repeat it to my readers, of primary importance, and the more they read history the more they will feel convinced of it.   The more extended the franchise is, the more it must likewise extend to those persons to whom time is of little value, to people who make a feast-day, perhaps a riotous day, of the election time.   They whose voting is the least desirable are the surest to be at the poll ; but the industrious mechanic, the laborious farmer, the man of study, the merchant and professional man—in short, all those who form the sinew and substance of the State, feel it a sacrifice of time to go to the place of voting, where they are not unfrequently delayed for a long time, by the other class, from depositing their vote, especially in populous places.   They are, therefore, the more imperatively called upon to keep constantly before their minds how important it is that they should vote, and not leave the election to be decided by those who have the smallest stake in the society.   Let no man be prevented from voting by the consideration of the loss of a day's labour, or the inconvenience to which he may expose himself in going to the poll.—*From Manual of Political Ethics, by Dr. Francis Lieber.*

C.—The total votes on the lists on which the elections of 1891 were run numbered in all Canada 1,132,201, of which 730,457 voted.   In 1887 the voters numbered 993,914, of which 725,056 voted.

D.—" The Council shall consist of 360 members—this will be a convenient number for sub-division.   If we divide the whole number into four parts of ninety each, we get ninety counsellors for each class.   (*Note.*   The Athenians were divided into four classes, according to their rated property.)   First, all the citizens shall vote for members of the council taken from the first class ; they shall be compelled to vote, and, if they do not, shall be duly fined. When the candidates have been elected, some one shall mark them down ; this shall be the business of the first day.   And on the following day the election shall be made from the second class in the same manner and under the same conditions as on the previous day ; and on the third day an election shall be made from the third class, at which every one may, if he likes, vote, and the three first classes shall be compelled to vote ; but the fourth and lowest class shall be under no compulsion, and any member of this class who does not vote shall not be punished.   On the fourth day members of the council shall be elected from the fourth and smallest class ; they shall be elected by all, but he who is of the fourth class shall suffer no penalty, nor he of the third, if he be not willing to vote ; but he who is of the first or second class, if he does not vote, shall be punished ; he who is of the second class shall pay a fine triple the fine which was exacted at first, and he who is of the first class quadruple On the fifth day the rulers shall bring out the names noted down, in the presence of all the citizens, and every man shall choose out of them, under pain, if he do not, of suffering the first penalty ; and, when they have chosen 180 out of each of the classes, they shall choose one-half of them by lot, who shall undergo a scrutiny ; these are to form the council for the year."—*From the Dialogues of Plato.   " Laws," Book 6.*

E.—Provisions of the election law of Denmark, of 1867 : Section 64.   Notice is given to the direct electors of the Landsthing of their being such, and of the time and place of election. . .   The electors are bound to present themselves on pain of penalty.

Section 74.   Every person appointed an elector of the second degree is bound to accept the trust, unless he can plead a legal objection.

Section 75.   Every elector of the second degree who makes default or abstains from voting is subject to a penalty of 20 rix-dollars--which penalty is absorbed by the poor-box of the commune or the municipal treasury.

Section 78. The electors of the second degree receive an indemnity of 48 skillings per mile, from their domicile to the place of voting for the Landsthing.

Section 80. The electors of the second degree and the direct electors must be present at the place and at the hour of election.

Section 92. Any person neglecting the duties imposed by the present law is subject to a fine of from 10 to 200 rix-dollars: unless a severer penalty has been imposed.

COMPULSORY VOTING.

By Sydney Fisher, in the Montreal Herald, May 24th, 1892.

I cannot agree with the view that this compulsory voting, will be an effectual or even partial cure. Such an expedient may force some few to an unwilling and unintelligent compliance with the law, but it will not in any way remove the cause of the evil, therefore cannot be effective. At the same time compulsory voting may easily cause hardship and may lower the morale of numbers of the electorate. It must be remembered in discussing the plan of forcing every man to vote that under our present laws a voter can only vote for one of certain duly nominated individuals and in consequence of the consent of the candidate being required and a large money deposit being exacted to nominate a man, it is not easy to secure the nomination of more than two or three candidates. Thus the average elector would be obliged to vote for a candidate in whose nomination he has had no part, unless indeed as one of the rank and file of a great political party, and of whom very probably he does not approve. Suppose for instance an honest voter who believes in protection finds two candidates nominated in his constituency, one a free trader and the other a boodler or a drunkard, consequently men neither of whom he can honestly support, nor does he consider either worthy to represent his views on public questions. Why, under such circumstances, should the voter be forced to cast his vote or lose his franchise or pay a fine? Suppose again a voter is a prohibitionist and finds no candidate who will agree to vote for Prohibition, why should he be forced to vote for a man who is opposed to what he considers the most important public question? It would be a hardship to make him lose his right to vote when other candidates are in the field. I see it is proposed by some that religious scruples shall relieve a voter from being forced to vote. I fear that in election times there would be great, if insincere, accession of religious fervour and I doubt the moral improvement of many of those who thus would shirk the vote. Another point which would largely nullify any benefit that might be obtained by compulsory voting is the secrecy of the ballot. It is something like the old adage, " One may bring the horse to water, but a hundred cannot make him drink." You may make the man go into the polling booth and go through all the motions of voting, but you cannot tell whether he votes or not.

I believe a better remedy would be to adopt an expedient by which the elector would have to appreciate his privilege in the franchise, and the only way I can think of to accomplish this, is to throw the responsibility of securing his right to vote on the citizen himself. Let only those vote who value the privilege sufficiently to make an effort, only a slight one but still an active step, to secure the privilege. This may at first sight appear reactionary as it is radical, but the mode I suggest of carrying the plan out is not reactionary at all. I would place the right to vote within the reach of every male British subject of twenty-one years of age who lives in Canada, but I would exact of him the active step of appearing personally before the proper official and entering his name on the list. If any resident of Canada be not willing to take so much trouble as this once a year to secure the right to have his say in the management of our public affairs, either he is so ignorant of the duties and privileges of citizenship that he is not competent to vote intelligently or he does not take sufficient interest in the affairs of the community to study them enough to vote properly. If a man has thus taken the trouble to obtain the right to vote, he is pretty sure to make use of it if he conscientiously can.

There are but few difficulties in the way of this reform, while nearly all the objectionable features of our present arrangememts would disappear. The scheme I would suggest, after considerable thought given to it during several years of active participation in election work is this : That in a certain month of the year, say May or September, the secretary-treasurer of the municipality, or in large cities an officer appointed for the purpose, should during certain hours of the day keep open a register for voters. Any man who would appear before him and make oath (the official being empowered ex-officio to administer oaths) that he was a British subject, twenty-one years of age, a resident in the municipality at that time, and that he had not registered anywhere else that year, should have his name entered as a voter. In case of confinement to the house by sickness during the whole of the month, a doctor's certificate under oath would entitle the applicant to registration without personal appearance, and absence from Canada during the whole month, properly established by oath would do the same. This list should come in force at the end of the given month and be valid for one year. The same process for a new list being gone through each year.

This list would cost hardly anything, there being no labor on the part of the officer to hunt up names, no enquiry into qualification, no revision. The man making oath would be liable to prosecution for perjury, if swearing falsely, which would be sufficient check on improper registration.

This plan involves the principle of one man one vote, which is the only true principle of a democratic franchise. No doubt at first the number of voters would be lessened, but it would be the indifferent or ignorant who would be left off, just the men who now either do not vote or put up their vote for sale.

A further enactment ought to go with this scheme ; namely, that paying a man for his time and trouble in registering or inducing him to register, would, in the first place deprive him of the right to vote, and also be punishable by a fine or imprisonment for either party to the bargain. I do not suppose that this or any other expedient will do away with bribery in elections until the voters themselves become honest, but I do believe that it would greatly lessen the evil of corrupt elections. The time of registration would not usually be in the heat of a contest and men would not be so easily induced to pledge themselves to an unknown candidate or to a future contest as they now are willing to sell themselves for cash down within a few days or a few hours of voting. A politician or a party even would not be so willing to pay out money to men for an uncertain return, and consequently bribery would be made more risky. This scheme is put forward as a reform, which I am confident would do more than any other so far suggested to improve our election work, while at the same time it would remove nearly all the expense and labor, and waste of time involved in the making up of our voters lists and so render corruption more difficult.

Certainly some reform in these matters is absolutely necessary if Canada is to be governed by her people in their own interests, and the most just and most effective mode is to shut out the ignorant, indifferent and corrupt from the power to control the election of the representatives.

POSTSCRIPT.

The foregoing excerpts present in a condensed form the views of many public men who have given much attention to the subject submitted for consideration. It is believed they will not be unacceptable to some of those readers who do not live within reach of public libraries, where they could have access to the original works.

While they were passing through the press, two articles have appeared which the writer deems it expedient to add to the list. The first in the " Week " of May 13th, by Dr. Wicksteed. of Ottawa, under the heading " Voting by Command;" the second in the " Montreal Herald" of May 24th, by Mr. Sydney Fisher, for many years member of the Dominion House of Commons, under the heading " Compulsory Voting." The first expresses the convictions of that section of the community which in order to obtain the voice of the people advocates the introduction of a law by which electors would be compelled to vote or be punished. The second takes a different view and with the design of shutting out the ignorant, indifferent and corrupt, from the power of controlling elections, submits a plan which he thinks would have that effect ; he is of opinion too that it would tend to raise the franchise so as to embrace chiefly, those who are sufficiently intelligent to value their political privileges and are patriotic enough to exercise them properly. These articles together with the introduction of a Bill in the Canadian Parliament to enact the principle of compulsory voting and the appointment of a special committee to consider the expediency of adopting the principle, are at least hopeful indications that among members of the House of Commons of Canada the feeling is arising that some amendment of our electoral system is imperatively called for. The Proportional Representation Society has already been alluded to (page 30) : a list of members of the British House of Commons who had joined this organization will be found at page 88, and in this list will be noticed the names of no less than twelve members who are, or were, ministers of the Crown, and of these, four ranked as " cabinet " ministers in Lord Salisbury's administration. Such facts attest that the public conscience in both countries is being awakened to the necessity of some radical change in electoral methods.

The writer is unable himself to recognize that any extraordinary results of a beneficial character would be achieved by the enforcement of a system of compulsory voting.   Taken by itself as explained in Dr. Wicksteed's paper, it would give no freedom of choice to the elector. Compulsory voting would not touch the real difficulty, which leads to party organization, and its outcome, the caucus system by which the choice is determined.   The candidates would be selected as at present, and as a rule by coteries of party politicians.   The ordinary independent voter would not have the remotest voice in the selection, and many will consider it a monstrous proposal that an elector should be forced by legislative enactment, under threat of fine, to vote for one of the two party candidates, in neither of whom he could place confidence.   For this is practically what he would be reduced to, if he were dragged in his despite to the polls, and compelled to choose between two evils.   His alternative would be to pay the penalty, or go through an empty form which would render his vote of no effect whatever.   Would not high minded men, rich and poor alike, feel themselves humiliated and degraded in being thus coerced?   If compulsory voting could be effectively enforced, its tendency would be to drive all composing the voting community, whether they will or not, to take sides with one party or the other.   It would by no means remove the evils of party government.   Its direct consequence would be to separate the community more completely than even at present, into two great political divisions.   In what way then would it effect good?   Would it not tend to intensify party bitterness?   Would it not consolidate and perpetuate the dualism which we deplore?   Would it not always leave unrepresented in parliament that great mass of the electors who had supported the defeated candidates?

High authorities have expressed the opinion that representative government is on its trial.   We may ask the question; has true representative government ever yet been tried?   The writer is profoundly convinced that our present duty is to make every effort to obtain this ideal government, and seek for nobler ideas of public life than now prevail, that is to say if we are to be freed from the political ills from which we suffer.   The issue, with greater accuracy, may be set forth that it is government by party which is on its trial.   Can we doubt what the verdict will be, when we have something better to take its place?

The foregoing pages indicate the views which begin to dominate on both sides of the Atlantic on this subject; the lesson is inculcated that we have reached the stage when we should aim to lay aside the spirit of *antagonism and wrong* which we have acquired by transmission from the distant past, and substitute the spirit of *amity and right*, in national, as we do in almost all other human affairs.   We recognize that we are in an age of evolution : the arts and sciences are expanding civilization in every sphere of activity, and it appears inconsistent with the law of progress that the domain of government should remain non-progressive or become retrogressive.

The evidence before us leads to the conviction that to enter on the path of progress, popular government must stand on a broader and sounder basis than that of party. We must hope for a political evolution which will enable every man in the land to feel that the acts of the government are his acts, that the laws made by parliament are made by those who represent him. We must look for a political development based on the fundamental principles of our constitution ; one which will bind every individual life, in the common life of the state ; a development which removing the causes of chronic internal dissensions, will benefit society, will give strength and stability to the commonwealth, and enable it the better to stand the test of time.

To determine the best means of effectively promoting this high public purpose is the end and object of the appeal which the Canadian Institute submits to the world of thought and constructive statesmanship. It cannot be doubted that this object will find earnest sympathy with every well wisher of his country.

S. F.

OTTAWA, May 26th, 1892.

CONTENTS.